CAMAS PUBLIC LIBRARY

P9-CCP-600

3 3277 00209 7280

STAINED
water damage
Pg 127-130
7/14

THE NEW TRADITIONAL GARDEN

THE *New* TRADITIONAL *G*ARDEN

A Practical Guide to Creating and Restoring
Authentic American Gardens for Homes of All Ages

MICHAEL WEISHAN

A Seth Godin Production

THE BALLANTINE PUBLISHING GROUP • NEW YORK

Camas Public Library

Published by The Ballantine Publishing Group

Copyright © 1999 by Michael Weishan

All rights reserved under International
and Pan-American Copyright Conventions. Published
in the United States by The Ballantine Publishing Group, a division
of Random House, Inc., New York, and simultaneously in
Canada by Random House of Canada Limited, Toronto.

Ballantine and colophon are registered trademarks of Random House, Inc.

www.randomhouse.com/BB/

LIBRARY OF CONGRESS CATALOGING-IN-PUBLICATION DATA
Weishan, Michael.
The new traditional garden : a practical guide to creating and restoring authentic
American gardens for homes of all ages / Michael Weishan.—1st ed.
p.   cm.
Includes bibliographical references (p. 321).
ISBN 0-345-42041-1 (alk. paper)
1. Gardens, American.   2. Historic gardens—United States.   I. Title.
SB457.53 .W45 1999
712'.6—dc21   98-46043
                                                                     CIP

Text design by Holly Johnson

Manufactured in the United States of America

First Edition: September 1999

10 9 8 7 6 5 4 3 2 1

To my grandfather, Eugene, who trusted enough to plant the seed;
To my mother, Carol, who watched over the crop through frost and draught;
And to my father, Richard, whose gentle wisdom
helped me bring the harvest home.

Sine vobis, nihil

. . . balance in the garden . . . architectural styles that influenced early gardens . . . the move toward a broader sense of "balance" . . . matching the style of your home to an appropriate garden style . . . the new formalism . . . adapting the best ideas of the past to suit your present needs

Chapter IV: Cohesion 76

Cohesion defined . . . the importance of boundaries . . . the dangers of neglecting internal divisions . . . creating "rooms" in your garden . . . the delineation of outdoor space according to function . . . the repetition of elements throughout your property . . . paths, walls, and fences . . . the importance of color . . . garden and house architecture joined

Chapter V: Details 102

The attention to detail in historic gardens . . . specific examples . . . fences as key offenders in the modern garden . . . how to improve them . . . the importance of structures such as pergolas, gazebos, and arbors . . . the deck craze of modern times . . . the use of smaller ornaments . . . decorative paving patterns and other ornamental features

Introduction

*L*ooking back, I find that I became a gardener by default. Most people who garden choose to do so deliberately, either as avocation or vocation, but neither of those pursuits was my conscious choice. I certainly never intended to make landscape design my career, nor did my passion for historic gardens and gardening make itself immediately apparent to me. In fact, I was trained in the classics and Romance languages, and I had had every intention of going into the foreign service, as my great friend and mentor, my grandfather, had done. His far-flung assignments always seemed to hold great glamour. Although my grandfather told me many times that the realities of diplomatic life were quite different, I was never one to be too bothered by such unromantic notions, and didn't pay much attention.

Thus I spent four years at Harvard studying Latin, Greek, Arabic, German, Italian, and French, along with the art, history, and literature of all these cultures. When all was said and done, I was an expensively educated young man, good at witty cocktail conversation in multiple languages, but seemingly without practical, or at least employable, skills. Nor was the prospect of my chosen profession, the diplomatic corps, looking too promising: the time period (the mid-1980s) was not exactly an ideal one for liberal-minded diplomats abroad, and in any event, upon closer examination, the day-to-day work of the average foreign service agent was beginning to appear as remarkably unappealing as my grandfather had described.

So I found myself in a holding pattern after college; I looked around for work and was fortunate enough to land a position as an editorial assistant at the Sardis Archaeological Expedition. This turned out to be a wonderful job, with a terrific boss who taught me all about the writing and editorial processes and gave me a chance to work on projects that most low-level editorial people never get to see. This first foray into the world of books was destined to bear a very late harvest, however, because a chance meeting soon took me out of publishing for many years. While I was at Sardis, I managed a small flock of student aides who helped us with the manuscripts. One of my unlikeliest "student" employees was a former Wall Street banker who had decided to give up the world of finance to become a minister. I was 20, you understand, and he was in his early fifties, a member of one of Boston's wealthy, old families.

His role in this tale is crucial, because one day he arrived quite late, profferring as excuse the problems he was having at his suburban house with the local landscape contractor. The property was large, with a rambling turn-of-the-century house; he and his wife felt that the plans they had commissioned didn't solve several important concerns. Oh, I said, why not try X, Y, and Z? Astonished, he asked how I knew anything about this subject. The answer was that besides a love of exotic travel and foreign lands, I had also inherited my grandfather's love of gardens and gardening. Gramps at one point had had quite an extensive garden, and between his other responsibilities, he had managed to find time to become a fairly well known grower of irises and daylilies. As a child, I had always worked with Grandpa in the garden—it just seemed the natural thing to do. This is what I meant when I said that I never really "chose" to garden. Grandpa gardened, I spent time with Grandpa, therefore I gardened. Besides, didn't all children spend hours helping to water and weed, dig and drag, then dash in precisely at three to see the latest edition of Thalassa Cruso's wonderful PBS series *Making Things Grow*? (I have always loved the title of that program—how typically, proactively British—things didn't grow of their own accord, you *made* them, but that's a whole other story.)

I spent many happy years in my grandfather's garden, learning how to plant and prune, to start new beds, to cultivate, and to harvest. We toured other people's gardens as well, and the two of us were something of a regular feature at the Boerner Botanical Gardens in Milwaukee. I think at one point I was the youngest-ever member of the American Iris Society. I took all this as a matter of course. Nor was Gramps the only gardener in our family—I have very distinct early memories of planting four-o'clocks with my mother by the back door, and of helping my father set up the wire cages for his precious tomatoes. I can see him as if it were yesterday, heading out to the garden with a salt shaker in hand to merrily munch his tomatoes (and doing his best to hide the shaker from my mother, who insisted he consumed too much salt). In my family, we all gardened. It was just natural. I helped at home with our garden, I helped Gramps with his, and I even tended my own: Gramps actually gave me my very own plot behind the garage, and at age 13, I laid out my first garden.

All this is a somewhat prolix explanation of how I discovered I was able to tell my minister friend how to fix his garden problems. All my study of history and the arts, and the thousands of hours in the garden with a master gardener, suddenly converged. At that moment, almost without my permission, my career in historic landscape design began. So delighted were my friend and his wife with the solutions I proposed that they invited me out the very next weekend to ask me to take on their project. Gardening had always seemed like such a natural activity for me that for some reason the thought had never crossed my mind that I might actually get *paid* to design gardens. What fun! So out I went on weekends and finished their project. Then they recommended me to their friends, who sent me to theirs, until suddenly I was having a very hard time fitting all this landscape activity around a nine-to-five job in publishing. With fond regrets and no little bit of trepidation at setting out on my own, I bid the archaeological world adieu and started my firm, GardenWorks Ltd.

That was in 1988, and since then my practice has grown tremendously, sending me all over the country designing, building, and restoring gardens. By inclination and training (by the latter I mean my background in European history and art), I had always favored a more traditional style of garden, but it wasn't until several years later that I began to specialize in re-creating the traditional *American* garden. And somewhere along the line, recalling the fun I had had at Sardis, it occurred to me that writing about old gardens would make an interesting adjunct to my practice. So I started a magazine, *Traditional Gardening*, which has grown from a small start-up into a nationally circulated quarterly providing practical information on every aspect of creating and restoring classic American gardens.

The New Traditional Garden is the culmination of all these experiences. At its simplest, the book deals with the development of a distinctly American style of gardening—the story of how we used to till, cultivate, and ornament our homes and grounds, and the lessons these old practices might teach us about our own yards today. For in my years of researching, writing about, designing, and building gardens, I have made a very important discovery: our own horticultural past can help make almost every modern American garden not only more beautiful and functional but also more useful and enjoyable, whether these landscapes accompany old houses or brand-new ones.

The New Traditional Garden will take you through the process of creating (or re-creating) a landscape that is not only pleasing and productive but at the same time is appropriate for your home. It is intended for every American gardener. And though I've made a special attempt to address the particular needs of experienced gardeners looking to re-create historic landscapes, someone completely new to the subject will likewise feel at home, as will the professional designer or landscaper. This book is not all-inclusive—a single work on such a vast subject could never be. But it is my firm belief that *every* gardener—from window-box planter to estate owner—can benefit from the knowledge of our American gardening past. As in all things, we have much to learn by looking backward from time to time.

The Story of
American *Gardening*

A number of years ago, I decided to return to Europe to spend several weeks touring gardens. Besides the obvious pleasures to be gained from wandering through these magnificent landscapes, my goal was to find new and interesting approaches I could use in my design practice. For years I had sensed that something was missing in the typical modern American landscape, especially after I had completed several "old-fashioned-style" gardens for clients that had far outshone others we had done that were more in keeping with modern practice.

So, in search of inspiration, I set off to tour European gardens. I was fascinated and awed by their magnificent expanses, manicured lawns, and ancient stonework. They all looked so wonderful, so appropriate in Europe, but what did these models have to tell us about gardens in Chicago, Los Angeles, or Boston? I boarded my flight home thoroughly sated from a tourist perspective but intellectually unsatisfied.

Then chance intervened and offered me a first-class window seat on the plane. Many hours later, I found myself circling Boston in what seemed like an interminable holding pattern. The weather was clear and the line of the coast perfectly visible. As we passed over the South Shore, I could just make out modern-day Plymouth and nearby the small, frail wooden buildings of Plimoth Plantation, hugging the shore.

I remembered my first trip to the plantation as a child with my mother, and smiled. What a different approach I was making to the New World than had those first settlers. The rigors of their ocean voyage are almost unimaginable for us today, as we speed across the Atlantic in a matter of hours, with decisions no more difficult than whether to have champagne or white wine with our lunch, and problems no more pressing than whether to watch the movie or take a short nap. In contrast to these sybaritic pleasures, the first ships to reach our shores had carried fifty to eighty men, women, and children crammed for three months into a space no larger than a modern two-bedroom house, along with everything necessary for a new life: food and supplies, assorted hardware, numerous domestic animals, and even the seeds for their gardens.

Yes, their gardens. I remembered those: Each house with its own little backyard garden. There was something so pleasant about those little plots; they seemed so right, comfortable, cozy. Then the notion struck me. The key

Left: What exactly the man in the tree hopes to accomplish is unclear, but this 16th-century Italian print gives a good idea of what small European gardens looked like during this period. Right: The first American gardens were not too dissimilar from their European counterparts. Note the neatly raised beds and the twig arbor in this 16th-century European garden.

This picture of a 16th-century French garden is revealing, as it shows both the older style of simple raised beds on the left, and the newly fashionable knot patterns on the right. Complicated designs became more and more popular throughout the 17th and 18th centuries.

to successful gardens for American houses new and old lay not in copying grand European models but in looking at these humble origins, where the interplay of need and resource had combined to create a unique style of Amer-

This garden, from a 16th-century German print, contains all the features that would eventually make their way into American gardens as time and prosperity allowed: a highly ornamental layout, elaborately detailed garden objects, even tender shrubs in pots. Note how the garden space and the buildings function as a single unit—it's hard to tell where the garden begins and the house ends.

An "old-fashioned" formal-style garden, which the English landscape movement almost entirely swept away during the 1700s, but which lingered on our shores for the next two centuries.

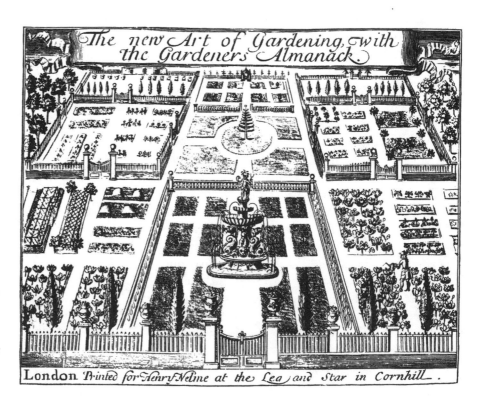

It was English gardens like this one that wealthy American landowners hoped to re-create in Colonial America. Note the use of fences, gates, and beds to give each area a distinct sense of enclosure.

ican garden perfectly suited to our architecture and lifestyles. As a country we had once had good gardens, even great gardens, as a matter of everyday fact, but now somehow we had lost them. The answer to improving today's landscapes, I realized, lay back in time, in the influences and forces that had shaped our land during the last three hundred years.

To begin to percieve the direction in which we need to go with our own gardens, we need to understand a bit about our gardening history. In the beginning there was nothing, at least as far as the European settlers were concerned. The first colonists to our shores were gardeners *by necessity*. Clinging to the edges of this strange, wild continent, they were well aware that the only sure source of supplies was what they could manage to grow and produce for themselves. (The generosity of the Native Americans they encountered, who shared with the Pilgrims their knowledge of foodstuffs and their methods of planting native crops, was providential, and completely unexpected.) Even before their houses were finished, the first settlers started to plant. Their gardens functioned as living larders, indispensable for providing their owners with food, medicine, and the materials for clothing.

Obviously these first gardens were not elaborate undertakings and were certainly not ornamental in nature. Very little actual evidence remains, but we know from views of the period and from archaeological research that the first American gardens were extremely modest affairs, inevitably sited near the house and constructed in an orderly, geometric pattern, often with raised plank-beds and an intersecting layout of paths between. These raised gardens sought to emulate, in their humble way, the neatly ordered formal gardens that the colonists had known in the time of Charles I. European garden practices and tastes were part of the baggage the settlers brought with them, along with their clothing, books, and beliefs, but the American garden was never just a European transplant. Almost immediately a distinctly new, more down-to-earth, more practical type of garden arose in response to American weather and soil conditions, to the availability of native crops, and to the pressing needs of an isolated people.

The 18th century brought a rapid progression of settlement and with it greater wealth and leisure that allowed the construction of more and more elaborate gardens, designed with an eye to pleasure as well as to practicality. Throughout the decades of the 1700s, American gardens grew in stature and complexity, and by the middle of the century, quite a number of intricate gardens had been constructed throughout the colonies. But interestingly enough, despite their increasing opulence, stylistically these gardens still followed the same forms and patterns of the previous century: largely geometric, cohesive spaces, notable for a strong link between house and garden, with an abundance of ornamental detailing and rich, mixed plantings of flowers, vegetables, and fruits. (Today we would label such a heterogeneous combination of plants a "cottage-style" garden.)

Montgomery Place,
on the Hudson River, was
typical of the expansive
park-like estates that became
fashionable in America
throughout the late 18th and
early 19th centuries.

By the time of the Revolution, the conservative nature of American gardens was much remarked upon by European visitors, who viewed our endeavors as marvelously provincial and "quaint," especially in light of what had been going on in England during the same period. There, this older, geometric, practical style of gardening had largely fallen out of fashion. Here, the colonists continued to construct their grounds as had their parents and grandparents. What appealed to them was not novelty but rather the comfort and security of their well-ordered, productive gardens.

At the dawn of the 19th century, American gardens still looked much as they had during the century previous: they were arranged in a largely formal manner, as befitted their European progenitors, yet with a distinctly American flavor of practicality and usefulness. New ideas were in the air, though, blowing in from the other side of the Atlantic. There, vast changes in agricultural practice, and the continuing general wave of social unease that had unseated so many monarchs during the last decades of the 1700s, eventually managed to filter into the realm of European garden design. The orderly, geometric layouts of the 16th and 17th centuries seemed outdated in light of this social upheaval, and expansive, naturalistic gardens, laid out in what was called the "landscape style," became the vogue throughout Europe. Enormous, parklike tracts were created to mimic the bucolic spirit of "nature un-

adorned." Lakes, meadows, classical follies, ha-has (a kind of moat that pre-
vented animals from crossing into the more cultivated areas of the garden but
that was invisible from the house), even whole forests were created where existing formal gardens, some centuries old, had been ruthlessly swept away.

Obviously only the richest of European society could afford to embrace
this garden style fully, but even the middle class designed or redesigned their
properties in a much freer, more parklike style, especially after 1800, when
landscape designers such as Repton and Loudon altered and adapted this
landscape approach to a more picturesque, domestic scale. In America similar
attempts began to change national taste. In 1806, Bernard M'Mahon, a
transplanted Irishman and noted seedsman, published *The American Gardener's
Calendar*, the first major landscape treatise published in the United States. He
proposed a freer, less geometric style with curving pathways, open lawn areas
framing the house, irregularly shaped flower beds, and naturalized boundary
plantings. In short, he advocated laying out the landscape in ways that better
conformed to the natural flow and appearance of the land.

*Andrew Jackson Downing,
perhaps America's most
famous 19th-century
landscape designer.*

Although M'Mahon had some notable admirers (Thomas Jefferson's gardens at Monticello owe much to his advice), his theories were slow to catch
on. Perhaps this was due to the fact that we Americans were by nature more
frugal than Europeans and more contented with the older, formal style,
which suited us quite well, thank you. Or perhaps vast tracts of "natural"
landscape seemed a little silly in a country still largely wilderness. Whatever
the reasons, M'Mahon's advice only slowly percolated through the American
gardening consciousness. Things did not really start to change until the
1840s, when Andrew Jackson Downing arrived on the scene and wrote his
first book, *A Treatise on the Theory and Practice of Landscape Gardening, Adapted to
North America; with a View to the Improvement of Country Residences.*

*Left: This illustration shows what Downing meant by "beauty." Note the symmetrical architecture and rounded plant forms, perfect for
the European garden. Right: Downing's "picturesque" required rugged forms in planting and architecture for a new, rugged land.*

Downing is one of the great figures in the history of American landscape design and one of the few people who can be credited with completely altering the way we gardened. Essentially, Downing took the work of Loudon, Repton, and M'Mahon and *Americanized* it, refining their ideas to suit the vagaries of American climate and attitudes. Not since the Pilgrims had the American landscape seen such a change.

Downing proposed that landscapes (and architecture) should strive to unify two essential characteristics: the *beautiful*, by which he meant the simple, classical, symmetrical, the *European;* and the *picturesque*—the stark, irregular, raw, *American*. Downing advocated an amalgam of the *beautiful* and *picturesque* in the landscape, resulting in a freer, more flowing style than had been seen in American gardens to that date. In practical terms, this meant that he favored looser, more naturalistic planting areas that often derived their inspiration from the wild beauty of the new continent. Geometry was not, however, completely banished from Downing's gardens. His designs did contain beds, terraces, and other features with straight lines and geometric forms. But the parts of the garden were scattered about the landscape, the various features no longer held in strict relationship to one another—*only to the house.* Although seemingly innocuous, this change marked a great departure from the gardens of the Colonial period and ushered in an entirely new period of American gardening.

Downing's ideas seemed more democratic, more American, than the royalist formality of the previous age, and many people, including a large portion of the design community, were converted. Large formal estates were redesigned in this "Downing style." More important, this type of garden seemed perfectly suited to the thousands of new buildings designed for the middle class that were springing up all over America, many in novel architectural styles, such as Gothic Revival, Italianate, and Tudoresque, which Downing also helped either to invent or to promote. (Downing's writings, by the way, make fascinating reading, and I highly recommend perusing any one of his volumes, if only for the extremely interesting engravings that so effectively illustrate his vision. His several works span the years from 1840 to 1850, and his literary output would surely have been more prodigious had he not tragically died while trying to save a friend's life when a river steamer on which they were traveling exploded and sank.)

Despite the sudden loss of Downing in 1852, the fledgling landscape movement he founded was well on its way. Perhaps the greatest of the next shapers of domestic American landscapes was Frank J. Scott. (I say "domestic" landscapes because another giant, Frederick Law Olmsted, was also active at this time, but the massive scope of his work was generally of a style and scale as to be of little relevance to the average homeowner.) Scott's opus, *The Art of Beautifying Suburban Home Grounds*, was published in 1870 and immediately became the major style book of the period. The very title is telling, in

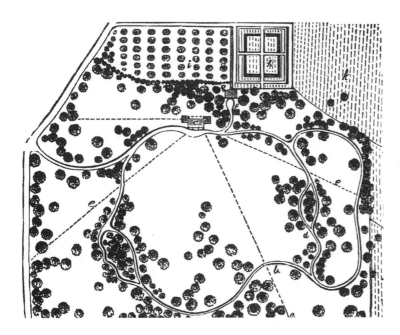

An illustration from Downing. The lines radiating from the house are the principal sight lines. The entire landscape is designed around its relationship to the structure.

that it reveals what was to become the focus of American gardens and gardening for the next century: the suburban garden. Scott felt a great dislike for the cramped urban environment, and he looked forward to a time when the cities would be "great working hives, but not homes, for a majority of their people." He proposed a "half country, half town," where one would find "streets and roads, and streams, dotted with a thousand suburban homes peeping from their groves." (A very appealing, romantic vision, as one can see from the figure on the next page, and certainly something that our modern developers would do well to remember.)

What is interesting to us today—and what was crucial to the development of modern American gardens—is that Scott was one of the first gardeners to argue that the landscape was by and large an artificial creation and that the goal of the garden was not to enhance *nature* but to enhance the *house*. Before this, the purpose of gardens had been to augment the natural world, whether through confining nature into strict geometric forms, as the colonists had done, or by improving it with further naturalistic effects, as Downing had advocated.

Under Scott, the garden became simply another means of domestic adornment, one that was subject to the same over-the-top love of ornamentation that was found in Victorian architecture and interiors. The layout of American gardens after 1870 became much looser and less symmetrical than that during the Colonial era. Curved lines were evident everywhere, in walks, drives, and border edges. Flower beds appeared in a profusion of shapes cut out of the lawn, often planted in what were called "ribbon beds," ever changing displays of annuals that were thought to resemble brightly colored ribbons. Distinctive specimen shrubs were also widely used, typically set out individually in the lawn, with each chosen for some interesting habit of flower or foliage—the Victorians especially liked weeping forms and plants with striking foliage color or variegation. For almost thirty years a joyful riot of color, form, and shape reigned in the American garden.

But as the 1900s dawned and Edward assumed the English throne, the Victorian desire for the purely picturesque and whimsical in overall garden design began rapidly to lose wind, like some damaged hot-air balloon. A movement to return to a more classical, formalized style, both in gardens and

This charming, idyllic view shows how Scott hoped all of suburban America would look—"half country, half town." How far we have strayed from his vision!

A typical Mid-Victorian garden in all its eclectic glory. The Victorians were fascinated with plants of contrasting texture and shape, each specimen placed so that it could be fully appreciated from all sides, like bibelots on a side table.

in architecture, spread again from England, led by Reginald Blomfield and espoused in this country by Charles Platt, Ogden Codman, and Edith Wharton, among others. (If at this point you think that we Americans have been totally captive to English thought and fancy throughout our gardening history, rest assured that we have had an equal or greater influence on the English garden, not so much in matters of style but in terms of plant material. Most modern English gardens contain substantial numbers of plants that came originally from this country—and in certain categories, such as plants for fall interest, they rely almost entirely on American imports.)

Accompanying this return to a more classical garden layout was a new movement in planting led by Gertrude Jekyll. Of all the names in the pantheon of English garden designers, hers reigns supreme. Born in 1843, this erstwhile painter, metalworker, and interior designer revolutionized gardens

What's old is new again as formalism returns to fashion in American gardens at the turn of the 20th century.

The quintessence of Gertrude Jekyll, and the ideal of legions of American gardeners, lives in this rose-covered garden.

in both England and America; she introduced (or, more precisely, reintro-duced) large herbaceous borders as an integral part of the landscape and pro-vided a theory of harmonious colors by which to plant them. Derived to a large extent from the old-fashioned, neglected "cottage-garden" style, these grand, labor-intensive borders were a major departure from the heavily annu-alized, geometric "ribbon" schemes then popular. Jekyll's books, along with those of William Robinson, heavily influenced late-19th-century American garden design, and Jekyllesque-style borders became a recurring feature in American gardens.

In the period between 1890 and 1940, some of the most incredible landscapes ever seen in this country were conceived. The booming economy of the late 19th and early 20th centuries, coupled with the enormous resources of the rapidly exploited continent (and no income taxes!), made large-scale garden building affordable, even to the middle class. And as a final shot in the arm, labor was comparatively inexpensive, which put quite elaborate gardens within the reach of all but the poorest homeowner. Towns all over the country quickly filled with ample houses in the Neo-Colonial, Colonial Revival, Tudor Revival, Beaux Arts, and a multitude of other "revival" styles, all of which were generally accompanied by fairly formal "revival-style" gardens. On a larger scale, fantastic estate gardens, some of a scope unimaginable to modern gardeners (not to mention their checkbooks), became almost commonplace in many areas.

Victorian gardens depended not only on lush plantings, but on beautifully crafted architectural features such as these stairs.

The advent of World War II brought this period to a complete and jarring end. For almost six years we stopped building gardens and turned our attention to defeating the menaces that had arisen in the East and West. Wartime meant little skilled labor, skyrocketing costs of goods, and Victory gardens in place of ornamentals—all of which spelled doom for many elaborate landscapes. By war's end, something fundamental had changed. It seemed that the old formulas were no longer valid. Certainly, beautiful individual gardens were created after the war. But for the most part, the nation had turned its collective back on the past and plunged headlong into an uncertain future.

The urgent need to resettle huge numbers of wartime personnel caused a rapid boom in suburban tract housing: tiny houses and tiny lots carved out of former farmland, often with no landscapes whatsoever. After the war, architectural style and aesthetic were constantly subjugated to general expediency and the search for novelty, and each subsequent decade brought further new terrors to the garden. The "Modernism" of the 1950s sought to streamline and minimize everything from cars to camellias. The '60s, '70s, and '80s brought us pink plastic flamingos, a plethora of pesticides, hideous subdivisions, and seemingly unending, ugly, urban sprawl.

Today, at the beginning of the new century, a collective desire for change is in the wind. For whatever reason—perhaps it is turn-of-the-millennium angst, or an awareness of how much we already have lost or destroyed—interest in and support for our past has reappeared with a fervor and has manifested itself in many ways. The nascence of the historic preservation movement, the major rehabilitation of old houses and buildings, the rebirth of decayed urban environments: each has shown that what is *old* can still be *good*—in fact, often *better*. This has become obvious in the garden as well.

So to end where we began: the remedy to our present gardening ills is quite simple. We need to turn to the past again, back to the gardens and gardeners of old, and learn from them. My purpose in this book is to identify the principles that made these old gardens work so well and to show modern gardeners how to incorporate them into today's landscapes. If we do this, our yards will be more useful and better-looking, our homes more appealing, and the overall appearance of our cities, towns, and countrysides more inviting. In short, we will once again enjoy that wonderful, distinctly American spirit that characterized the garden of old.

Archaeology in the Garden

Gardening and archaeology may not seem to have anything in common, but increasingly today the tools of archaeology are being used to study garden history. The idea of analyzing a garden archaeologically took a giant step forward at the Roman town of Pompeii, which was completely buried by volcanic eruption in A.D. 79. Before these excavations, which took place during the 1960s and '70s, the shape and extent of historic gardens and grounds had often been determined by locating remains of a site's architectural features. The content, however, was a different matter. Scholars could only guess from secondhand sources, such as written accounts or pictures, what had actually been grown in the gardens. At Pompeii, scholars led by Wilhelmina Jashemski discovered that although the original plants had long since decayed, the imprints of their roots were frequently preserved in the undisturbed soil. By taking casts of these root cavities, researchers could get a good idea of what plants had been grown in the atrium gardens of Roman houses and how and where the gardens had been planted.

That great bane of allergy sufferers, pollen, is also an invaluable tool to garden archaeology. The shape of each plant's pollen grains is unique and acts like a fingerprint at a crime scene: although not proof positive that an individual plant was present in a specific spot (pollen is often carried far afield by the wind), by identifying pollen grains in the soil scientists *can* be certain that the plant in question was "loitering" nearby.

> ### THE UNBEARABLE EXCITEMENT
>
> *Then came the spring, and the almost unbearable excitement—which can only be enjoyed in an ancient garden—of discovering where the previous owners had planted their bulbs. Of all the treasure hunts in which men have ever engaged, this must surely be the most enthralling ... to wander out on a February morning, in an old garden which is all your own and yet is still a mystery, and to prowl about under the beech trees, gently raking away a layer of frozen leaves in the hope of finding a cluster of snowdrops ... to scan the cold hard lawns in March for the first signs of the fresh green blades of the crocuses ... to go through the orchard with a thin comb, putting a bamboo to mark every fresh discovery of daffodils.*
>
> —Beverly Nichols, *Merry Hall* (1951)

Another method that has recently become widely used in garden-history research is the study of phytoliths. Many plants absorb silica from groundwater, which slowly deposits in the veins (vascular system) of the plants, forming a blueprint of the tissue in which the silica collects. When the plant dies and decays, these accretions, called phytoliths, remain in the surrounding soil (or rock formed from that soil), sometimes for millions of years. By analyzing these structures and developing a library of known forms, scientists can determine with a great degree of accuracy what plants were present in the garden during a certain period.

With the rise of enabling technology, the archaeological exploration of the garden has become the goal at most historic sites around the country and has caused substantial rethinking and revision in many historic gardens. So what does this mean to the average homeowner? Well, not much without a large budget, as archaeological digs are prohibitively expensive. But if your site has considerable historic significance, it is worthwhile to contact the state historical commission or a local university to inquire whether funds and resources might be available for such a project. Oftentimes these types of digs make excellent training projects for student archaeologists, for example. There are also several private companies that specialize in garden archaeology. But bear in mind that if you are considering using professionals, you should forgo the temptation to dig around yourself. Amateur exploration frequently destroys a site for professional purposes by removing materials from their context: once separated from the strata in which it belongs, a unique object becomes just another artifact, telling us nothing about how it fits into the overall picture of time and place.

RESTORE OR EVOKE?

The issue of whether to exactly duplicate a period landscape or to simply evoke the feeling of a particular time is one that comes up frequently and often stirs debate. In some ways, new-house owners are lucky—they don't have to account to anyone but themselves. Old-house owners, however, inherit considerable historical baggage. Many times sensitive owners feel guilty for not restoring or exactly duplicating historic features, as if somehow they are cheating themselves and the past. My personal opinion is this: in a museum-like setting, historical accuracy is not only desirable but essential. For other old houses, especially those of historic or aesthetic importance, owners should by all means strive to preserve and protect whatever has managed to survive into our time. We are, after all, merely trustees of our properties, and we owe it to ourselves and our children to preserve and protect this heritage.

Nevertheless, certain facts of modern living must be taken into account. In the same way most of us would demand indoor plumbing instead of an outhouse, we must make certain choices outdoors to accommodate the modern lifestyle. It is important to remember that our forebears did not consider their homes or gardens sacrosanct either: with each new innovation, out went the old, so much so that today we are often forced to undo their "modernizations." What is important to keep in mind is that any changes you plan in your landscape should be sympathetic in style and feeling with the property as a whole.

In the Beginning: The Gardens of Plimoth Plantation

For those interested in our earliest horticultural beginnings, Plimoth Plantation is a mecca. The tiny wooden houses and simple gardens have been re-created, as closely as possible, to reflect the lives of the people who lived in them. And an easy life this was not: Unaccustomed to the colder climate and strange growing conditions, the European settlers failed miserably with their initial plantings and barely made it through their first few winters. Only the assistance of the Native American inhabitants saved the day, and even with this unexpected aid, the colonists lived hand to mouth for years afterward. By dint of great effort though, they eventually learned the secrets to successful gardening in this new land.

The landscapes at Plimoth were not pleasure grounds by any means of the imagination. The Pilgrims constructed no-nonsense gardens of practicality and utility that functioned as living larders. Intimately linked to the tiny thatched houses by a rough fence of wooden pales, each yard was carefully subdivided into small, rectangular beds, with 3- to 4-foot dirt paths between them. The garden beds were just wide enough to be weeded easily from either side, and raised with rough-hewn planks or stones brought from the nearby shore. Crammed into these beds were a wide selection of plants both for medicinal and culinary use, as the gardens were expected to maintain the family until the main field crops came in, as well as to provide food additives and medicines throughout the year. To assure this supply, before leaving the Old World each family had gathered together seeds or sometimes even live plants to make their new garden. Given the difficulty of the journey, each plant had to have a specific use or function to justify its passage. By looking over one of the Plimoth plant lists, you can see how much the early colonists depended on their gardens for their day-to-day existence.

To guarantee high yields in such small spaces, the soil was carefully enriched. All wastes—human, animal, and vegetable—were carefully hoarded, composted in piles, and added to the gardens when ready. Another common practice was one we would today call "overseeding." For example, onions, which are slow to germinate, were overseeded with lettuce, which is quick to mature. As the lettuce grew, it was removed, allowing space for the onions and providing a double harvest from a single space.

Flowers abounded in Plimoth gardens, but not as deliberate additions. Although the colonists greatly appreciated their beauty, blooms were incidental in these first gardens; plants were chosen for their usefulness, not their aesthetic value. If flowers occured, all the better. It wasn't until much later that more prosperous circumstances permitted the luxury of planting solely for beauty's sake.

So what can we learn from these first, simple gardens? Many things, but perhaps most important, the value of space—the idea that each and every garden area should justify its existence and should produce something for the greater good of the landscape, whether of a practical, tangible value or a purely aesthetic one. Too many parts of our modern landscapes merely exist without purpose or definition. This is ridiculous, especially given the ever-shrinking and ever-more-costly nature of our land resources. "Waste not, want not" goes the old adage, and it's never been truer than in today's gardens. It's time, again, to concern ourselves with how we relate to our land and how it relates to us.

A 2,000-Year-Old Tip From Plimoth

Ancient Indian lore tells how the crow brought corn to man as a gift from the gods thousands of years ago, making Native Americans this continent's first gardeners. In fact, it was the Wampanoag Indians who showed the first European settlers at Plimoth how to plant and sow

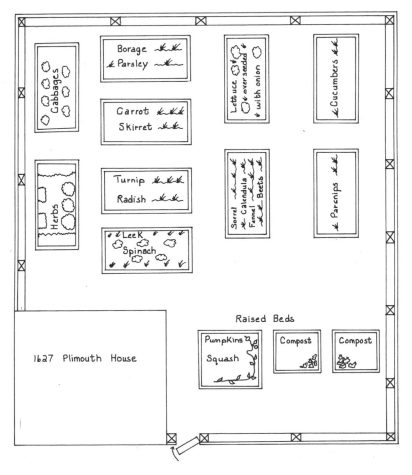

A typical garden plan from Plimoth Plantation. (Illustration by Penny Delany.)

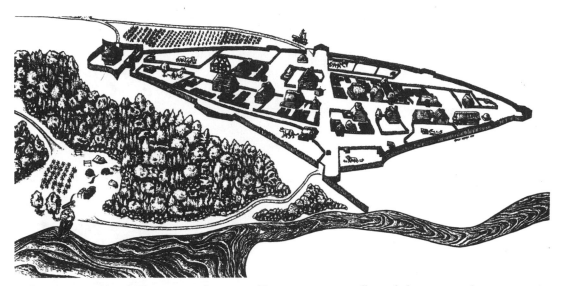

In this overview of Plimoth Plantation, garden space and house space are practically equal, demonstrating the importance of these gardens to the first settlers.

corn, without which they surely would have perished during their first tenuous years. The Indian method of planting was completely different from the European way, as the Native American system managed to take from the land without polluting or depleting it, demanded much less work, and produced much greater harvests. I was fascinated to learn about this ancient tradition at the Wampanoag village at Plimoth Plantation. Not only is their system extremely clever, in that it incorporates the best aspects of what we would today call "companion planting," but it also produces a highly balanced and nutritious crop of beans, corn, and squash, all from the same square-foot mound and without chemicals. Small garden owners take note: If you have always wanted to grow corn in your garden but avoided it because it would take up too much room, try this: You'll be happy you did.

First, dig a 6-inch-deep hole and throw in a dead fish or several fish heads. (Fish emulsion fertilizer will work well enough for the fishless, though I must say, having tried it both ways, the real thing works better.) Cover up the fish (or fertilizer) and form a mound about 5 inches high. Make as many mounds as you wish and space these about 3 feet apart. Plant your corn in the center of the mound. Modern varieties may be used, but you may want to experiment with some of the interesting heirloom types now available. When the corn has reached hand-height, plant pole beans (any variety of climbing beans will do) immediately around the corn, and then plant squash around the outside of the mound. Now here's the neat part: You have just planted a perfectly balanced miniature habitat. As the corn grows taller and takes nitrogen from the soil, the beans, which add nitrogen to the soil, use the bare lower stalks of the corn as a natural trellis. In the meantime, the prickly-haired, large-leaved squash (or watermelons, or pumpkins—all were traditionally grown) happily spreads out along the ground from the base of the mound, keeping the soil naturally moist and shaded, preventing the growth of extraneous weeds and discouraging animals (and children) with their scratchy leaves. By autumn, you'll have a rich harvest of corn, squash, and beans and an enriched garden, all from a single 2,000-year-old tip. What more could you ask?

SCHEMATIC LAYOUT OF A 1627 COLONIAL KITCHEN GARDEN AT PLIMOTH PLANTATION

Cabbage (Coles)	Cabbage: *Brassica oleracea var. capitata* Cauliflower: *Brassica oleracea var. botrytis*	Annual	A basic staple of the English diet. Coles also include cauliflower and coleworts.
Angelica	*Angelica archangelica*	Biennial	Used in food and medicine. Grows 3- to 6-foot with interesting yellow-green flowers and seeds.
Mustard or Garden Cress	*Brassica juncea*	Annual	A typical addition to salads in the period.
Borage	*Borago officinalis*	Annual	A much-beloved and beautiful plant with blue star-shaped edible flowers.
Calendula	*Calendula officinalis*	Annual	Edible yellow, gold, and orange cress-like flowers. Also called pot marigolds.
Parsley	*Petroselinum crispum*	Biennial	A basic kitchen staple recognized for its diuretic properties.
Carrot	*Daucus carota sativa*	Biennial[1]	Often found in its early white form.
Skirret	*Sium sisarum*	Perennial	Today an heirloom, this root crop was common throughout the 17th century.

Turnip	*Brassica rapa*	Annual	An early New England staple root crop.
Radish	*Raphanus sativus*	Annual	Eaten with salt and bread or added to salads. Radish "cods" or seed pods were added to salads and pickled.
Leek	*Allium porrum*	Annual	Sometimes planted as a "companion" border around a bed of tender salad greens to keep out garden pests.
Spinach	*Spinacia oleracea*	Annual	Common salad herb eaten both cooked and fresh.
Onion	*Allium cepa*	Annual	Staple root crop used in food and medicine. Also companion planted to keep out "garden fleas" (aphids) from tender salad plants overplanted in the same beds.
Lettuce	*Lactuca sativa*	Annual	The Cos and Romaine varieties were common salad ingredients.
Cucumber	*Cucumis sativus*	Annual	Common vine plant eaten fresh, in salads, or pickled. Planted on hills or mounds
Beet	*Beta vulgaris*	Annual	Used for greens, as well as the roots.
Fennel	*Foeniculum vulgare*	Biennial or Annual	Common culinary and medicinal plant with edible leaf, seed, and flower.
Sorrel	*Rumex acetosa*	Perennial	One of the first "roots and buds" of spring. Culinary and medicinal. Lemon-flavored leaf used in salads, soups, and sauces

Parsnip	*Pastinaca sativa*	Annual	Staple root crop. Culinary and medicinal.
Pumpkin	*Cucurbita pepo*	Annual	New World vine fruit adopted early into English diet.
Hyssop	*Hyssopus officianlis*	Perennial	Medicinal and culinary herb used for its properties as an expectorant and for flavoring.
Gillyflower	*Dianthus caryophyllus*	Perennial	Fragrant edible and medicinal flower fondly known as pinks or clove gillyflower.
Rosemary	*Rosmarinus officinalis*	Perennial or Annual[2]	Medicinal, pot herb, culinary, and ceremonial were common.
Burnet	*Poterium sanguisorba*	Perennial	Later known as Salad Burnet. Used for culinary, medicinal, salad, and pot herb purposes.
Feverfew	*Parthenium chrysanthemum*	Annual	Self-sowing. Added to food for its medicinal properties, to aid digestion and ease migraines
Thyme	*Thymus vulgaris*	Perennial	Creeping favorite with edible leaves and flowers for culinary and medicinal uses.
Violet	*Viola odorata*	Perennial	Early garden favorite. Leaves and flowers used in salads, fragrant oils, and medicines.
Sage	*Salvia officinalis*	Perennial	Edible leaf and flower. Pot and medicinal herb. Sage buds used in butter or sage ale.

Rue	*Ruta graveolens*	Perennial	Silver-blue foliage with yellow flowers. Used medicinally.
Winter Savory	*Satureja montana*	Perennial	Savory pot herb with edible leaf and flower.
Elecampane	*Inula helenium*	Perennial	Stately 5- to 7-foot medicinal with yellow flowers. Root used to treat deep cough and phlegm.
Southern Wood	*Artemisia abrotanum*	Perennial	Fragrant strewing/worming plant also used to keep away moths.
Tansy	*Tanacetum vulgare*	Perennial	Medicinal and culinary herb, also strewn to keep away ants.
Wormwood	*Artemisia absinthium*	Perennial	Tall silver-gray medicinal plant.
Marjoram	*Origanum vulgare*	Perennial	Pot herb with edible leaves and attractive pink-purple or white flowers.
Blessed Thistle	*Cnicus benedictus*	Annual	A medicinal bitter herb used for digestive ailments.
Houseleek	*Sempervivum tectorum*	Perennial	Currently known as Hens and Chicks. Used like aloe during the Colonial period. Also used to patch holes in roofs.

[1]Harvested as annual.
[2]Depending on climate and care.

Historic Garden

A Question of History: Colonial Williamsburg

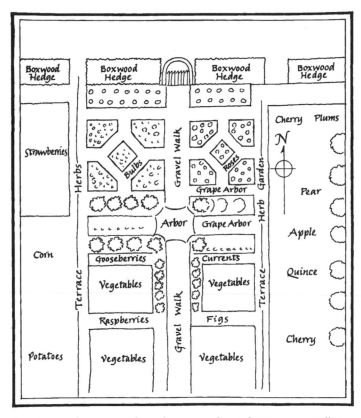

Sometimes garden memories last a long time—late in life Benjamin Waller's great-great-granddaughter Luty drew her grandmother's garden, which had been designed after Waller's. Amazingly, archaeological research in Waller's garden revealed that her sketch was quite similar to the design discovered by the excavations, though far less elaborate than the garden as actually restored (see page 25). (Courtesy of Princeton University Press. Used by permission.)

One thing to keep in mind when talking about studying the history of American gardens (or gardens anywhere, for that matter) is that it is not by any means an exact science. By their very nature, gardens are transitory, ethereal creations, and very, very few—if any—remain much as they were originally designed. The natural cycles of life and death, if nothing else, have seen to that. And, of course, the farther back we go in time, the shakier our knowledge becomes. Garden history is to a large degree based on assumptions and indirect documentary sources, such as period engravings, correspondence by the garden owners, plant lists made by individuals and nurseries, and a scant handful of sourcebooks. Thus, except in a few rare cases, historical garden re-creation is an exercise in interpretation of the probable—an evocation of the past, not a duplication of it, and subject to revision as new information comes to light. There is no better example of this than the gardens of Colonial Williamsburg.

To a large extent, the gardens of Williamsburg have come to represent the idea of the "Colonial garden" to many Americans. Each year, hundreds of thousands of visitors to this living museum wander through landscapes of undeniable beauty, full of intricate topiaries, box-edged beds, flower-filled

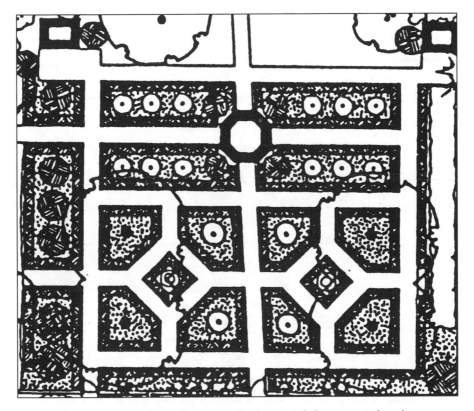

A section of the Benjamin Waller garden as restored. The octagonal above corresponds to the arbor in the illustration on the previous page. Notice how much more ornate the restored garden is than the original. (Drawing by M. Kent Brinkley, ASLA, used with permission. © 1996 Colonial Williamsburg Fdn. All rights reserved.)

borders, and elaborate fences and gates. They then return home and seek to duplicate a "Colonial" garden in their own yards. But how accurately "Colonial" are these Williamsburg models?

The short answer is that in terms of layout, the gardens of Williamsburg are quite historically accurate. Extensive archaeological work has revealed the path locations, placement of principal features and outbuildings, and the like. In effect, the "bones" of the gardens are true to Colonial form. These

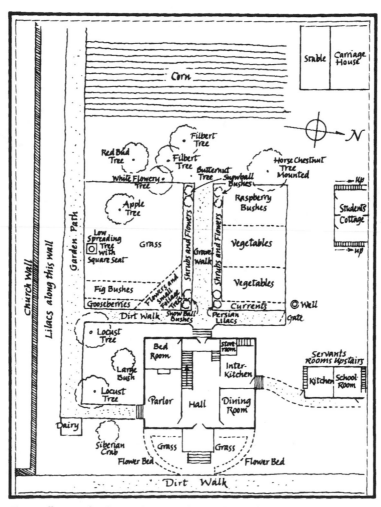

Kate Millington, daughter of the owner, drew a plan of the George Wythe house garden between 1837 and 1848. If you compare this plan to the garden as it was actually restored (see next page), you'll notice how the modern garden has been substantially improved by the restorers—a tendency that is often hard to avoid.

(Courtesy of Princeton University Press. Used by permission.)

results have also been validated by various other historical sources, such as letters, maps, and family archives, which have helped to fill out our understanding of these landscapes.

But the horticultural aspect of the Williamsburg gardens—that is, what was planted where and why—is much less clear. While we have fairly detailed plant lists from the period, we do not know exactly how these plants were used or the effects gardeners were trying to achieve with them. What we do

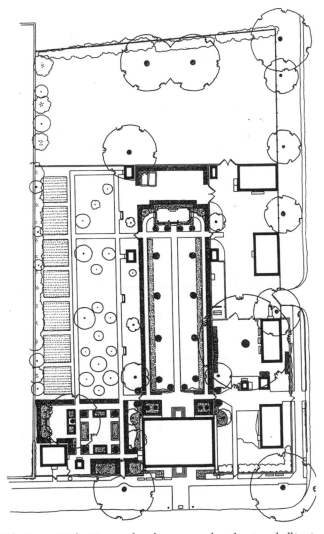

The George Wythe House and garden as restored, with a formal allée of shrubs and lawn replacing the more humble garden of mixed flowers, vegetables, and shrubs. (Drawing by M. Kent Brinkley, ASLA, used with permission. © 1996 Colonial Williamsburg Fdn. All rights reserved.)

know is that in terms of planting and effect, the restored gardens of Williamsburg have as much to do with the Colonial Revival style of the 20th century as they do with the Colonial period itself.

This makes a great deal of sense if you think about the changes that have occurred in the American landscape since the Revolutionary era. Early travelers to Williamsburg describe approaching the town through a series of rolling fields, with the cityscape visible from miles away. Individual houses and gardens also enjoyed these vistas, and the latest research indicates that many Williamsburg gardens were designed to take advantage of views through neighboring gardens into the general landscape beyond.

Of course, when Williamsburg was restored in the late 1920s and the 1930s, the original townscape was long gone, and the Colonial center was surrounded by what the museum's founders considered unsightly Victorian buildings. A deliberate attempt was made to isolate the restoration from any modern influence with large buffer groves and plantings. With the rampant urban growth in the area during the last few decades, this trend has only intensified.

This practice of enclosure and isolation managed to permeate the designs for the restored gardens as well. The re-created gardens followed the footprints of the old—walls and outbuildings were restored to their original condition, paths replaced, beds located as close as possible to their earlier sites—but the whole design concept was changed. The original outward-facing, open 18th-century landscape orientation gave way to gardens that were turned inward. Each landscape became an individual, distinctly independent garden setting, more in keeping with the 20th-century aesthetic of the garden as a private, intimate, personal space. The re-created gardens of Williamsburg are much more heavily enclosed, much more prettified, much more detailed than were the original gardens that occupied these sites. They are in effect Colonial *Revival* gardens.

Does any of this take away from the beauty and pleasure of these gardens? Certainly not. The gardens of Williamsburg teach important lessons about efficient space layout, unity of house and garden into a single unit, and division of space into logical, effective units. In their Americanized version of 18th-century European gardens, Colonial Revival gardens remain some of the most beautiful ever created in this country—and perfectly suited to many of the houses built from the late 18th century to the present era.

How-to: Finding the Ghosts in Your Garden

Before you do a thing—make a plot plan, buy a bush, or plant a petunia—do your garden a big favor. Go outside and take a hard look at what you have. Look especially for the venerable old presences in your garden—plants or features that have been there for a long time.

Some will be obvious—apple trees, oaks, and sprawling lilac bushes are all hard to miss. But some will be overgrown or covered over—these are the ghosts in your garden, and they're not only wonderful, they are important clues to your garden's history. Archaeologists know that one of the best times to look for ghosts in the garden is in high summer during the dry season. Buried and forgotten objects or features of your garden such as old foundation walls, walks, and drives will typically retain moisture long after the surrounding areas are dried out. The grass that covers them will remain visibly green, in contrast to the surrounding browned-out sections. The placement of old trees often gives valuable clues as well—chances are, if you have a line of old oak or apple trees, they once marked a boundary or drive of some sort.

As you review the various existing features of your garden, keep in mind a lesson I first learned from Thalassa Cruso, the great garden guru of the 1960s and '70s, who saved me from one of the biggest mistakes of my gardening career. In her book *Making Things Grow Outdoors*, she relates a story about how she was tempted to cut down a large tree on her property shortly after moving in because it darkened the house. She thought better of it, though, and decided to wait awhile. Thank goodness she did, for that very tree had been carefully planted to shield the house during the summer—the shade that had seemed so unwelcome in the early spring actually kept the house from turning into an inferno during the warmest months.

I had a similar situation here in Southborough, Massachusetts, shortly after I moved into my 1852 house. There were two large spruces about 25 feet off the north side of the house that at the time seemed stranded in the middle of nowhere. My immediate temptation was to take them down and design a new garden in that area. I had just reread Cruso's work, however, and I decided to wait and follow her advice. The following winter proved her point: not only did those two spruces shield the house from terrific northerly blasts all winter long, they also provided vital interest and refuge for a host of wildlife during the winter. As the Romans said, *festina lente!*

The point is, you need to determine what you have to begin with in your garden and treat it as the framework for your improvements. This does not mean that you can't cut something down just because it's old. It does mean that you need to move cautiously. Here is some good advice on the subject, which is as true today as it was when it was written centuries ago.

One is often in great straits when an old garden is to be set to rights without wholly destroying it. In such a case, an exact plan should be taken, and every part of it examined one after another before we condemn it. Above all, we should conform the buildings, wall basins, and canals, already made, unless they are exceedingly ill-placed and without destroying too much, in order to rectify every fault, redress only those that are most necessary, preserving as much as is possible, especially the Wood, Hedges, and Walks of High Trees, which are long in raising and which in this renewal should be looked upon as sacred, and be very little, if any at all, meddled with. This indeed requires a very provident and skilled hand, not such as are for cutting down and destroying everything to make way for their whimsical designs, of which one sees too many sad instances.

—Dezallier d'Argenville, *The Theory and Practice of Gardening* (1709)

Finally, keep your eyes open for other features of your garden that may be more reclusive. Certain plants are extremely long lived and often give indications of what the garden looked like years ago. Once when I was doing a historically correct garden plan of an 1870s Italianate mansion in Boston, I was faced with considerable uncertainty as to the historical accuracy of my final design, since very little documentary evidence existed for the property. I had first seen the property in winter, and I returned to meet with the clients on a beautiful March day, brisk but sunny.

As I approached the house in my car, I noticed that there were a few small white specks waving in the lawn. Curious, I got out of the car and in the still-brown grass found circles of the tiniest snowdrops. There was no clue in the current lawn that there had ever been beds, nor were there any old pictures of the house that we knew of. But there, like silent ghostly witnesses, stood the hardy little snowdrops, still blooming after almost a century of neglect. When viewed from above, the pattern of bulbs showed that there had existed an elaborate layout of beds along what had once undoubtedly been a semicircular drive. With this evidence, I was able to recreate the original layout with complete confidence, all due to the faithful testament of those tiny snowdrops.

So be on the lookout for something old in the garden—you never know when it may teach you something new.

Snowdrop

*U*nity

Of all the important principles that made old gardens so successful, the first and broadest was the unity of house and yard. Historically, the entire property, buildings and garden together, was considered a single element. The grounds were as important as any room in the house and worked with the structure to better the property as a whole. The particular ways in which this unity was constructed in any one garden depended on climate and on the owner's taste, needs, and (of course) budget.

A good example of this is the garden illustrated on the next page, drawn by Arthur Shurcliff (or Shurtleff, before he Anglicized his name), one of the greatest historical landscape architects of the 20th century and the person responsible for laying out the gardens at Colonial Williamsburg and Sturbridge

Village. Although not of a specific site, the plan is an excellent composite of many Colonial gardens in towns throughout the Virginias. This lot is approximately 100 by 250 feet, with the house sitting cozily more or less front and center. The multiple independent outbuildings were a unique feature of southern gardens. As the winters were not severe, southerners tended to design their gardens with a large number of separate secondary structures scattered along the garden's edge, which removed most of the practical (read: hot and smelly) work areas—the dairy, smokehouse, privy, and often even the kitchen—from the main house. This arrangement helped to unify garden and house into a single unit, as day-to-day functions could only be accomplished by passing constantly from house to garden, garden to house. Each part of the landscape related to the other, and all parts related to the house.

Instead of plantings immediately around the house and outbuildings to link the architecture to the garden landscape, a series of right-angled paths (perhaps edged in boxwood at more prosperous homes) provided intimate communication between house and landscape. The flower areas were intermingled with the more practical areas of vegetable and fruit growing, which were an integral part of almost every Colonial garden and were set near the house for viewing and tending. The lot was fenced off from its neighbors, which also helped to tie the house to the landscape.

The gardens of Colonial New England were similar in style, but their design was looser than that of southern gardens and was more adapted to the harsh climate of the rolling, rocky countryside. In the North, the symmetrical alignment of house and garden was less important than in the South: although designed in the same geometric style, the garden often lay to the side of or at an angle to the main house. Independent outbuildings were also less common in the North, where the cold-winter climate by necessity joined the functions of farm and family more intimately together.

This arrangement can be seen prominently in the plan of the Daniels/Freeman farm in Cornish, New Hampshire. The property dated to about 1800 and was studied by Shurcliff in

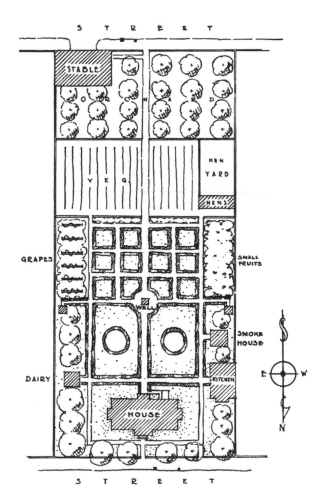

While this plan is a composite of several gardens, it gives a very good idea of the features of early Colonial gardens in the South. Note the many outbuildings scattered throughout the garden.

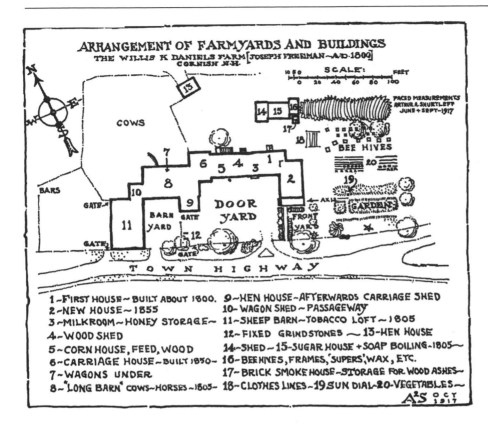

ARRANGEMENT OF FARMYARDS AND BUILDINGS
THE WILLIS K. DANIELS FARM [JOSEPH FREEMAN~A.D.1800]
CORNISH N.H.

1~FIRST HOUSE ~ BUILT ABOUT 1800.
2~NEW HOUSE ~ 1855
3~MILKROOM ~ HONEY STORAGE~
4~WOOD SHED
5~CORN HOUSE, FEED, WOOD
6~CARRIAGE HOUSE ~ BUILT 1850~
7~WAGONS UNDER
8~"LONG BARN" COWS~HORSES~1805~
9~HEN HOUSE~AFTERWARDS CARRIAGE SHED
10~WAGON SHED ~ PASSAGEWAY
11~SHEEP BARN~TOBACCO LOFT~1805
12~FIXED GRINDSTONES ~ 13~HEN HOUSE
14~SHED ~ 15~SUGAR HOUSE + SOAP BOILING~1805~
16~BEEHIVES, FRAMES, SUPERS, WAX, ETC.
17~BRICK SMOKE HOUSE~STORAGE FOR WOOD ASHES~
18~CLOTHES LINES~19 SUN DIAL~20~VEGETABLES~

Owing to the harsh winters, Northern gardens were often structured around a rambling house, which united all functions of the property—house, sheds, gardens, and even barns—in close, covered proximity.

1917 while it was still fairly intact. As was typical in the region, the various buildings of the farm were all joined together to afford sheltered passage between them during long, snowy winters. The house was placed extremely close to the road to allow the easiest access possible when the town "broke out" the snowbound roads with ox ploughs. Although remarkably simple in design, this farm shows how closely the house was linked to garden, work areas, and pastures. In this working landscape, form followed function. All the needs and necessities of living were provided for in the garden: yard area for animals and farm chores, drying space for clothes, vegetable plots, flower gardens.

Nor did the North lack for more sophisticated, purely aesthetic gardens. The figure on the next page shows the plan of a town garden in the Salem-Newburyport-Portsmouth area, again drawn by Shurcliff. The structure of this garden is a little more carefree than that of the Virginia garden. As Shurcliff put it: "[In keeping with their Puritan creators,] the garden patterns are all rectangular and relate in the most frugal way to the boundaries of the lot. . . . There is no effort at display here. The grounds were arranged conveniently for the pleasure of the family and to secure the least cost of upkeep."

Obviously not all gardens in the Colonial period were exactly like these

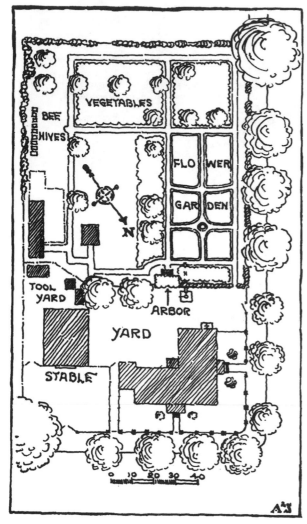

VEGETABLES

BEE HIVES

FLO WER

GAR DEN

N

TOOL YARD

ARBOR

YARD

STABLE

0 10 20 30 40

A'J

Even on difficult sites, where the hilly terrain made the garden layout difficult, there was always a very clear relationship between house and garden. Notice how in this Colonial garden plan the main axis of this property extends from the front door, right through the house, through the arbor, and up the garden path.

examples, and it is true, too, that both the Virginia and the Salem gardens belonged to people in the wealthier segments of society. What is clear, though, is that even in the humbler gardens, such as the one at the New Hampshire farmhouse, much care and thought were given to the layout of the grounds in order to enhance the important relationship between house and garden.

Since from the beginning of our gardening history the house and landscape were inextricably linked, changes in one meant adaptations in the other. The two worked together to produce our idea of home, cityscape, and countryside. This continued to be true as the Colonial period ended and we entered the 19th century. As Victorian architecture became more free-form and less symmetrical, so did Victorian landscapes. This looser design was perfectly acceptable for these houses, and indeed even appropriate, because the style of house and the style of garden complemented each other and together formed a whole.

Suburbia was born during this period, thanks partly to the ideas and vision of the great 19th-century designer Frank J. Scott. To decorate the new suburban houses, he proposed a landscape style that was the "art of picture making and picture framing, by means of the varied forms of vegetable growth." Reasoning that good gardening "renders the Dwelling the central interest of a picture," Scott asserted that decorative gardening and competent architecture would produce homes "with an air of extent and domesticity that so many of the box-like suburban houses of the day are totally wanting in." (Valuable advice much ignored today!)

Scott's plan (see next page) shows what this meant in practical terms for the Victorian homeowner. By far the most striking characteristic, in comparison with landscapes today, is once again the complete linkage between the house and the garden. The faint dashed lines radiating from the house are sight lines, which appear in almost all plans of the period. These sight lines indicate important views and focal points in the landscape—as seen from the house. Although quite simple, sight lines seem an almost foreign concept today, given the way most landscapes are constructed—from the outside, passing through them, with the garden and the house as two separate entities. These days gardens are mistakenly planned by well-intentioned homeowners and designers as a series of miniature, unrelated vignettes—plantings to be viewed from the street, shrubs around the pool, a flower bed along the walk. These mini stage sets were important to the Victorians as well, but only as part of the larger picture. First and foremost came the house and its relation to the garden. This is crucial to understanding American gardens of this period and also to diagnosing the sorry state of American landscapes today. For the Victorians, the "home grounds" were an essential part of the house itself, carefully designed to link the work of man with that of nature.

On Scott's plan, the house is tied to the grounds

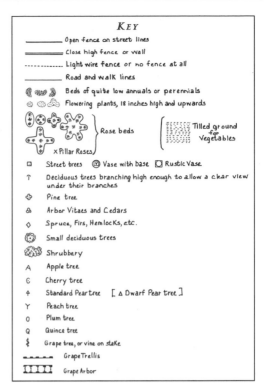

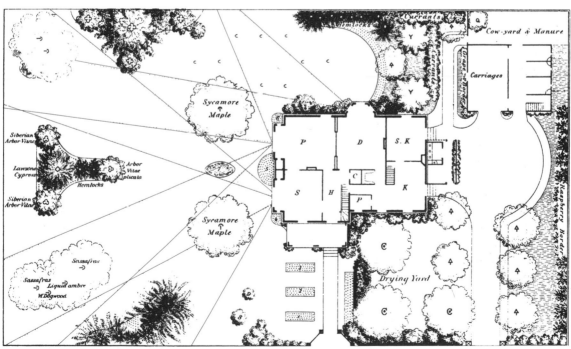

In this 1870 Frank Scott garden, you will find all the elements prized by the Victorians: good sight lines from the house, well-placed trees, shrubs, and annual beds, beautifully laid-out walks and drives—even a special lawn for croquet, complete with wickets!

with wide and ample walkways, in much the same way as the Colonial Virginia house was. Carriage drives flow up to and around the structures, locking them in place. Wide paths allow free and easy access from house to garden, where ample areas are set aside for flowers, vegetables and fruits, select ornamental shrubs, gaming, and even more utilitarian needs. (You can even see a privy, the four-hole structure attached to the rear of the house and shielded by grape vines. Privies were common features in most American gardens until the beginning of the 20th century—and are usually the one garden feature not even the most avid historical gardener talks about re-creating!)

As the century progressed and the later Victorian architectural styles arrived, the important relationship between house and garden remained: each showcased the best aspects of the other. Gertrude Jekyll and William Robinson in England introduced a new approach to flower gardening, replacing the large, artificial bedding-out schemes with complicated, more "naturalistic" borders filled with perennials and flowering shrubs. Despite these changes in flower-planting materials and style, the concept of a unified house and garden remained in place, on grand estates and humble properties alike, until after World War II.

Today our properties look distinctly disunited, and this is one of the reasons our yards have lost so much character. If you drive through any of our towns and suburbs, you are likely to see vast, unused areas, covered in an amorphous mass of grass, with no rhyme or reason for their existence and no apparent relationship to the house. If individual elements of the landscape do exist, generally they are thrown together higgledy-piggledy, as if some giant child had tossed toys in the air and left them wherever they fell: a clump of trees here, a pool there, perhaps a barbecue there; flower border slung off to one side, walkway to nowhere on the other, and a few miscellaneous garden ornaments thrown in for good measure. Many elements exist in today's gardens simply because at one point they were required, or someone liked them, or the contractor had a few extra on hand, without any consideration about how they relate to the house and to the property as a whole. This is contrary to how American gardens were once laid out, and it is certainly something to be avoided today.

This idea of unity is fundamental to understanding what is awry in the American landscape. House and garden have historically been one, and we need to think again of the inside and outside functioning as a single, united entity, each part complementing the other's best aspects and each helping to ameliorate the worst parts of both.

So how to begin? The first step in this process is to take a careful look around the landscape, and begin to chart out your house and garden so that you can take a look at your property as a whole, which is the subject of the how-to sections in the next chapters.

 The Urban Garden

Given the number of people gardening in cities these days, there is a lot of interest in what urban gardens traditionally looked like. Unfortunately we don't have many accurate models, due as much to the rapid pace of change and reconstruction in urban environments as to the rarity of urban gardens in the first place. Until well into the 20th century, you were much more likely to find a servants' work area or an ash heap in the backyard of a small city house than some sort of garden hideaway. The reason for this was simple: when the boundaries of cities and towns were only minutes from the unspoiled countryside (and I do mean real countryside, not the awful suburban sprawl we have today), there was much less of an incentive to garden in a difficult urban environment. Also, it was much more common for the wealthier classes, historically the biggest promoters and creators of gardens, to have another, "country" house to which they retired when bucolic pleasures beckoned.

That is not to say, however, that urban gardens didn't exist; since Roman times there have been inveterate gardeners who have overcome the challenges of city gardening to achieve their mini-Edens. And there are a few American models that tell us something about the city gardens our Colonial ancestors grew. In general they were simply miniature versions of larger country gardens. The compact, formalized plans of Williamsburg, Salem, and Savannah show us that small urban gardens of the 18th and early 19th centuries followed the same trends and styles as did their bigger country cousins, perhaps even more successfully, as the generally square lots and immediate presence of the house forced a close and intimate relationship between home and garden.

As the Victorian period opened, though, growing city populations without recourse to country gardens accelerated the urban gardening movement, and city green space became

Left: A small Victorian front garden invites the guest to enter. Note the ample paving and decorative clay edging tile. Right: This New York City garden shows the lush exuberance many Victorians aimed for in their planting beds. Not one inch of space is left unadorned.

much more common. A desperate New York City gardener wrote to the editor at *Vick's Illus-trated Monthly Magazine* in 1878 and complained:

It is pleasant to read your books and dream of the country, and what can we poor folks do but dream, who are shut up between brick walls, with only perhaps twenty feet square of back-yard?

The reply was quick:

Do! why almost anything that is undertaken with a will. Only a short time ago we received a photograph of a garden "in the heart" of the great city, and we have had it engraved to show our correspondent that something can be done besides dreaming about gardens, even in the great metropolis (see previous page, illustration on right). The sketch was accompanied by the following remarks: "I enclose a stereoscopic view of a back yard, 18 × 30 feet, showing what can be done in the way of beautifying a home, even in the heart of the city of New York. At a very small out-lay for bulbs and seeds, we had flowers all summer, and were never at a loss to make up a very fine bouquet. The yard has been admired by every one who has seen it, and from a distance had the appearance of one vast bouquet of flowers and variegated foliage. The subtropical system [presumably the writer massed large quantities of tender plants together fairly randomly] *works much better in a place like mine than the ribbon or other sys-tems of planting* [that is, organized geometric beds]. *Cannas, Ricinus, Caladiums, Coleus, Dahlias, Gladiolus &c., do all very well in a city yard, and with some care taken in planting them a very fine effect can be produced, even on a small scale."*

Viewing this picture today, what may amaze modern readers is how many plants and dif-ferent garden features are crammed into such small spaces. This really shouldn't surprise us, though, given the gilded-to-the-hilt nature of authentic Victorian interiors.

So how do you go about restoring or re-creating a historically correct urban garden? You proceed in the same way you would in a much larger suburban or country plot, with a few ad-ditional caveats. The first is that you must make sure that every portion of garden space ful-fills at least one purpose. There can be no slack in tiny gardens: every section has to do double, often even triple, duty. The existence of any empty space must be justified.

Second, it is *especially* important that the garden layout and elements are in complete sym-pathy with the house—in the urban garden, you are right on top of the architecture, so it is essential that there are no clashes in style, shape, color, or texture between house and garden. (We'll discuss specific examples of clashes and how to avoid these later on.)

Finally, it is crucial that a small garden appears to be a seamless extension of the indoors, not an individual, separate unit: entrance and egress must flow effortlessly between inside and out. This is the case with larger gardens, too, but once again infinitely more important in the small-scale garden. One of the best ways to achieve this is to make sure that the plantings soften the lines of the hardscape (the nonliving elements of the landscape), thereby blurring the division between house and yard. Vines are perfect for this but are often overlooked in modern gardens. A water feature is something else you might consider—the tactile, auditory, and visual pleasures of moving water have made it an important part of urban gardens for over two thousand years. Whatever elements you use, with a little determination and a bit of elbow grease, you, too, can create your own urban oasis.

Historic Garden

The Unified Whole: Washington Irving's Sunnyside

An early view of Irving's Sunnyside. (Illustration courtesy of Historic Hudson Valley, Tarrytown, New York.)

After spending many years abroad as America's first man of letters, in 1835 Washington Irving returned to his beloved Hudson River valley, where he had spent his youth and set many of his works. It was there that he chose to make his personal Eden, next to his "grand and noble" river. Irving bought a run-down, 10-acre farm along the water's edge near Tarrytown, New York, and immediately began to push out the walls of the simple 17th-century cottage he had found there. (The original house had been built in 1690, but enchanted by everything old, and never one to hesitate telling a tall tale, Irving had *"1656"* emblazoned in large iron letters on the gable overlooking the river and often delighted in telling gullible visitors fictional accounts about the previous inhabitants.)

By the time he was finished, Irving had created an elaborately gabled Dutch Revival cottage complete with a Spanish tower and with a picturesque landscape that captured the ideals of the Romantic movement. For the intellectuals of this group, the new industrial age of the early 19th century held little aesthetic appeal: the old simple country ways, which had previously provided a direct and heartfelt communion with the natural world, seemed a much better model. In their view, *nature* reigned supreme in the world; the works of man reached their acme only when they imitated the flow and pattern of nature itself. Thus it was not surprising that Irving, following the advice of landscape architect Andrew Jackson Downing and many others in this coterie, carefully constructed a picturesque landscape to reflect the Romantic ideal.

Prior to Irving's tenancy, the parcel had been working agricultural land. Although Irving did succeed in gathering the occasional harvest (managing the "roughs," as he called it), the acreage quickly developed into a *ferme ornée* (literally a "decorated farm") where each element was carefully crafted to cre-

Irving encouraged publicity about Sunnyside, sensing that it would secure his fame as the preeminent American Romantic. This illustration, published in Harper's New Monthly Magazine *in December, 1856, captured the idyllic vision of the Hudson. The train, which in reality so bothered Irving, is here just another picturesque element.*

The Cottage – South view.

Sunnyside became a popular tourist destination and frequently appeared in tourist guides and books on the Hudson region. This drawing was published in the 1800s in Sketchbook Leisure Hours *by Evie A. Todd.*

ate the almost dreamlike effect of a landscape untouched by humans. The more practical elements of the landscape—the large kitchen garden, service courtyard, orchard, and farming areas—were tucked discreetly out of sight. Irving's house and grounds became famous in their day, the epitome of the genteel rural existence espoused by so many writers of the era.

The melding of artificial and natural elements into a seamless, unified whole is the pervasive theme at Sunnyside. The house sits quite deliberately at the *bottom* of the slope, hugging the hillside so as not to call attention to itself. The structure, unlike most others of the day, was almost completely covered in vines. Irving had intentionally planted wisteria and trumpet vine, which at the time were both recently imported novelties, to give the house an impression of age, along with English ivy from Melrose Abbey, the home of his idol, Sir Walter Scott. Throughout, the structure was intimately commingled with the outdoors. Large windows and French doors looked out over the majestic Hudson, and a little Gothic "piazza" off the main sitting room allowed for the easy flow of people in and out on warm evenings. Irving managed to link even that most protean element of the landscape, water, to the dwelling: besides perching his house just above the river's edge, he diverted one of the many runnels on the property to form a large pond, which he called the "Little Mediterranean." From this, several streams embraced the approach drive on their way past the house to the river, while an elaborate gravitational system of piping brought this same crystal-clear springwater directly into the kitchen—quite an innovation for its time.

Sunnyside's fame was such that it even appeared in advertisements. Here buxom ladies were added to the landscape to spice things up for a 19th century tobacco lid.

From the house, the landscape rolled romantically up the hill, revealing meadows, woodlands, rustic seats, and narrow stone bridges leaping over rushing brooks. The material for the latter two elements was all completely natural—wood from the forests and stone from the hills, constructed in a simple, rustic style. Only the fencing was visibly artificial. (Although despising the industrialized world, many of the Romantics, like Irving, didn't hesitate to embrace the latest innovations: Irving's fencing was a clever system of modular iron components that could be easily taken apart and reconfigured into a different fence line as needed.)

Although the landscape was designed to look completely natural, it is amazing how much contrivance the carefully thought-out and executed design actually required. Trees were planted just for their aesthetic weeping appeal; vistas were opened, or closed, and framed as needed; water was channeled and land completely recontoured. (Only one man-made intrusion couldn't be overcome: soon after Irving purchased the property, the train line was put through right along the Hudson shore beneath his house. Irving tolerated this situation for the sake of the view, simply moving his own bedroom to the far side of the house.)

Today Sunnyside is a perfect example of the Romantic landscape design that was so prevalent in the early part of the 19th century. Although the scale and scope of the estate are beyond today's average homeowner, the landscape still teaches valuable lessons about the charming effects to be achieved when house and landscape act as one.

Climbers

Exactly why vines have become so neglected as useful elements in the American landscape is puzzling, since no garden from the Colonial era onward would have been considered complete without them, nor should our gardens today. Viewed as the garden's "draperies," vines were an integral part of the overall landscape scheme, either linking disparate sections in a profusion of foliage or else hiding unsightly portions from view. As visual aids, vining plants are invaluable—no other type of plant material does this job so effectively.

There are numerous ways to use vines in the landscape—hiding old stumps, climbing up trees, shading trellises and arbors, covering fences with flowers, and, the most classic of all, growing up walls of houses.

If you are one of those people who think that vines

This delicate Chinese wisteria, which arrived on our shores in about 1816, has been gracing American gardens ever since.

The magnificent iron arbor shows not only the decorative possibilities of vines in the landscape, but also the value of well-designed garden structures.

aren't good for houses, you're wrong. You just need to take some precautions. Most vines can be classified in one of two groups: vines that twine around a support in order to remain upright and vines that use "holdfasts," a type of modified root, to attach to the wall. It's these latter that have given house vines a bad name, because the holdfasts may damage the house's wooden siding. If your home has wooden clapboards, then choose one of the shorter twining vines and provide a separate means of support. Select a very sturdy trellis, and before you install it, place "feet" on the back of the four corners and in the center to keep the trellis an inch or two off the house, which will prevent the buildup of moisture and rot. (Old wine-bottle corks screwed onto the back of the trellis work well for this. Think of it as a good excuse to drink more wine!) Then hang the trellis on several hooks and be sure to secure it at the base so the wind can't get behind the whole assemblage and rip it from the wall. When the clapboards need repainting, the whole trellis can be lifted off the house, vines and all, and laid flat on the ground. If your house is made of brick, stone, or stucco or is sided, then you needn't worry; either the twining or holdfast varieties will work fine.

The following table gives some information on the best vines for landscape use, along with their approximate dates of introduction to this country. Those that climb by holdfasts are noted. If you are interested in learning more about the growing habits of these vines, Donald Wyman's *Shrubs and Vines for American Gardens* is a classic. For more historical information, including other vines and changes in nomenclature, Leighton's works are also invaluable. (See bibliography on page 321.)

Woodbine on a small-town church. Also known as Virginia Creeper, this vine has been a favorite for covering buildings since the Revolution.

Botanical Name	Common Name	Description	Zone	Year of Introduction
Actinidia kolomikta	Kiwi vine	This 15'–20' climber often pictured in garden catalogs has leaves striped with pink and white—*if* you can find a male plant and *if* it finds calcareous soil to its liking!	5	1855
Adlumia fungosa	Climbing fumitory	This biennial vine, grown as an annual, has pinkish blossoms in a loose cluster. Great for hiding unsightly views. Best in semishade. 15'.	Annual/ biennial	Native; since early 1800s
Akebia quinata	Fiveleaf akebia	Charming twiner. One of the best foliage vines according to Wyman. 30'–40'.	4/5	1845
Aristolochia durior	Dutchman's pipe	Huge, roundish leaves and long, pipelike flowers make this one of my favorites. Note: Leaves are poisonous if consumed. Twiner. 30'.	4	Native; since Colonial times
Bignonia capreolata	Cross vine	A popular vine in the South that climbs by tendrils. Profuse orange-red flowers in late May and reddish green leaves in the fall. 60'.	6	Native; before 1800

Botanical Name	Common Name	Description	Zone	Year of Introduction
Campsis radicans	Trumpet vine	Brilliant orange-red flowers in midsummer. 40'. Climbs by holdfasts.	4	Native; before 1800
Clematis paniculata	Sweet autumn clematis	Loads of sweet-scented flowers in the fall. Twiner. 15'.	5	1864
Dolichos lablab	Hyacinth bean	This lovely annual with purplish green leaves and long purple-and-white flowers was a favorite of Thomas Jefferson's. To 10'.	Annual 9	Late 1700s
Hedera helix	English ivy	Evergreen vine that suffers from winter damage north of Zone 6. Climbs by holdfasts. 30'.	5/6	Early Colonial times, with many later introductions
Ipomoea purpurea	Morning glory	Lovely vine in a variety of colors.	Annual	Early 1800s
Ipomoea quamoclit	Cypress vine	A tropical grown as an annual in the North, this tendril climber has scarlet, tubelike flowers that bloom from August to October.	Annual 9	Early 1800s
Lonicera flava	Yellow honeysuckle	Twining vine with fragrant orange-yellow flowers in June. 20'–30'.	5	Native; since Colonial era; other varieties introduced later
Lycium halimifolium	Boxthorn	With small lilac-purple flowers in late June and red fruits in the fall, this is not actually a vine but a rambling shrub.	5	Early Colonial era
Mina lobata	Crimson starglory	This exotic, with its lovely foliage and exquisite flowers that turn from yellow to red, is one of the best of the annuals. To 20'.	Annual 10	Late 1800s
Parthenocissus quinquefolia	Woodbine Virginia creeper	Climbs by tendrils. Great for houses or arbors. Brilliant red fall color. To 50'.	4	Native; since Colonial era
Parthenocissus tricuspidata	Boston ivy	Lustrous leaves and dark berries. Great for clinging to wall or stonework. Rootlike holdfasts. To 60'.	3/4	1862
Phaseolus coccineus	Scarlet runner bean	The bright red flowers and subsequent bean pods make this twiner a hit with the kids. To 15'.	Annual	Early 1800s
Polygonum aubertii	Chinese fleece vine	This hardy tendril climber may grow 20' in a season. White blooms appear in late summer, hence the common name. 60'.	4/5	1899
Thunbergia alata	Clock vine	Native to South America, this vine is treated as an annual in the North. White to orange flowers with purple throats. 15'.	Annual 10	Early 1800s
Wisteria species	Wisteria	Fragrant flowers dangle in lovely racemes from this romantic twiner. 50'–60'.	5	*W. sinensis*, 1816; *W. floribunda*, 1830; many later cultivars

How-To: Sizing Up Your Property, Part One

The importance of planning can't be overstated: "draw twice, dig once," as my grandfather used to say. This gardener has drawn a big plan, framed it, and taken it outside to consult as he works.

Before you move your first spadeful of dirt, you need to begin with a good, accurate plot plan. Don't scrimp on this—it's really important. The easiest way, of course, is to hire a landscape professional to chart out the property. But it's not very difficult to draw your own plan, and even if you decide later to engage a designer, you will save yourself considerable time and money, not to mention get a better garden, if you do some of the groundwork yourself.

First, you'll need to gather a few things: some sharpened pencils; graph paper in various sizes (a pad 8$^1/_2$ × 11 and several sheets as big as you can find); measuring tapes, one 50–100 feet and another 25 feet (the new handheld electric measurers are great for this type of work); a compass; a yardstick; a mortgage plot plan (this will save a lot of time); and house architectural plans, if available.

Begin by looking at your house, as it is obviously the focal point of your property. What architectural style is it? This is crucial to selecting the type of landscape that is ultimately appropriate for your home. One absolutely fantastic resource, and a book no old-house buff should be without, is *A Field Guide to American Houses* by Virginia and Lee McAlester. It contains everything you need to know to pin down exactly what style your house is, and it will also give you the name and purpose of that little thingamajig on the roof that you always wondered about.

If your house is new and seemingly not of any one style, take a look at its architectural details and try to find hints or features of a specific period. Many modern houses, for example, are simplified derivations of Colonial forms and do well with more geometric types of landscapes.

Once you understand more about your house's style, try to spend some time learning its particular history, especially if it is more than 50 years old. You would be amazed at the stories a simple deed search at your local registry will reveal—tales that may go a long way to explain various idiosyncrasies of your house and grounds. (You'll also be able to get a plot plan at the registry, if you don't already have one.)

Before you step outside, sketch or trace the borders of your property and the house from the plot plan onto another sheet of paper. (You don't want to damage the original.) If you don't have the plot plan available, take a moment and sketch out very roughly the general layout of the house and lot. At this stage, you just want to get an approximation of the house and how it sits on the land, one that you can carry around with you outside without fear of water or other damage.

Next, take accurate site measurements of the house and the main existing features of the garden. This sounds complicated, but it really isn't. It just takes a bit of time—generally several hours, and *very* worthwhile ones at that. Taking your time and being as accurate as possible, begin noting the house measurements on your plot plan. If you have the architectural plans of the house in your possession, you're lucky. All the house measurements are already there—the only thing you have to do is scale them from the drawings. If you don't have the architectural plans, you'll need to take out tape and yardstick and measure the foundation outline, or *footprint*, of your house. Start at one corner and continue around the perimeter. As you proceed, note the exact locations of all doors and of any windows that feature principal views of the yard. Often the easiest way to do this is to take what are known as running measurements (see figure at top of page).

Once you've accurately drawn the house, move on to the principal features of the property as a whole. A quick look at the "Symbology of Plans" diagram (next page) will give you some idea of how to draw the various features you encounter. These symbols are reasonably universal and are used by amateurs and professionals alike to render their landscapes. Mark down the locations of all existing principal features: ponds, streams, outbuildings, trees, flower beds, terraces, decks—whatever plays a role in your yard.

To determine the location of an object such as a tree or an outcropping in relation to the property borders (most important!), a method called triangulation is useful (see figure at right).

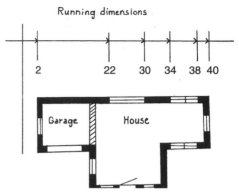

Once you've taken your property's measurements, do a clean drawing (or use your computer) and then make several copies. (Illustration by Penny Delany.)

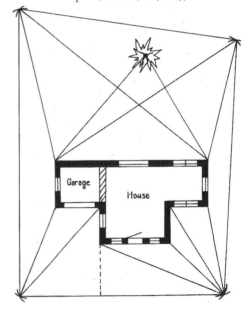

The triangulation method will save time and aggravation in plotting distant features in your landscape. The process is based on the fact that two measured arcs can intersect only at a unique point. Here the corners of the lot and landscape features are located by measuring from points on the house. Just be sure these base points are correctly located on your plan, or your subsequent measurements will be incorrect. (Illustration by Penny Delany.)

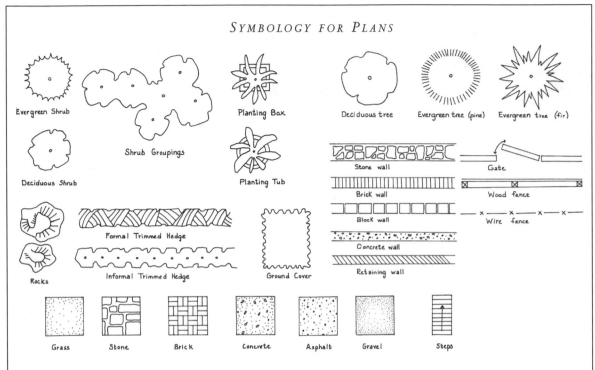

SYMBOLOGY FOR PLANS

Evergreen Shrub

Shrub Groupings

Deciduous Shrub

Planting Box

Planting Tub

Deciduous tree

Evergreen tree (pine)

Evergreen tree (fir)

Stone wall

Gate

Brick wall

Wood fence

Block wall

Wire fence

Concrete wall

Retaining wall

Formal Trimmed Hedge

Informal Trimmed Hedge

Rocks

Ground Cover

Grass   Stone   Brick   Concrete   Asphalt   Gravel   Steps

When you start to draw your property, you will find these standard symbols helpful. They are used by landscape designers to show various features of the property in plan view, and to give a good idea of the size, shape, and texture these objects will have in the actual landscape. (Illustration by Penny Delany.)

It's really quite basic, and it works on the geometric rule that two lines can intersect at only one unique point. Using two known base points, measure the distance to the object from each of the points, and note it on your plan. When you go to make your first draft plan, simply swing a measured line from each point with a compass. This will form two arcs that will intersect at one point and one point only—thereby locating your object on the plan. (Note: Your measured distance cannot be greater than the full extension of the compass. If necessary, start with a smaller scale and transfer the plan to a larger scale later.)

Once you've measured all the primary features of your property, it's time to plot out your yard on graph paper (if you have access to one, you can use a computer software package). Keep in mind that the greatest dimension of your property will determine the scale required to fit on paper—for instance, if your lot measures 200 by 100 feet, 200 feet is the longest dimension, so you will need at least a 50-inch sheet of paper to use 1/4-inch scale (1 inch = 4 feet), 25-inch paper for 1/8, 12 1/2-inch paper for 1/16, and so on. Make as large a drawing as you can (it will make things easier later), and be as accurate as possible—the time you spend now will save a lot of hassles down the road.

When you have finished the plan of existing features, use it to make another copy, this time omitting those features you may not want to keep and drawing out only the house, the lot lines, and the elements you wish to save. The first plan becomes your base, allowing you to see the current state of the landscape, while the second, more simplified version will allow you room to chart out all the changes you will want to make.

Next, consider sun and shade. The amount of sun various parts of your garden receive will be the single most important issue for determining how well plants will do. You need to pay attention to the labels that come with plants at the nursery. They are not just decorations or general guidelines—"full sun" means at least 8 hours of full, direct sun a day. And "part sun" does not mean dappled sunlight—it means at least 5 hours of full sun per day. Every gardening primer reminds us of this, but I've noticed an amusing (and expensive) tendency to ignore these directions whenever possible!

Chart out the areas of sun and shade in your yard and note them on the plan. Pay attention to seasonal differences as well. (See figures below.) Usage patterns likewise will be determined to some extent by sun and shade patterns: after all, there's no point in putting that new pool in the part of the yard that never receives any sun.

Equally important, though often overlooked, are general wind patterns. These are a little harder to chart, because you generally need considerable experience with the house and land to know how the wind has a tendency to blow. For starters, watch

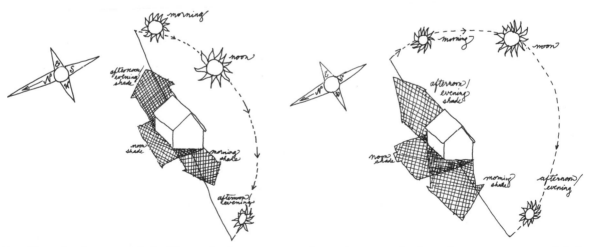

Left: The sun's path in winter. Right: The same landscape in summer. Our gardening forefathers knew the importance of sun and shade in their garden, and situated their houses and gardens accordingly—something we need to pay more attention to today. The sun's path is closer to the horizon in the winter than in the summer, so an area may be sunny for several hours each day in midsummer, but in chilly shadow throughout the rest of the year. So pay close attention to the sun patterns in your yard. (Illustration by Lea Richardson.)

how the winter winds blow the snow—do the drifts pile up in any one place, or is one area particularly windswept in the spring? This is important because windy areas are much harder on plants. Warm early-spring winds desiccate plants such as evergreens at the time they can least tolerate it—when the ground is still frozen. As the leaves lose moisture due to the wind and sun, the plants die because they can't pull water from their still-frozen roots to replace it. This process, known as winterkill, is perhaps the most common cause of plant failure. (Wind is a consideration for humans, too: sitting on a terrace in a particularly breezy spot can be a bone-chilling experience!)

Water runoff is something else to keep in mind. How does the property drain? Low or boggy areas are obviously not good choices for outdoor living areas, nor are they good, somewhat surprisingly, for artificial pools and fountains, because water and mud flow into the pool, dirtying it terribly. Natural ponds do well in such spots, though. Soil conditions in damp or wet areas will also restrict the type of plants you can use in such locations.

Next, note the primary views from the house. Is there a spot in the yard that you look out on every time you stand at the kitchen sink? Is there some eyesore that you wish to hide, or some distant view you would like to frame? If so, note it on the plan. Stand in each one of your principal windows and doors and try drawing the main sight line in pencil on your diagram, like the ones in Victorian garden plans. These lines will help you remember what views are important and will aid in the process of planning the location of special features and focal points. Also, take a walk around the property and look at your house and yard as others do. What areas are seen most? Which are in need of some privacy? Note this on your plan as well.

Now is the time to give some consideration to how you move through your property. Is there a constant muddy path where the kids, dogs, and mail carrier regularly cut across the lawn? Chances are you may need some type of path there. Are your current walks and drives suitable to your needs? Can you get the car in and out of the garage easily? Is there ample parking? Does your house have an orphaned front door with no means of entrance or egress? Are there areas of the property that need better access? If the answer to any of these questions is yes, give some thought to how to improve these areas, and ponder various design options. This is the ideal time to let your imagination roam over your property, envisioning this, removing that—while any mistakes are only an erasure away from correction!

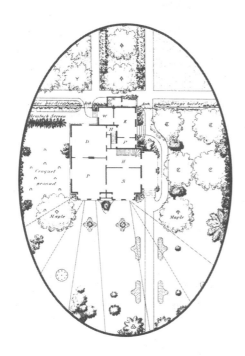

Order
and *Balance*

It is an accepted axiom in landscape history that gardens reflect the time, place, and most of all the philosophy of their creators. A quick look across history demonstrates the truth of this. What better shows the Romans' love of domestic life than their enclosed villa gardens centered around hearth and home? What reveals more about medicine, science, and belief during the Middle Ages than a monastic garden? What could be more telling of the Sun King than his garden at Versailles, radiating

These two figures clearly illustrate the ideas of symmetry and balance. In the first house, the facade is balanced; in the second, the facade is symmetrical.

for miles from a single point, his throne? American gardens have also been closely linked to the philosophies of the people who built them.

Our founding fathers, men so dedicated to a controlled system of checks and balances that they fought and won a war to establish these principles, built gardens imbued with the same spirit—measured, balanced order. In this Age of Enlightenment, where rational, reasoned thought was valued above all else, and garden making was considered one of the highest forms of civilized behavior, their precisely planned and laid-out landscapes easily became a metaphor for a well-ordered, balanced world.

The two guiding concepts behind these gardens—order and balance—are closely related.

Order is the logical arrangement of diverse elements. Balance is a slightly more nebulous concept. In the garden, when we refer to balance, we mean the equal weighting of mass on each side of any given view. Balance can be symmetrical, where one side is the mirror reflection of the other. The figures above, from Andrew Downing's first book, *Cottage Residences*, provide a good way to visualize this notion. In the first figure, an irregularly shaped building is divided by a central line, marked *a*. Although the left and right sides are not the same (one has a tower and the other a large gable), the general feeling of the structure is in *balance*. One side appears to have as much *visual weight* as the other, even though the elements of the two are quite disparate. In the second figure, the right and left sides are identical, so this building is not only balanced but also symmetrical.

In even the most loosely designed old gardens, a deliberate sense of order linked different garden areas to each other and allowed a rational relationship between the grounds and the dwelling. Depending on the style of the structure, this order was achieved either with a strict symmetry or with a more general concept of overall balance. Because of these principles, old gardens made sense to the viewer. The layout was reasonable, unlike the random placement of garden features that we see too much of today.

Order, balance, and symmetry are all visible in the composite Colonial property illustrated on page 32. The garden is directly related to the house structure, centered on the house and aligned with the front and rear doors on an imaginary line, called an *axis*. On either side of the axis, the various parts of the garden are balanced or, in some cases, symmetrical. For instance, in the garden area around the well, one side mirrors the other, and the symmetry of the *garden* as a whole mirrors the symmetry of the *house* as a whole. (The house architecture is not represented, but assuredly it was some type of Federal style with a symmetrical facade.) The larger garden also exhibits a well-conceived balance; although each side of the main axis is slightly different, the shapes and massing of the two echo each other nicely. If you could whisk yourself magically into this garden, you would feel an innate sense of the rightness of the design. This feeling is hard to describe, but when gardens (and architecture) are in balance, one somehow feels on an unconscious level that the garden is "correct."

This type of harmonious relationship between house and garden was common all through the Colonial period. The architectural styles of the time—early Colonial, Federal, Georgian, and later Greek Revival—were all based on classical elements, which were in turn based on strict geometric relationships among circle, square, and triangle. Given this mathematical genesis, it is not surprising that all these house styles lent themselves easily to this kind of balanced, geometric garden treatment (as do their modern reincarnations and derivatives, often referred to as "Contractor Palladian"). When house and garden are based on the same underlying principles, a palpable harmony resonates between them.

Simply because these landscapes were geometric doesn't mean they were rigid applications of circle and square. There was a certain carefree genius to these American Colonial gardens; they were flexible and less fussy than their British counterparts, and each maker adapted the ideas of balance and symmetry to their particular site. Consider a plan of the manor house that gave its name to the Bowery in New York City (this page). Notice how the site precluded a perfectly symmetrical alignment of the garden to the house. No matter,

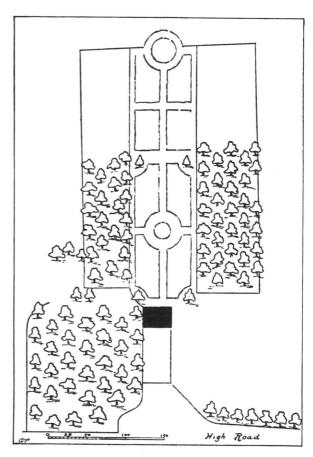

Colonial gardens sometimes show a charming disregard for strict adherence to the rules, as long as the overall effect remains the same. Here the main axis of the house and garden show a slight shift to accommodate the site.

the garden was shifted over slightly and the inner symmetry of the garden maintained. What was important was that the ordered, geometric nature of the garden matched the architecture of the house.

Nor was the idea of symmetry and balance neglected in the Victorian era. At the beginning of the 19th century, with the rise of "Romantic" house styles, the idea of perfect symmetry in both landscape and architecture gave way to the broader concept of "balance." This was entirely appropriate to the new styles of architecture, which were much freer and much more flowing. The best gardens of these houses reflected that trend as well. The figure

A balanced approach to the landscape was crucial to the success of this amazingly detailed plan. Even the three-seater at the rear of the house is shown (suitably covered by grapevines)!

(Key to illustration by Penny Delany.)

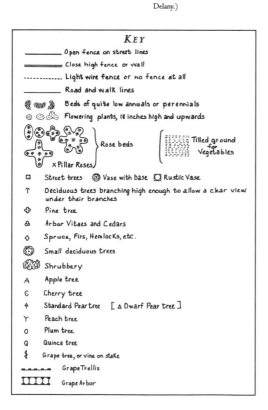

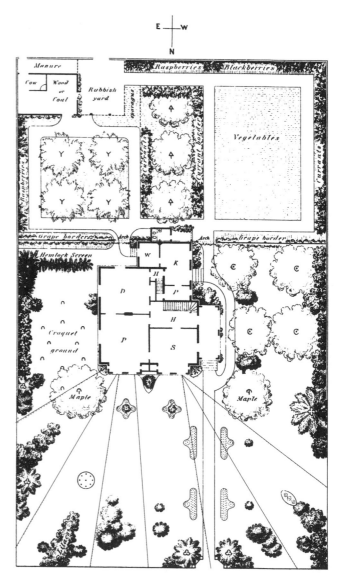

on page 54 shows the floor plan of a typical house of the period, probably one in the Italianate, bracketed style. Notice how different the landscape is from the Colonial model—nothing is at all symmetrical, and at first glance, certain elements seem to be scattered about randomly. But a subtler hand is at work here. Note how the individual elements are balanced, one side to the other. Orchard echoes vegetable garden, the croquet ground balances the mass of the cherry planting, and so on. The various flower and shrubbery elements are placed so that no part of the property is too heavily weighted with vegetation. There is an internal balance. Not symmetrical, not rigidly geometric, but once again parts of the garden are in harmony with themselves and with the house.

For the owner of a home built in the Colonial style or one of the Colonial Revival styles, a garden based on symmetrical models is a good bet. Likewise, the owner of a picturesque Victorian would do well to follow the model of the freer, more eclectic garden, keeping in mind, however, that the secret of success in even these gardens is a balanced design. But what about the owner of a postwar house on an acre or two in the average suburb? Surprisingly enough, the answer may lie in a modified type of the formal garden, a style I like to call *New Formalism*, which takes the best elements of the past and adapts them for today's lifestyle. This style is a looser version of the whole-property design common in the Colonial period, and even in the Victorian era it was commonly used for flower and vegetable areas.

No word in the garden vocabulary is more misunderstood than *formal*. Almost inevitably, when I suggest to a client that some sort of formal approach might be appropriate, the response is: "Oh, we really don't want anything too formal in this garden. The house [or our lifestyle] doesn't warrant it." This almost knee-jerk reaction against formalism, I believe, has its roots in the modern American predilection to reject anything that might limit personal comfort or freedom. "Formal" seems to suggest uncomfortably dressed ladies and gentlemen perched on hard, unyielding garden furniture, sweating through interminable teas. Or sometimes people think that formalism in gardens is appropriate only for grand mansions. But the "formal style" dates back to the subsistence gardens of Plimoth and Jamestown and has suitably accompanied both simple country cottages and great estates.

In a garden, the term *formal* means a fair amount of symmetry and orderliness, as opposed to a natural or wild look. This style of garden is suitable for many modern houses. The figure on page 57 shows a house in one of Boston's wealthiest suburbs. The architectural vocabulary is almost entirely classical—the quoins on the sides of the facade, the Ionic-style arch with a Palladian fan over the door, the absolutely symmetrical relationship of the windows. This "Contractor Palladian" style has become very common in this country. You can't do much about the derivative architecture of these houses, but you can help the overall visual integrity of the property by laying out the

IN DEFENSE OF
FORMALISM

*Is the house to be considered in relation to the
garden, and as an integral part of a design
which depends for its success on the combined
effect of the house and garden; or is the house
to be ignored in dealing with the garden[?]
. . . The formal treatment of gardens ought,
perhaps, to be called the architectural treatment
of gardens, for it consists in the extension of
the principles of design which govern the house
to the grounds which surround it. . . . The object of formal gardening is to bring the two
into harmony, to make the house grow out of
its surroundings, and to prevent its being an
excrescence on the face of nature. The building
cannot resemble anything in nature, unless
you are content with a mud-hut and cover it
with grass; but on the other hand, you can lay
out the grounds, and alter the levels, and plant
hedges and trees exactly as you please; in a
word, you can so control and modify the
grounds as to bring nature into harmony with
the house, if you cannot bring the house into
harmony with nature.*

—Reginald Blomfield
The Formal Garden in England (1892)

grounds in a more or less orderly, balanced fashion. This goes far in uniting house and landscape into an aesthetic whole, providing visual balance and logic.

It is interesting to note what happens when this advice is ignored. Look at the modern house again and notice how this completely unbalanced, un-pleasant-looking landscape takes away what little appeal the house itself has to offer. To the left we have a strange hillock that flows down the hillside like some mud slide after a storm, threatening to swallow up an inadequately sized walkway. Next to the walk sits a giant concrete pineapple, further weighting the already heavy left side of the house. Joining this ugly mass is some type of Victorian-style iron fence, which is completely inappropriate to the classical elements in the facade. And beside all of this, clustering to the house like lost children to their mother, is a motley collection of shrubs (with the inevitable yews!), which add absolutely nothing to the house or landscape.

What a waste! The real tragedy here is the cost. Each of these elements is individually quite pleas-ant—and quite expensive. (The iron fence and stone wall alone must have cost a princely sum.) Used properly and appropriately, each element would have been an excellent addition to some land-scape—but used together, they form a very costly horror show. The point of all this is that if you are going to spend money on a landscape, why not spend money on one that complements and en-hances your home, instead of one that fights with it? It's time that we as homeowners take back our landscapes from the hands of incompetent contrac-tors and second-rate landscapers. It's our land, our homes, and, after all, our money—we are all made the poorer both financially and mentally by having to put up with such inferior results.

You may be worried that the overall look of this "New Formalism" gar-den will be too fussy. This is not necessarily the case. A strict geometric relationship within the garden is really most noticeable when one looks at the plan. The bones of the garden—the paths, terraces, focal points, pools, and so on—are indeed laid out in some sort of ordered or geometric way. But the garden itself can be as carefree and loose as a cottage garden (which looks

While it will never win an architectural prize, this example of "Contractor Palladian" would be more inviting if the landscaping had been designed to complement the house.

(Illustration by Penny Delany.)

very natural but, with its orderly square beds and central focal point, is quite formal) or as tight and restricted as the landscape at Versailles.

This is precisely the essence of the New Formalism: we can take advantage of the many benefits offered by architectural-style gardens and then make the plan and planting as formal as we want. If you'd like a boxwood-edged garden, with fountains and borders, go ahead. If you prefer a wide-open landscape with ample space and a quiet, simple palette, bravo! You can have both, or either, within this formula. The important thing is not to turn away from the sense and wisdom of a historical geometric approach simply because it seems at first glance to be too stiff or rigid. In the garden, *you* control the degree and amount of formality—you are free to pick from a wide range of related historical elements to suit your personal taste and lifestyle. The caveat here is that the individual elements must have a similar feel and style—obviously a Federal fence, Victorian arbor, and turn-of-the-century walk lumped together would not make the best possible combination. A safe choice is to limit your selections to a set time period: usually elements from a given age (or reproductions thereof) will resemble each other in look and feel sufficiently to be compatible. For the more aesthetically ambitious, elements from different styles can sometimes be successfully combined, especially if they share similar materials or means of craftsmanship. The key here is that the elements must be sympathetic with each other and work well together. The best advice I can give you is that if you have any real doubts about an element's compatibility with your overall garden, don't use it. A few well-designed elements are always better than lots of conflicting, mediocre ones, both indoors and out.

The last argument in favor of the New Formalism is a very important and practical one: garden cost and maintenance. It is true that an architectural-style garden is often initially more expensive to design and install. These gardens are by nature more complicated than their naturalistic cousins and require more "hardscaping"—structures, paths, ornaments, and the like—which are quite costly. However, these gardens are cheaper to maintain, and given the cost of labor today, they typically are the *less* costly option in the long run. Generally, increased complexity means increased maintenance, but formal gardens are the exception to the rule. Because they rely heavily on geometry and architecture to achieve their effect, formal gardens are by their very nature more static and durable than a less structured garden that depends solely on a wealth of bloom and foliage to please the eye. This is something to keep in mind when you are considering the bottom line.

THE MYTH OF THE MEADOW

Meadow gardens promise beauty, ease, and thrift, all at once—"a can of seeds is all you need." But unless you have a very large, open site measured in acres, meadow gardens not only are unfeasible, but they look completely inappropriate as well. Wild or naturalistic grass areas depend for their aesthetic appeal on large amounts of land and sweeping, uninterrupted vistas. They are not effective otherwise, and a half-acre is about the barest minimum that will work. Anything less looks simply like an unmowed plot of weeds.

Also, true meadows are *a lot* of work—despite the general perception that they, like other wild areas, are low maintenance. Meadows are actually a transitory state in nature, a quick stopping point between bare ground, which nature abhors, and forest, which nature prefers. To get the meadow to look good and flower every year, it must be mowed at least three times a season with a special mower, and then the tons of grass that are produced must be laboriously gathered and composted—or you must have animals to eat the grass. Without this upkeep, the meadow rapidly reverts to scrub and, eventually, woodland. Meadows *are* undeniably beautiful, and where appropriate they should be encouraged. Just keep in mind that they are *not* the low-maintenance solution so falsely promised and are not a viable solution at all for the average small lot.

The Art of Victorian Shrub Planting

Like the plush, ornate interiors of Victorian houses, late-19th-century gardens reveled in color, intricacy, and pattern. Until that time, gardens had been designed largely in response to nature—as a way of taming the encroaching wilderness, as the Colonials did with their enclosed, geometric plots, or as a romanticized version of it, as practiced by Downing and his coterie. During the last thirty years of the 19th century, however, the garden became something more: another form of domestic adornment. In these landscapes, the textured fabrics, ornate woodwork, and bold colors typical of Victorian architecture and interiors found their living counterparts outside—ribbon beds of brightly colored annuals, elaborate garden structures, and the meticulous display of specimen shrubs and trees.

This little grouping is typical of the type of plantings Victorians located at curves or forks in a path. They liked to give the impression that there was a reason for a detour, other than the aesthetic appeal of the winding walk itself.

When we look back at period illustrations today, the busy appearance and seeming randomness of the plantings may defy our modern, more restrained sensibilities. But who can blame the Victorians for their enthusiasm? Like children in a candy store, gardeners of the late 19th century must have found the dizzying range of newly available plant material irresistible. With their characteristic penchant for the decorative, Victorians deliberately chose their plants for unique form, foliage, or flowers and set these plants apart in the landscape to highlight their most prominent qualities. Among their favorites were shrub and tree specimens with weeping forms and striking foliage or variegation. To a large degree, Victorian planting schemes reflected the sheer horticultural exuberance of the time and the irrepressible need of an upwardly mobile class of gardeners to show off their new, prized possessions.

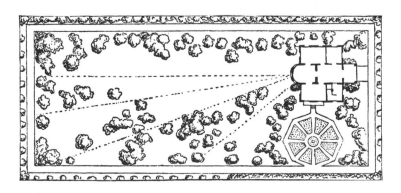

Victorians placed great emphasis on the internal vistas of the lot. Shrubs were located in precise groupings designed to allow framed, window-like views through the property, and beyond.

For those who have a Victorian home and would like to replicate some of the period's horticultural opulence, it will be of some comfort to you to know that there was indeed a method to the apparent madness of Victorian shrubbery plantings. Granted, the placement looks a bit random to our eyes, but once you understand some general guidelines common to the period, it all begins to make sense.

As far as shrubs were concerned, the design philosophy can be summed up in six "rules" published by Frank J. Scott in a chapter of his *Art of Beautifying Suburban Home Grounds* entitled "Arrangement in Planting." Scott made the rules general enough to be applicable to a variety of planting schemes and to accommodate individual tastes and space restrictions, and despite the passage of over a hundred years, they are as valuable today as they were a century ago for those wanting to capture the spirit of the Victorian landscape.

RULE 1 *"Preserve in one or more places (according to the size and form of the lot) the greatest length of unbroken lawn that the space will admit of."*

Scott believed that the house should be set as far as possible from the street or other perimeter, with at least one section of uninterrupted lawn to enhance the sense of space within the garden and to allow for an unobstructed view from the house to the street. This concept, of maximizing the interior space and fortifying the perimeters (albeit with "windows"—see Rule 2), is equally valid for landscapes from any period, Colonial to modern.

RULE 2 *"Plant between radiating lines from the house to the outside of the lot, so as to leave open lines of view from the principal windows and entrance porches; also find where, without injuring the views to and from the house, the best vistas may be left from the street into the lot, and from one point to another across the grounds, or to points of interest beyond."*

Victorians loved to see and be seen. The notion of privacy that we so cherish today in our cramped urban and suburban spaces was not an issue for them. The ultimate design goal was to maximize the vista from the house—whether of the garden itself, as in Rule 1, or of the landscape beyond. To that end, Scott suggested planting along axis lines, with sufficient gaps in between to allow for unobstructed views to and from the house. (If you look closely, on most period landscape plans you will notice these dashed axis lines—the sight lines—clearly indicated. See the figures on pages 35, 54, and 59, for example.)

RULE 3 *"Plant the larger trees and shrubs farthest from the center of the lawn, so that the smaller may be seen to advantage in front of them."*

Although we tend to favor large, blended plantings with muted color schemes, Victorians wanted to be able to appreciate plants individually—for their shape, size, and color. Scott provided the design rationale for this showcase mentality. He proposed planting in smaller groups, each with "not less than twenty species of trees and shrubs," with larger trees in the center and the smaller specimens arranged "in such a manner that each may show its peculiar beauty without concealing any of the others and at the same time." The object was that all the plants should be "seen at once . . . each growing to a perfect development of its best form."

RULE 4 *"On small lots, plant no trees which quickly attain great size, if it is intended to have a variety of shrubs or flowers."*

The emphasis here is on eventual scale. Too often (then as now), small houses in time came to be completely buried in overly large plantings. Scott was an advocate of closely matching plants to the extent of the yard and urged gardeners "to endeavour to develop another type of beauty for small spaces: that of artistic elegance in the treatment of small things."

RULE 5 *"In adding to belts or groups of trees or shrubs, plant near the salient points, rather than in bays or openings."*

Most Victorian shrubbery plantings were arranged not in straight lines but in highly effective groupings of varying thickness and densities that projected into the lawn area like peninsulas along a coastline. Here Scott is commenting on the tendency to dilute the visual effectiveness of this scheme by adding too many smaller satellite beds in the "bays"—the spaces between these projections. Doing so, he warned, meant "breaking up the lawn . . . into insignificant fragments" and "changing the sunny projections and shadowy bays of a shrubbery border into a lumpish wall of verdure." Flower beds, he felt, were particularly misused in this manner and that in general they should be located "either near walks or the *points* of shrubbery projections, not individually in the spaces between."

RULE 6 *"Shrubs which rest upon the lawn should not be planted nearer than from six to ten feet from the front fence, except where intended to form a continuous screen of foliage."*

Although he notes that this rule is not always practical for small lots, Scott is here advising against cramming shrubbery tightly up against a fence. The plants should be given enough room to grow naturally and to be appreciated from all vantage points.

A Victorian Front-Yard Makeover

The front of this Italianate Victorian is one of the most engaging projects I have ever done. The house itself is spectacular—thanks in large part to the homeowners, who waged a two-year war to bring the house back from the brink of collapse to an almost museum-quality restoration. The first time I saw the landscape, the house was completely covered in huge, gloomy evergreens and almost none of the facade was visible. The very first thing to do was to remove these overgrown plantings and get a look at the architecture of the house.

Once the marvelous front was uncovered (revealing at the same time the water damage that those large plantings had caused to the wooden siding), I had the opportunity to assess the house and yard as a whole. Like many older houses, this one had once occupied a much larger site, which had subsequently been sold off and developed. Enough land was left, however, even in this dense urban location, to allow for an evocative re-creation of a Victorian-style front garden, an idea that the owners actively embraced.

There was no surviving map of the original garden, so the owners and I decided to use period plans to give us an idea of what we should do. In terms of layout, there were two options: a semicircular walk across the front, or a curved layout leading from the drive. Both had historical precedents, but the clients preferred the second approach. In either design, a key element was the walk—it had to be in keeping with

Victorian Front Yard: Before

Huge plantings completely overpower the house. (Illustration by Penny Delany.)

Victorian Front Yard: After

The landscape is restored to the original proportions and intent. It is important to note that the foundation plantings here have already reached their mature, maximum height and will never grow to overwhelm the house. (Illustration by Penny Delany.)

the large porch and reflect something of the house design. Thus we installed a new, six-foot-wide brick walkway with an exuberant herringbone pattern—an appropriate choice of material in light of the urban setting, the elaborate architecture of the house, and the fact that the town has been a famous brick producer for over a hundred years.

As the clients wanted to have an abundance of flowers, we chose to interpret the garden in a late Victorian style, with flower borders that lapped the walks, foundations, and fence lines. These beds were planted out with a large selection of old-fashioned perennials such as foxgloves, delphiniums, peonies, black-eyed Susans, iris, and daisies as well as with a yearly addition of annuals to extend the flowering season.

Finally, the high foundation of the house was lightly "dressed" in the Victorian manner with flowering deciduous shrubs and vines, such as antique roses, deutzia, clematis, and even an upright blueberry bush or two, which are very ornamental plants and produce a great crop, with just enough evergreen boxwood to provide some winter interest. All these plantings, however, were carefully chosen so that at their mature size they would never again overwhelm the front facade, even without pruning. The end result is a romantic front garden, which welcomes visitors to the house, cheers passersby on the street, and enhances the property as a whole.

Historic Garden

The Gardens of Portsmouth, New Hampshire

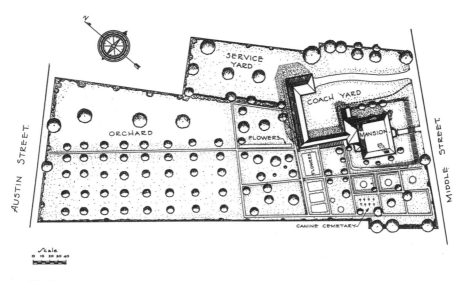

The Rundlet–May House and Garden on Middle Street.

The historic city of Portsmouth, New Hampshire, would be a charming place to visit even without the added attraction of its many centuries-old gardens. Situated on the Atlantic at the mouth of the Piscataqua River, with an excellent harbor and easy access to interior waterways, Portsmouth rapidly rose to wealth and prominence as a center for the lucrative trade in fish and timber. Merchants, bankers, shipbuilders, and craftsmen flocked to the city during the 1700s, constructing many large homes with fine gardens. Although Portsmouth's fortunes were somewhat diminished by the Revolution, the period after the war and the early years of the 19th century only increased the city's prosperity. In fact, it was not until the era when the railroad superseded ships as a means of efficient inland transportation that the city's importance began to fade.

From the late 1800s onward, Portsmouth started a slow decline into genteel poverty that was not fully reversed until the 1970s. What was a disaster for the economy, however, proved a blessing for the historic fabric of the city: a large portion of Portsmouth escaped destruction through "renovation" and "urban renewal" long enough to allow the growing historic-preservation movement to mobilize and save a large number of structures. Today

Portsmouth boasts an intact historic center full of 18th-century buildings, wonderful stores, restaurants, and museums, and, of course, some very interesting gardens.

A quick look at two of these gardens will help illustrate some of the ideas of order and balance we have been talking about. The first garden, at the Rundlet-May house (see illustration on previous page), has the claim of being the oldest garden in Portsmouth still on its original site. Built in 1807 and probably designed by the owner himself, the garden remains today almost unaltered in its basic layout. In typical American fashion, Rundlet wanted an ordered garden, one that matched the classic lines of his new Federal-style house, but the site didn't quite conform to a perfectly symmetrical layout. His ingenious solution was to design a garden that seems to be built around a series of right angles and regular beds, even though there's hardly a true 90-degree angle anywhere.

Constructed on a site that slopes slightly away from the house, the garden is divided by gravel walks into a series of terraces and compartments. The plan of this garden clearly reveals walkways that aren't perfectly aligned with the house, but when you are in the garden, everything appears amazingly straight and square. This is because the path layout follows a clever visual trick of appearing to be at right angles to whatever part of the house guides the eye. The whole is a triumph of visual deception, and an extremely effective one at that: the garden's three original areas—upper garden, kitchen garden, and orchard—flow in a logical, unified sequence from a line that

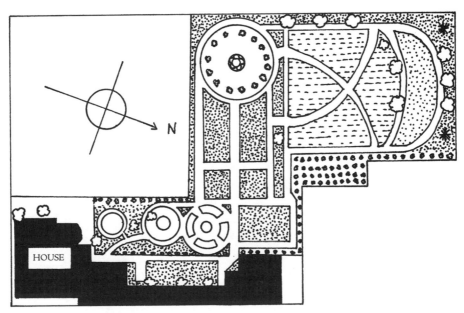

The Sarah Goodwin Garden in Portsmouth, drawn from a 19th-century plan. (Illustration by Penny Delany.)

leads all the way from the front door to the rear of the property. An ordered garden for an ordered house.

Another fine example of order and balance can be found in the Sarah Goodwin garden, which is now part of the Strawbery Banke Museum. Although the house has been moved from its original site, the diaries, notes, and plans of the garden's creator, Sarah Goodwin, were so voluminous and spanned so many years (1832–1896) that curators at the museum were able to replicate the layout and planting of her garden in meticulous detail. The plan on the previous page dates from the mid-1860s and shows a garden in full Victorian style. Although very different in character and feeling from the Rundlet property, the garden works because it exhibits the same concern for order and balance. The space is divided into three distinct areas by ample gravel paths: a flower garden with circular beds near the house; a larger, more extended flower area centered on a large urn; and a wild area off to one side. A close look at the plan reveals that the whole series of circles and arcs is actually based around two principal intersecting axes, one parallel to the house and one at a right angle to it. Masses in the garden are carefully balanced. Roses rise on rustic arbors, punctuating the garden like a series of classical columns; an urn sits in the midst of an elaborate annual planting; a wild garden is separated from the more formal areas by a living arch of hemlocks. The result is a perfect example of a whimsical yet ordered Victorian layout, showing the pleasing effects to be found when order and balance reign in the garden.

MAKING THE MOST OF
WHAT YOU HAVE

We start, as gardeners always have, with ideas of squares, rectangles, and curves. But we are growing rigid in our conceptions, one fears; at any rate, one hears of a "true" line, a "true" circle, as if it were more virtuous than a bent line or an oval shape. The Colonists adjusted their forms gracefully to existing objects: used them as opportunities to create changes and varieties in designs that otherwise might have been too prim. So should our side paths follow property lines regardless of "true right angles." Where symmetrical patterns are wanted, stick to the plan where possible; but if the garage gets in the way, yield the design to the inevitable. Get around as best one can, and then go on again. Instead of unsightliness, the result is fairly sure of having unexpected charm. For it shows common sense and ability to make the most of what we have—both agreeable qualities.

—Fletcher Steele, "The Colonial
Garden Today," *Colonial Gardens* (1932)

A Master Plan for Re-creating a Victorian Yard

To illustrate his ideas, and for maximum practicality and service to his readers, Frank J. Scott filled his *Suburban Home Grounds* with numerous plans and planting schemes for lots of varying sizes. Here is one such plan, which illustrates many of his favorite design concepts (see following page), complete with the original plant list and Scott's accompanying text, along with some modern interpretations.

One thing to keep in mind is that the horticultural nomenclature has changed considerably since Scott's day. Therefore exact translation to modern-day varieties is not always possible. The modern re-creator of this garden would do well to check the hardiness of the varieties listed and make appropriate substitutions for his or her climate, as well as to consider using some of the newer cultivars available, especially of plants such as rhododendrons and azaleas, if absolute historical accuracy is not an issue.

We have here an inside lot of sixty feet front, occupied to the depth of one hundred and thirty feet by the house, the walks and the ground embellishments.... The house is stretched out to correspond with the form of the lot, which is supposed to have no desirable ground connections with the adjoining lots, yet not so disagreeably surrounded as to make it necessary to shut out by trees and shrubs the out-look over the fences from the side-windows of the bay. The style of planting here shown is such as would suit only a person or family of decided taste for flowers, and the choicest selections of small shrubs. In the rear left-hand corner is room enough for two cherry trees (marked C), under which the lawn forms a sufficient drying-yard, and a convenient currant-border utilizes a space next to the fence. Besides the cherries, no large trees are to be planted except hemlocks (marked H), which are gracefully shrubby in their early growth, and can be so easily kept within proper bounds by pruning, that they are introduced to form an evergreen flanking for the rear of the house, and back-ground for the narrow strips of lawn on either side of it. In time they will overarch the walk, and under their dark shadows the glimpse of the bit of lawn beyond, with its bright flowers, will be brought into pretty relief.... Nearly all the shrub and tree embellishment is with small evergreens, flowers of annuals, and bedding plants. Flowers are always relieved with good effect when seen against a background of evergreens. It will be observed that the close side-fences are, much of their length, uncovered by shrubbery. They must, therefore, be very neatly, even elegantly made, if the proprietor can afford it. They then become a suitable backing for the flowers that may be made to form a sloping bank of bloom against them. By finishing the inside of the fence en espalier, it may be covered all over with delicate summer vines whose roots, growing under it, will interfere little with planting and transplanting seeds, roots, and bulbs in front of them. In naming the trees intended for this plan, it must not be supposed that other selections equally good, or better, may not be made by a good gardener. The following is suggested as one of many that will be appropriate to the place:

A, A. Two hemlocks [*Tsuga canadensis*] planted two feet from the fence and from the walk to form an arch over the gate when large enough.

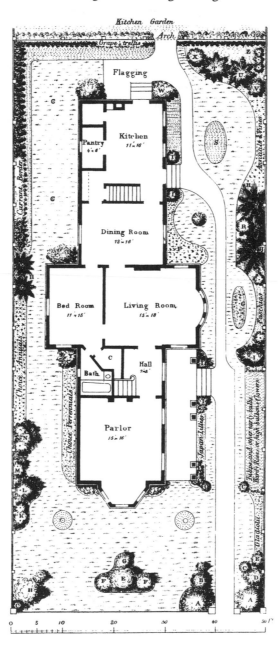

A typical landscape plan from Scott for a small lot.

B. Parson's dwarf hemlock [probably *Tsuga canadensis* 'Nana', the dwarf hemlock] two feet from the walk and six feet from the fence.

C, C, C, C. Irish junipers [*Juniperus communis* 'Stricta'] two feet from the walk.

D. Space between juniper and corner post on the right may be filled with mahonias [probably *Mahonia aquifolium*], English ivy [*Hedera helix*] and azaleas that love shade.

E (next to the fence). Dwarf weeping juniper [*Juniperus communis* 'Oblonga Pendula'].

E (in the center of front group). The pendulous Norway spruce [*Picea abies* 'Pendula'], the central stem of which must be kept erect by tying to a stake until it is from six to eight feet high. [**Editorial note: This is probably not the world's best choice here—with all respect to Scott. These trees get huge; a good substitute might be *Pinus flexilis* 'Glauca Pendula' (white weeping limber pine) or *Pinus strobus* 'Pendula' (weeping white pine), both of which are much easier to keep under control. If you are not a stickler for exact historical accuracy, it would behoove you to investigate (with the counsel of good nursery staff) what modern, more compact cultivars may be available today that would give you the same Victorian look and feel without some of the work involved in keeping these beauties in check.**]

F, F. One, the dwarf Norway spruce [*Picea abies* 'Gregoryana'—see note above] and the other the dwarf silver-fir [*Abies alba* 'Compacta'].

G (in front of the group). Golden arbor-vitae [*Thuja occidentalis* 'Lutea'].

G (opposite bow-window of living-room). A bed of assorted geraniums. [**Editorial note: Scott means here the "bedding" geraniums so common to the period but now very rare; commonly available varieties will do, especially any with variegated foliage.**]

G (opposite dining-room). A single plant of coleus [*Coleus blumei* var. *verschaffeltii*]. [**Editorial note: This old variety is dark red; some of the old varieties of coleus (now lost) would grow to almost 4 feet—thus Scott's "single plant." Today's varieties are now mostly limited to 18 inches; thus I would substitute a massed planting here.**]

H, H, H. Hemlocks; for the left-hand front corner use Sargent's hemlock—its main stem to be kept tied to a stake until it has a firm growth six feet high. [**Editorial note: *Tsuga canadensis* 'Pendula'; one of the other compact varieties might also be a good choice.**]

I, I, I (on the left side of the walk). Dwarf-box for clipping. [**Editorial note: This was probably *Buxus sempervirens*, the "clipping" referring to its use in holiday decorations.**]

I (on right side of walk). The weeping arbor-vitae [*Thuja occidentalis* 'Pendula'] and the dwarf weeping juniper [*Juniperus communis* 'Oblonga Pendula'] (planted close together to form one clump).

J. *Podocarpus japonica* [**Editorial note: Probably *Podocarpus macrophyllus*, the Japanese kusamaki—Scott notes it should be protected in the winter, and it is hardy only to Zone 8. A dwarf Japanese yew or mugo pine might be used in colder climates.]

K. Parson's arbor [*Thuja occidentalis* 'Compacta']. These are to be planted two feet from the fence, with a golden arbor-vitae [*Thuja occidentalis* 'Lutea'] between K and L. [**Editorial note:** *Thuja occidentalis* **'Compacta' is no longer listed. However,** *Thuja occidentalis* **is the common arborvitae, and several dwarf cultivars are available.**]

L. A pendulous silver-fir [*Picea abies* 'Pendula'] four feet from the fence [see E]. Directly back of it, midway between it and the fence, the erect yew [*Taxus baccata* 'Erecta'], whose deep green winter foilage will contrast well with the golden arbor-vitaes near it, and as its hardiness in all localities is not so well proved as that of the other trees near it, its placement back of them, and near to the fence, will serve to ensure its safety from cold.

M. Irish junipers [*Juniperus communis* 'Stricta'] and Swedish junipers [*Juniperus communis* 'Suecica'] near the fence.

N. The dwarf white pine [*Pinus strobus* 'Compacta'] four feet from the fence; and behind, on each side, small rhododendrons. [**Editorial note: Perhaps** *Rhododendron catawbiense* **var.** *compactum;* **many more-recent cultivars have been introduced that are much in keeping with the Victorian spirit, such as** *R.* **'Boule de Neige'.**] Four feet above the pine, near the fence, plant a common hemlock [*Tsuga canadensis*], and when it is large enough to form a back-ground for the dwarf pine—say from eight to ten feet high—keep it well clipped back to prevent it from spreading over the dwarfs, and taking up too much of the lawn.

O, O. Round beds for verbenas or other creeping flowers of constant brilliancy.

P. Bed for favorite fragrant annuals or low shrubs.

Q (by the side of the kitchen). Bed for flowering vines to train on the house, or, if the exposure be southerly, or southeasterly, some good variety of grape-vine. Whichever side of the rear part of the house has the proper exposure to ripen grapes well, cannot be more pleasingly covered than with neatly kept grape-vines; which should not be fastened directly to the house, but on horizontal slats from six inches to a foot from the house [trellis]; and these should be so strongly put up that they may be used instead of a ladder to stand upon to trim the vines and gather the fruit.

R. Rhododendrons [various compact varieties].

S. Bed of cannas, or assorted smaller plants with brilliant leaves of various colors.

T, U, V, X, Z. A bed of rhododendrons [various compact varieties].

Y. Rhododendrons [*Rhododendron canadense, R. catawbiense, R. maximum,* and *R. ponticum*] and azaleas [*Rhododendron arborescens, R. nudiflorum, R. viscosum,* etc.].

W, W, W. May be common deciduous shrubs of any favorite full-foliaged sort.

How-to: Garden Voyeurism

One of the most productive things I do before actually implementing a garden design is to take a walk around the neighborhood where the project is located. As my mother is fond of saying, there is nothing new under the sun: chances are you will see challenges very similar to the ones you face in your own garden during a quick tour around the block. By looking at how your neighbors have handled the same problems, you can assess the success of their solutions without having to repeat their costly errors. Here are some tips to keep in mind as you peer into other people's gardens.

Avoid large plantings that overwhelm the house and/or weight one side of the lot. Look at the front of this house: see how heavily the large tree draws the eye to the left side of the lot, obscuring the house and making the entire property seem unbalanced? To correct this situation, the owners are faced with the difficult decision of either cutting down a misplaced, albeit handsome, tree (in this case a rare Monkey Puzzle) or living with a seriously flawed landscape. The smaller plantings in the rest of the yard are also overgrown and should be removed. You can avoid this situation by making sure your plantings stay in scale with your house and do not grow so large as to hide the facade.

Keep in mind relative scale. Where's the house in this picture? The shrubbery in front of this house dominates the scene, overwhelming a beautifully crafted facade. Not to mention the fact that these overgrown, heavily pruned bushes are very costly and time-consuming to maintain. Also unsettling is the way the hedge terminates so abruptly and without reason. Hedges, like fences, need to begin at a logical starting point and end equally logically, not just dangle in space. The only solution here is to replace the whole ensemble with a much simpler yet more interesting planting to complement the house. A word to the wise: It's much easier to choose plants that will not outgrow their space and require extensive pruning than to try to control the situation after the fact.

Don't forget to make sure the style of the planting matches the style of your house. While the informal mix of perennials, small shrubs, and rustic fence seen here would have been appropriate for a country cottage, the overall effect when placed in front of this very formal front facade merely appears weedy and overgrown. Remember: House and garden need to share a similar and complementary style.

When in doubt, less is more. One of the most common landscaping mistakes is to add "just one more thing." Here, too, many different elements—ornamental trees, shrubs, hedges, house, and drive—compete with one another and make the scene a chaotic jumble. Keep a tight rein on the number of different elements that vie for your attention in any given area of your landscape. You can never go wrong with simplicity in line and clarity in conception. If you change your mind later, it will be much easier to add elements than to take them away.

Just because something is pretty in and of itself doesn't mean that it's appropriate for your yard. The story is an old one: In an elegant little boutique you see the "perfect" garden ornament. But before you pay all that money and lug that heavy piece of lead or stone home, consider whether the style and feeling of the piece conforms to the rest of your landscape. Will its beauty work *for* you or *against* you? In this example, two very large sculptural pieces are tossed into the middle of an otherwise unassuming landscape. The result in this case is gaudy and theatrical. "Think twice and buy once" should be your watchwords.

Make sure the materials you choose to construct your garden with are similar in style to those found in your house. Nothing makes a garden plan go awry faster than using materials in the garden that clash with those in the architecture. If your home is built of smooth, tan-colored brick, for example, you may not want to use rough, red brick in close proximity to the house. Instead, try pulling similar textures and colors from the structure into the garden. If you aren't sure which materials go

best with what, ask your local supplier for some samples to take home, and place them up against the house. If they don't look good close up, chances are they won't look good where you want to put them. Keep in mind the impression that different surfaces and textures can impart as well. For instance, a rough farmer's wall lends a countrified air that would not be appropriate for a town house. Conversely, an intricate wrought-iron fence would look silly next to a simple rustic cottage. Decide on the theme your house and landscape best impart, then stick to it, using a limited palette of materials and adding subtle, complementary variations for variety and effect. In these three examples, it is easy to see how the fences and walls installed in front of these houses conflict in style and feeling with the architecture behind them.

Cohesion

In traditional American gardens, the property was seen as a series of individual spaces (or "rooms"), each with its own purpose and identity yet with a *cohesive sense of design* that linked it to the rest of the yard. This cohesion is the third and most specific of the guiding principles that we need to resurrect in our gardens.

On small lots today, the demands of living in close proximity to neighbors often force owners to define boundaries with a fence, hedge, or other means. Given slightly more room, though, we have a tendency to neglect enclosure. But a landscape without a boundary is like a picture without a frame—even an exquisite canvas looks better with some kind of border. This is not to say that the area needs to be completely enclosed. The border needs only to be suggested. Traditionally, if there was an interesting prospect beyond the immediate landscape, the vista was framed with some type of intermittent boundary, such as hedges, gates, or large trees, so that the owners could peer out past the foreground into the distance as if through some large picture window. Once again the idea of framing the view is borrowed from art. Space, no matter how large, requires definition to be effective. This premise is valued in interior design, but for some reason outdoors, the need for visual enclosure is rarely given much consideration nowadays. Think of the boundaries of your garden as the walls of your house—defining your space, keeping unwanted elements out, and letting pleasant elements in.

Equally important is the use of space *within* each portion of the yard—the internal divisions, if you will. Your house has rooms, after all; so should your garden. Historically, our gardens were always separated into different areas by their function—pleasure grounds were distinct from work areas, carriage yards from vegetable gardens. Obviously this had the practical advantage of keeping unwanted animals, sights, and smells away from the more recreational areas of the landscape. But there was more to this separation than day-to-day concerns. Outside spaces *look better* when distinctly different parts are delineated in some way. Our Colonial forebears knew this, and as they carved out their house plots, farms, and fields from the virgin continent, they subdivided the space internally into a logical series of room areas, giving equal accord to the dictates of activity and overall aesthetics.

A good example of this type of room division is the garden of the Dr. Barraud house in Colonial Williamsburg (see figure on page 78). This garden is particularly interesting, as it is one of the few that came into the 20th century with its design still reasonably discernible. As already discussed, many of the gardens at Williamsburg are largely theoretical landscapes that have been re-created in styles appropriate for the houses. The Barraud garden, however, was the subject of considerable archaeological research, which revealed not only the foundations of the missing outbuildings but also a very complete picture of the paths that linked the various rooms of the garden.

Dr. Barraud's garden is today divided into four overall rooms: practical workspace, garden area, pleasure garden, and a wilder, less formal woodland area. The work area was definitively identified during excavations by the marled paving fragments. Written records indicate that the property also possessed a large vegetable garden, and probably a more ornamental area, but which of the existing areas it was is not completely clear. The important point is that the property, only half an acre or so, was in fact divided into

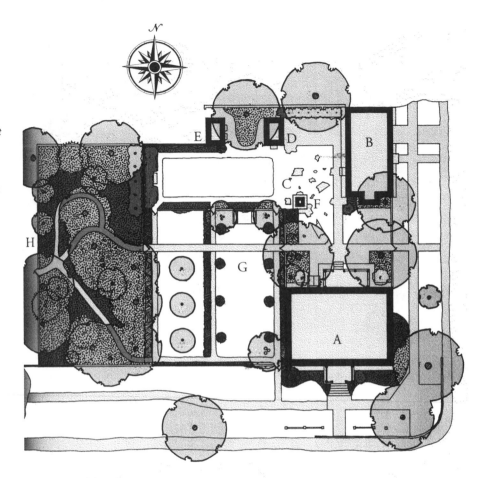

One of my favorite places at Williamsburg in terms of design, the Barraud House garden is a great illustration of how a property can be divided into coherent, functioning rooms. (Drawing by M. Kent Brinkley, ASLA, used with permission. © 1996 Colonial Williamsburg Fdn. All rights reserved.)

KEY TO THE PLAN
A. Dr. Barraud House
B. Kitchen

C. Well
D. Smokehouse
E. Privy

F. Kitchen Yard
G. Pleasure Garden
H. Natural Garden

logical compartments organized by function, each with a slightly different feel and character but all linked in such a way as to form a pleasing whole.

There are many different ways to achieve this effect, and which you use depends on the style of your garden and your house. Obviously the idea is to choose a manner of delineation that is appropriate to the overall feel and look of your garden. Also, the degree of separation you require is a factor—a 6-foot brick wall will, of course, give a much greater feeling of enclosure than a low row of boxwood. In the Barraud garden, low box hedges and pathways delineate each space. Lines of trees, flower borders, fences, walls, or simply changes in level (such as descending terraces) were all common means of subdividing and defining space.

One very crucial caveat must be mentioned here: As important (and historically correct) as it is to logically divide and arrange your garden space, be careful not to go overboard and subdivide your garden to such an extent that it becomes a series of chopped-up little spaces that cease to function as a whole. Each division should be justifiable and, most important, should seek to *maximize the internal space available in each area*. If you are lucky enough to have a large field or open space, for example, don't subdivide it into three or four little sections unless there is a very good reason for doing so. Similarly, in very small gardens, a good general rule is to fortify the exterior boundaries and to maximize interior space wherever possible. In the same way that the rooms of your home should appear large and spacious, so should those of your garden.

The idea of making functional sense of your landscape is almost so basic as to be common sense; yet for some reason, it has been almost completely neglected in the modern American landscape. Today individual bits and pieces of our yards all flow together into one large amorphous mass, totally devoid of purpose or personality: our landscapes simply *exist* in some nebulous way, rather than playing a viable and useful role in our lives. A typical American property will have completely separate front, side, and back yards, without any unifying elements to make the overall layout cohesive. This is one of the main reasons that our houses look so remote and unsympathetic. Each part of the yard is unrelated to the other, with the poor house sitting in the middle like some architectural schizophrenic desperately trying to relate to so many dissimilar personalities. It's as jarring as if the inside of your house had a kitchen decorated in High Victorian Gothic, the adjacent dining room in Southwestern Adobe style, the living room in Louis XIV, and the front hall in Bauhaus with a Medieval stair thrown in just for effect!

The different areas of your garden should relate to each other just as the rooms of your house do. This is *cohesion* in design. One of the easiest ways to achieve it is to *repeat* elements or aspects of the garden, especially with some variation, throughout the different areas of the yard. The simplest form of repetition is the use of a single type of construction material throughout the garden. For example, in the Barraud garden, pathways of the same brick and marl (a type of clay) wind throughout the design, even into the less formal areas of the garden. This recurrence of construction material is an effective way to link even quite disparate parts of the landscape.

Paths are important to think about, because they are frequently the main offender in poorly designed modern gardens. When faced with the prospect of laying a walk or a path from one area to another, many people are tempted to use a little bit of brick here, some stepping-stones there, perhaps some bluestone or cobble hither and yon. Try to avoid this. Instead, carry the same material, perhaps with different patterns or layout, throughout the garden.

The same is true of walls or fences—people use a bit of this for a few feet along the side, and then in the front, something entirely different. What most people don't realize is the extent to which we take in and judge our surroundings on a subconscious level. Although you may not be aware that the fence in front is white picket and the side portion chain link, when you pass through your garden, something strikes you as amiss. We are happy when things mesh on a visual level and ill at ease when they don't.

Using wildly different materials in one space is as bad outdoors as it is indoors, and successful gardens throughout our history avoided this pitfall, sometimes more by coincidence than by design. Our earliest forebears were frugal folk and generally had neither the time, patience, nor money to experiment with exotic materials in the garden. If the region was stony, so be it: stones appeared in the walls, in the paths, even in the foundation of the house. If wood was abundant in the area, paths were often formed of planks, and both house and garden structures were made primarily of wood. In the South where clay was readily at hand, brick prevailed. Using native material joins your work in the garden with nature's and makes the man-made part of the land itself. This is one aspect of the inner harmony you feel when you enter some of these grand old gardens, and it is something that we should certainly strive for today.

Repetition can be taken to the extreme, as these two examples from Vicks illustrate. While mimicking architectural forms in the landscape can produce dramatic results, overuse of this technique is monotonous.

Similarly, repeating plants throughout the garden is a common feature of most old American gardens—a horticultural theme and variation, if you will. In the Barraud garden the clipped boxwood hedges simultaneously define the different areas and conduct the visitor from one space to another, framing and delineating each along the way. Boxwood is perfect for this; its dark evergreen foliage easily links even the most disparate elements into a unified whole. (See Boxwood Basics on page 89.)

Repeating plant material is an effective means of defining and linking sections of your property, but you do not have to repeat the same plant again and again to achieve the desired effect. Plant material of the same *shape* or *color* can also be used to link various parts of the garden. This idea was probably brought to its acme during the Victorian era, when gardeners sought not only to repeat the shapes of plants in various parts of the garden but even to echo the architecture of the house with the planting itself. A perfect example of this is the use of large, conical evergreens to mimic the many gables of a Gothic Revival house. While this level of visual sophistication might seem a little extreme to people today, the Victorians used it quite often.

The general premise of echoing the architecture with plants is quite sound, and if used on a limited basis this can be an excellent method of uniting house and yard. The danger is (and was) overuse, as you can see from the figures at left. In both examples the same form was repeated so often that house and garden disappeared into a jumbled mass. The average homeowner should try to use similarly shaped plants in different parts of the property. For example, if you have a lovely weeping willow in the back, by all means think about including a weeping cherry or pear to echo that somewhere else.

Color is another element that is easy to repeat in the garden. Choose a color you like as a theme, and plant annuals, perennials, trees, and shrubs that will repeat it (or shades of it) all around the yard. Variegated plants—those whose leaves are a mix of colors, including green, cream, yellow—are good candidates for this, and I use them throughout the properties I design. Not only are they interesting in themselves, they're terrific foils to the usual solid color of most plants. Plants with red, yellow, or blue foliage can also be used very effectively to join sections of the garden. A sand cherry (*Prunus* × *cistena*) in the background of a perennial border can beautifully echo a large red maple (*Acer atropurpureum*) behind it, for example. One caution, however: Although the Victorians unabashedly adored strong color contrasts and thought nothing of locating many multicolored plants together in the garden, this practice may appear rather garish today. A little colored foliage goes a long way—like cayenne pepper in chili, it should be used sparingly until you are sure you like it!

Before we leave the subject of repeating design elements, I would like to

This cleverly designed Colonial garden seems completely symmetrical when viewed from inside, but there is not a single true angle in the entire design. The unity of house and garden was achieved through careful manipulation of visual perspective, and the repetition of design elements between house and garden.

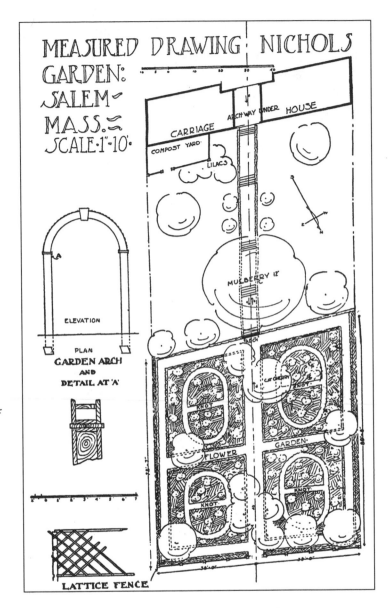

MEASURED DRAWING NICHOLS GARDEN: SALEM MASS. SCALE 1"=10'

The elaborate knot gardens in the lower portion of the garden were documented in 1911 and were probably installed when the house was built around 1800. The overall garden plan is shown on the previous page, while the turn-of-the-century photos on the next page document this garden's thoughtful design.

point out a clever trick that I've noticed in a number of old gardens, including the Nichols garden in Salem, Massachusetts (see figures on this page and on pages 81 and 83). The house and garden on Federal Street were built between 1782 and 1800 and—this was rare—were both designed by the same architect, Samuel McIntire. This fact probably accounts for the unique cohesiveness between house and landscape. All the traditional elements were present in this property. The gardens logically flow around the house and the service buildings, linking architecture to nature. And despite a fairly difficult

Wouldn't you love to be able to walk into this Colonial garden? That allure is in large part due to the repetition of familiar themes and variations which draws you from the house into the garden. You are in comfortable territory here: the curved top of the gate echoes the archway in the carriage house, the curved window tops, and the arch in the garden; even the architecture of the cascading stairs unite the garden to the house beyond. Unfortunately, while the house is now an outstanding museum in Salem, Massachusetts, only a pitiful fragment of the garden remains, a plight common to many historic sites throughout the country.

lot shape, the grounds were laid out to echo the strict order and symmetry of the house itself. (According to the 1911 issue of *Landscape Architecture*, which fortunately documented this property while the grounds still contained their 18th-century plantings, the layout was so cleverly designed that when in the garden you could not tell that the various sections were not perfectly squared.) Finally, the overall landscape was visually cohesive and moved logically from one area to another with ease.

The clever trick in this garden was that the repetition was *architectural*: elements from the house structure itself were carried outside. The garden was divided into a series of short terraces by the repeated use of short stairs, like landings in a hall. Even more interesting, the garden arch over the main path exactly mimicked the larger arch in the service buildings; house and garden were joined together.

This inventive type of linkage is not as difficult to achieve as you might think. Look for elements of your house's architectural detailing, and find some way to echo them in the garden. For example, with a Colonial house, try repeating the capitals and columns used in the front porch on a fence gate. With a Gothic Revival, instead of simple clay pots on the terrace, use planters that repeat the Gothic arches of the windows. With an Arts and Crafts house, use furniture on the terrace or in the sunroom that repeats the style and color of the woodwork inside. I'm sure you get the point—whatever type of house you have, integrate it with the garden and avoid the horrible mix and match of styles so often found in our landscapes today. (For more on this subject, see the next chapter.)

Finally, there is one last traditional design idea that you should keep in mind. Given the logic of viewing your property as a series of outdoor rooms that relate to the house, it stands to reason that each *room*, like those inside, should have some *internal* logic or organizing principle. In practical work areas, or in those parts of the yard used primarily for transit from one space to another, this is easy. The hard-surface workspace or walkway forms a principal point of interest, and all the other areas logically fall into place around it. The Low House in Savannah, built in 1848 by Andrew Low, a British cotton merchant, is a good example. The wide stone walk (interestingly, paved with flagstones brought as ballast from England) provides access to the front door and subdivides the front space into two equal sections, each occupied by an elaborate bed in the style common to the period. Had this been a Colonial house, the front planting would have been simpler and more geometric. A modern structure might have two grass plats with side borders of small trees, flowering shrubs, and perennials. In all these cases, though, the idea is the same. The practical elements of the design determine the theme and focal point of the space; all that is needed is some artistic embellishment appropriate to the style of the house.

Here in the 1848 Lowe House in Savannah, the symmetrically placed walkway forms the organizing principal for the front yard.

This unfortunately is not the case with most other areas of your yard. These sections are blank slates, without distinct personalities or purposes, *until you give them one.* Oftentimes, the boundaries between areas are not defined. In these cases you have to seize the bull by the horns and do the whole job yourself. It's not too hard if you remember the points of the third lesson from our gardening past: like indoor rooms, garden spaces must have a cohesive, logical *layout*: defined exterior borders, internal divisions determined by usage and purpose, a rational decorating scheme that relates one room to another, and some sort of center or focal point to each space.

☀ A Farmhouse Front-Yard Makeover

The front of this house (which happens to be my own) once presented many of the problems typical to old houses. Large overgrown shrubbery that dwarfed the house, an "orphaned" front door, poor car access, and the house's proximity to what had once been a dirt lane and is now a heavily trafficked two-lane thoroughfare: all of these challenges demanded substantial changes to the front of the property. As the rapid urbanization of the area had made re-creation of the original farm-scape impractical, I decided that the grounds around the house should be evocative of the period, not an absolutely accurate reproduction. Thus the goal was to solve the problems and still maintain something of the antique feel of the property.

The typical modern solution would have been to use a large fence or a dense front planting to screen the house from traffic, but this would have been completely out of character with the architecture, and it would have relegated what was left of the front yard to an unused, and unusable, space. Instead, I followed the Victorian precept of *fortifying the perimeter and opening up the interior*. The large, overgrown evergreen shrubbery (once again, mostly poor abused yews planted in the wrong location) was removed from the foundation, which immediately increased the light to the inside of the house and restored a sense of proportion to the facade. In their place, low-growing, flowering deciduous shrubs were installed, which gently nestle the stone foundation in greenery, bloom in three seasons, and provide a pleasant, light silhouette during the winter.

To solve the problem of the orphaned front door and to improve car access, I installed a semicircular cobblestone driveway. There was some indication that a drive or path had once existed in that shape, but the choice of cobble was purely a personal, not a historical one. Although cobble drives existed in the mid-19th century when this farmhouse was built, the rural setting and social status of the inhabitants (farmers) would have made this choice unlikely. For the 20th century, however, cobbles are ideal: their antique look and feel blends well with almost all architectural styles and provides a sympathetic all-weather paving surface that avoids the look of an asphalt parking lot. To help afford both sight and sound protection from the street, without completely hiding the house, a line of narrow, upright European hornbeams *(Carpinus betulus)* was installed, with low shrubbery along the base. (I initially underplanted with antique roses, which thrived for a few years until the trees grew denser and began to shade them. I then moved the roses and replaced them with the more shade-tolerant *Stephanandra incisa*, which has a decorative, serrated leaf, Victorian in feel, which complements the front of the house.)

Finally, during the construction of the garden I found evidence of a low stone farmer's wall in front of the property. I decided to rebuild it myself, doing small sections as time permitted. Though quite arduous, working with stone is quite a joy, and certainly

Farmhouse Front Yard: Before

Farmhouse Front Yard: After (Illustrations by Penny Delany.)

negates any need to go to the health club! This wall, now completed, greatly helps absorb traffic noise, as well as giving the front garden a crisp, defined look.

Taken together, these projects have transformed the front of the property from an unused and unloved space into a practical, enjoyable part of the landscape that complements the house as a whole.

Boxwood Basics

Boxwood was one of the first ornamental shrubs imported to our shores, and it has been in constant use ever since, for several reasons. First and foremost, common box (*Buxus sempervirens*) is a long-lived yet fairly rapidly growing shrub that is extremely easy to shape into a wide variety of forms. The dwarf type, Buxus sempervivens '*Suffruticosa*', is perfect for edging beds and borders, grows at the infinitesimally slow rate of ½ inch a year or less, and at maturity is no taller than 18 inches. Another distinctive feature of boxwood is its scent—when the sun heats the leaves, the oils in them release a delicious fragrance, which for me always recalls images of summer afternoons in great gardens.

Box gardens were extremely commonplace in this country, especially in the South, until the time of the Civil War, when the labor required to shape and maintain these extensive and elaborate gardens became too "expensive," as one old book put it. This, of course, is a euphemistic way of saying that the "labor" had been emancipated, as it is an undeniable fact that many gardens throughout the United States, north and south, relied heavily on slaves for their upkeep at one point or another in their history. A perfect example of an antebellum boxwood garden is Valley View, outside of Carterville, Georgia (see page 90). The house and garden were built by Col. Hame Caldwell Sproull in the 1840s, and despite the vicissitudes of war and fortune (Sherman passed right by), the garden remained

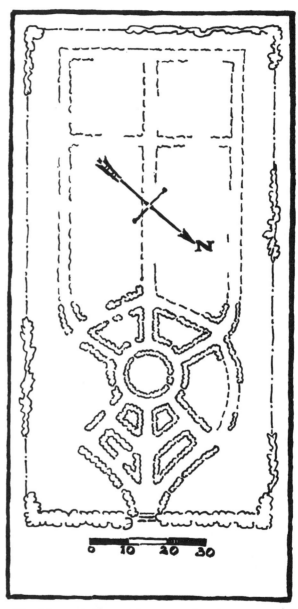

Although boxwood does much better in southern climes, it was not unknown in the North, even at the very edge of its range. This elaborate Colonial boxwood pattern survived long enough outside of Portsmouth, New Hampshire, to be documented by Arthur Shurcliff in the early part of the 20th century.

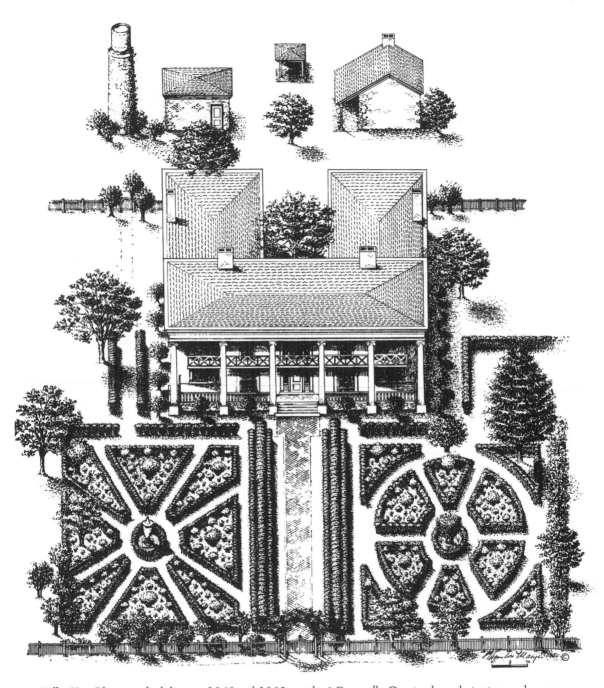

Valley View Plantation, built between 1848 and 1863 outside of Carterville, Georgia, shows the intricate garden patterns that can be achieved using boxwood edging. This type of elaborate front-yard treatment was common in the South before the Civil War. (Illustration from *Garden History of Georgia, 1733–1933* by the Peachtree Garden Club, 1933. Copyright © 1976 Garden Club of Georgia. Reprinted with permission of Garden Club of Georgia, Inc.)

reasonably intact into the 1930s, when it was documented in *The Garden History of Georgia 1733–1933*. Although it is somewhat more elaborate than other gardens of the period, its formal borders are actually fairly typical of antebellum plantation gardens. Note how box is used throughout to both define the various sections of the garden and unite the diverse elements.

The Garden History of Georgia, from which this illustration comes, is careful to record that the boxwood at Valley View was brought by the owner's wife from her old family home in South Carolina. You will find this charming practice of passing boxwood from one generation's garden to the next in garden histories all over the country; it is a tradition that ought to be maintained today. For me, it's truly life-affirming to have a piece of someone else's garden to remember them by, perhaps because through these living gifts, in some small way a part of the person lives on. In my own garden there are many such "remembrance" plants. In particular, I am privileged to have some of the descendants of my grandfather's bearded irises, ones that my aunt lovingly saved and shipped to me after his death. Every time I look at those irises I smile, as they remind me of a wonderful man who managed to be grandfather, mentor, and dear friend and who was in large part responsible for my earliest interest in gardening. There is something almost magical about visiting a garden and knowing that a certain tree or shrub is a living memory of a long-lost time. Imagination is somehow quickened, and images fly: can't you just envision that early pioneer on her journey to the then wilds of Georgia, carefully guarding her mother's precious cutting of box to start a new garden far from home?

If you would like to use boxwood in your own garden, it's not hard to do. Boxwood is readily available at most nurseries, although it's certainly not inexpensive, at least around Boston, where one good-size shrub will make quite a dent in your wallet. If the idea of a box border appeals, but not the huge expenditure, why not carry on the tradition and start your own from a friend's or relative's garden? Boxwood roots readily from cuttings, which is why it was so easily carried from place to place even before modern transportation. To start a new box bush, simply take a 3- to 4-inch cutting of boxwood from the end of a branch, strip off the lower leaves, dip the cutting in rooting hormone, pot it in a soilless mix, and place the pot in the shade. A month or so later, roots will have formed, and voilà, you are part of a centuries-old tradition!

Common box is hardy to Zone 5B with protection, but take care after heavy winter storms to knock the snow from the bushes, or the branches will break off and leave unsightly gaps. Spraying with an antidesiccant in fall will also help immensely to keep the shrubs, especially the dwarf varieties, healthy over winter. There are a number of other, newer and more hardy boxwood varieties available for gardeners who live in more northerly climes.

Know Your Zone

Plant labels supply a lot of information that is ignored at your (and your plant's) peril. Perhaps the most important piece of label information, after size and light specifications, is the growing zone, or hardiness information. Plants are almost always labeled "Hardy to Zone X," indicating the geographical limits of their range. To find out what growing zone your garden is in, consult the map below: the coldest zones are those with the lowest numbers. Many maps further divide large zones into several half zones, labeled A and B (B being the warmer). In general, plants can survive in zones with numbers greater or equal to their minimum hardiness zone. Although there are some exceptions to this rule (some plants have an upper limit to their heat tolerance—their labels will read hardy to Zones 7–9, for example—while others can sometimes be coaxed by experienced growers to accept a colder zone or half zone), the beginner would be wise to accept a plant's hardiness rating as a given. Occasionally, however, even the label will attempt to fudge: a classic example is "minimally (or "normally") hardy to Zone 6," which, for the wise beginner who doesn't want to replace their plant, should be read as "hardy to Zone 7"!

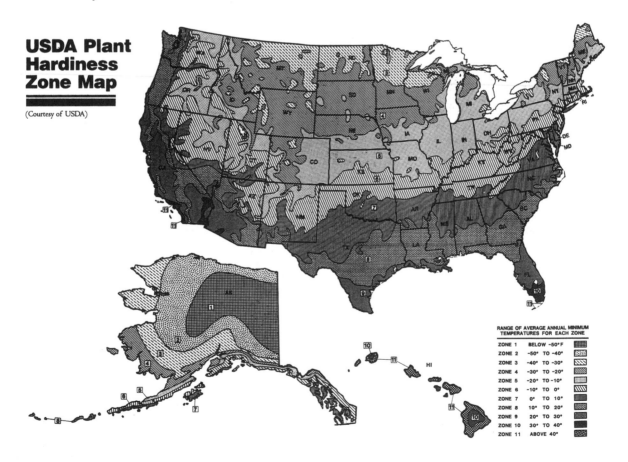

USDA Plant Hardiness Zone Map

(Courtesy of USDA)

RANGE OF AVERAGE ANNUAL MINIMUM
TEMPERATURES FOR EACH ZONE

ZONE 1	BELOW −50°F
ZONE 2	−50° TO −40°
ZONE 3	−40° TO −30°
ZONE 4	−30° TO −20°
ZONE 5	−20° TO −10°
ZONE 6	−10° TO 0°
ZONE 7	0° TO 10°
ZONE 8	10° TO 20°
ZONE 9	20° TO 30°
ZONE 10	30° TO 40°
ZONE 11	ABOVE 40°

Historic Garden

Fort Vancouver, Washington

The restored garden at Fort Vancouver, showing the palisade and the fort buildings beyond. (Photo by Rick Edwards, courtesy of Fort Vancouver National Historic Site.)

> *We were soon conducted . . . into the garden, and be assured that we were not a little surprised to see west of the Rocky Mountains, where we did not expect to meet scarcely the first buddings of civilization, such perfection in gardening.*

This would be rare praise for any garden, but it is nothing short of extraordinary when you consider the date and location: 1836, at the end of the Oregon Trail, where one day would rise the city of Vancouver, Washington. Here stood Fort Vancouver and, just outside its palisades, a remarkable garden created at the insistence of a remarkable man, Dr. John McLoughlin.

First, some background. Despite its name, Fort Vancouver was not a military establishment but rather one of the numerous trading posts built by the Hudson's Bay Company throughout the Northwest. Established in 1824, the fort had three purposes: to provide a principal base of operations for the company's enormous trade in beaver pelts and furs, to strengthen the British claim to the area, and to discourage American settlement of what was then called Oregon Country through a devious strategy of monopolizing the fur trade. While the economic theory behind Fort Vancouver was sound, it failed to take into consideration the dynamic and forceful personality of the fort's head administrator, the doctor-turned-fur-trader John McLoughlin. A wise businessman with an uncanny knack for anticipating trends, McLoughlin disagreed with his superiors back in London. He strongly believed that the area's future lay more in farming than in fur trading. And he did not feel that increased American immigration posed the threat to company profits that many claimed it did.

In fact, McLoughlin chose the fort's site on the Columbia River not so much for its trading advantages as for its being "a place where we could cultivate the soil and raise our own provisions." He slowly proceeded to shift the fort's economic emphasis from trading furs to producing the foodstuffs and supplies that would be needed by the area's growing population. As it turned out, McLoughlin was right on the mark: by the mid-1840s, when fur production had fallen to almost nothing owing to overhunting, the fort was turning over a healthy profit from raising grain, milling flour, breeding livestock, processing salmon, and producing goods as varied as milled lumber and dairy products. By 1846 the fort had almost 1,500 acres under intense cultivation; of these, the pride and joy of Fort Vancouver was McLoughlin's kitchen garden.

Situated just outside the fort's walls, the 7-acre garden was the first formally arranged planting west of the Mississippi. In typical early-19th-century fashion, the purpose of McLoughlin's garden was twofold: a pleasure garden for himself and the other company officials, and a place to produce delights for his table. Everything grew there in profusion: vegetables ("too numerous to mention," noted one early visitor); fruits on bush and vine—muskmelons, watermelons, citrons, grapes, gooseberries, currants, raspberries, and blackberries; fruits on trees—plums, nectarines, cherries, peaches, pears, quinces, and pomegranates. Even oranges, lemons, and figs grew in protective frames. Flowers were everywhere, mixed in around the vegetables: love-lies-bleeding, poppies, delphiniums, foxgloves, old roses, cosmos, sweet peas, and dahlias, then a great novelty, even in Europe. McLoughlin used the company's vast resources to import material from all over the globe for his garden. In fact, most of the fort's original stock came from England and Scotland, as did the fort's full-time gardener, Scotsman William Bruce.

The reason this profusion of plants functioned so well together and was so admired by visitors was because of the garden's cohesive design. Every important design element we've discussed was present: a cohesive, logical layout; defined exterior borders; internal divisions determined by usage and purpose; a rational decorating scheme that related one room to another; and some sort of center or focal point to each space. McLoughlin's garden was rectilinear, separated from the areas around it by a wooden fence. Internally, ample paths, lined with strawberries, divided the garden into nine smaller rectangles. Although each area had a slightly different layout, the beds shared enough common elements to form unity. Garden ornaments—the wellhead, fences, trellis, arbors, and benches—added the required focal points and provided pleasurable spots from which to admire the floriferous garden.

The very fact that some semblance of McLoughlin's garden exists today is a tribute to the National Park Service and in particular to Ranger Rick Edwards and his staff, who have meticulously researched and helped to restore the garden, mostly through volunteer effort. The fort was designated a historic site in 1948. Restoration and rebuilding began in earnest in 1961, although efforts to reproduce the gardens did not get under way until the late 1980s. (The current buildings and gardens are re-creations, as the structures

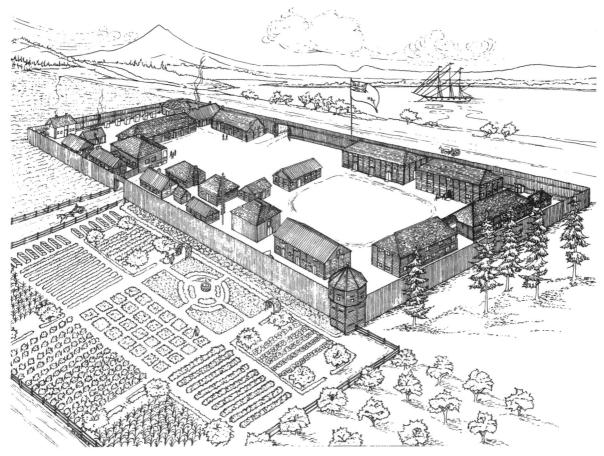

A modern rendering of McLoughlin's garden, pieced together from firsthand accounts and sketches, shows the site as it may have appeared in 1845. (Drawing courtesy of National Park Service, Fort Vancouver National Historic Site.)

and gardens had disappeared rapidly after the Hudson's Bay Company abandoned the fort in 1860.) While what garden visitors marvel at today is only a fraction of the original kitchen garden's 7 acres, the re-creation done by Edwards and his staff is nothing short of remarkable. Heirloom plants grow in organic abundance, showing not only the possibilities of period plantings but also an environmentally friendly approach to modern gardening. Plans have been formulated to restore the garden to its former site and size, and if adequate funding is provided, visitors may one day again be able to wander through this marvelous masterpiece of cultivated, cohesive garden design.

Fort Vancouver Old-Fashioned Favorites Recommended by Fort Vancouver's Gardening Ranger, Rick Edwards:

1. **Cinderella pumpkin** (Rouge Vif d'Etamps): This is a wonderful heirloom that dates back to the 18th century. Besides its remarkable orange-red appearance and heavy ribbing, which makes it look like the coach from those wonderful old engravings of the Cinderella tale, Rouge Vif d'Etamps makes one of the best pumpkin pies I have ever tasted.

2. **Cardoon** (*Cynara cardunculus*): We first planted this southern European native back in 1988, and its gray-green leaves, which often reach 6 feet, have been a real attention-getter ever since. William Cobbett, the author of *The English Gardener* (published in 1829 and one of the books used to re-create the Fort Vancouver garden), was not especially fond of the plant and said that if you must grow it, it should be planted near the back of the garden so as not to overpower the other plants. Personally, I think it's spectacular.

3. **Carrot 'Scarlet Horn':** This tasty little carrot gets its name from the reddish hue that develops at the top, near the surface of the soil. A great carrot for general growing conditions.

4. **Watermelon 'Moon and Stars':** I first learned about this wonderful heirloom from Kent Whealy of the Seed Savers Exchange. Even though the melon dates from a later period than the 1840s, we have chosen to grow it because of its remarkable appearance: a dark green skin covered with yellow spots that are said to resemble the moon and the stars. This plant was near extinction ten years ago, but thanks to a few dedicated growers, it now can be seen in county fairs throughout the country.

5. **Marigold 'Lemon Gem':** This beautiful little annual is reminiscent of the original Victorian marigolds, before they were hybridized almost beyond recognition. 'Lemon Gem' produces masses of single flowers that many don't even recognize as marigolds. They can be planted in clumps and borders to produce a very pleasing appearance. Its foliage is quite fragrant and looks wonderful planted with lobelias like 'Crystal Palace'.

6. **Tomato 'Pomme d'Amour':** This gem we came across recently from Select Seeds. This plant does wonderfully in the Pacific Northwest, producing groups of five to seven medium-size tomatoes that are clustered on the end of the vine. It reminds me of the hothouse variety that you spend around $3 a pound for in the gourmet produce markets. You also have to love the name "Apple of Love."

7. **Black hollyhocks:** A favorite of Thomas Jefferson and our visitors alike, this hollyhock is a real showstopper with a very dark maroon flower that almost looks black. Sometimes it produces a double flower that only adds to the visual impact.

8. **Bean 'Scarlet Runner':** Every year I plant these favorites on May 24, Queen Victoria's birthday, along the fence on the end of the garden. By late summer, the vines make a great screen with masses of red flowers. No old garden should be without it.

9. **Zinnia elegans:** Although introduced around 1900, this flower has such an old-fashioned look and feel that we always include some in the cutting bed. It is very easy to grow and never fails to put on a colorful show.

10. **Hops** *(Humulus lupulus)*: This plant was important in 19th-century gardens for several reasons: the primary, of course, was for making beer, but hops was also a key ingredient in the production of yeast for bread. The young shoots are very tasty, too, and can be steamed like asparagus and served with a butter-parsley sauce. Hops vines are also a wonderful plant for shading a sunny terrace or arbor seat.

How-to: Sizing Up Your Property, Part Two

Now that you've already charted out your property, noted down its principal features and areas, and made a general assessment of what you've got and what you want, your next step is to roughly block out your property into logical areas, generally determining the purpose and extent of each "room." For some areas this is rather easy. Other places on the property present more difficulties, especially when there doesn't seem to be any obvious purpose or reason for their presence, other than the fact that they *exist* and it would be nice to use them.

Every property poses its own challenges that require their own solutions, so perhaps the easiest way to go about this is to follow the creation of an actual plan I did for a client on the South Shore of Massachusetts (see figures below and on next page). This particular home was built around 1840 and located about a block from the seashore, in a quaint section of an old whaling village. The house was a simple late Greek Revival structure, of the type called Farmhouse or Carpenter Revival. Although this house was an antique, the house's simple, rather generic detailing and plain white clapboards make it not altogether dissimilar from thousands of houses all across America, both new and old. Also, its tiny (8,000 sq. ft.) lot presents the same challenges faced by many of today's gardeners.

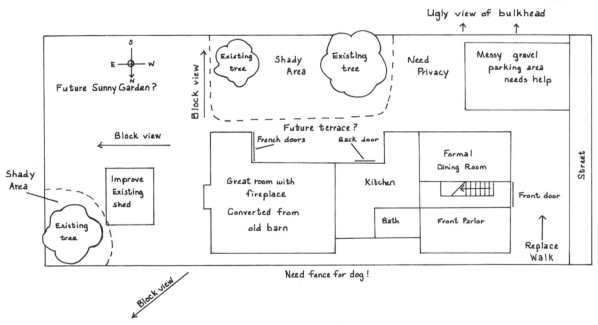

The initial overview of this garden shows many of the problems common to old landscapes: stranded front doors, poor sightlines, limited (or nonexistent) outdoor sitting space, run-down garden areas, and no provision for parking. (Illustration by Penny Delany.)

The owners had purchased the property to use as a summer/weekend residence, and after substantial restoration and remodeling of the interior, they were ready to tackle the outside. Because this was a part-time residence, the owners wanted an adapted version of the original landscape—something that would evoke the romance of the period and complement the house, without being too fussy and consuming of valuable weekend time. The garden also had to accommodate the demands of modern living.

Off-street parking, for instance, was essential, because there were times of the year (most of the winter, in fact) when street parking was prohibited. Obviously the need for parking had not existed when the house was built; the original owner kept two horses down the street at the local mews when he wasn't sailing the seven seas. The most recent owners had simply thrown down some gravel in a sloppy, lazy way and parked their cars on what was once the front lawn. As neither distant parking nor a messy lot was an acceptable solution to my clients, some compromises to exact historical accuracy had to be made. The trick in these situations is to find a solution that blends as harmoniously as possible into the existing architectural and landscape fabric, respecting the past as well as the needs of the present.

To begin, I drew up a basic plot plan. As you can see from the first illustration, there wasn't much to work with. The lot (55 by 130 feet) was essentially flat, with grass, a gravel parking area, and few old trees and shrubs. Next I noted the current problems and conditions. An immediate problem was that the front door was "orphaned," stranded without a walkway. This is a typical occurrence in many old houses: as the car gained importance, the entrance nearest the garage or parking area was the one most used and the front door was seldom if ever opened. With the decline of foot traffic, homeowners were often reluctant to spend money to repair an unused walkway and found it simpler to remove it entirely rather than replace it.

The lack of privacy was another major problem. The house was hemmed in on three sides by the neighbors' lots; the boundaries were so completely undefined that we had to have the place surveyed to find out exactly where they lay. (An important issue: Make sure the improvements you're planning are on your own land. You would be amazed how many times people undertake a project, only to find out that all or part of their effort is actually owned by someone else, with all the attendant ramifications.) Whatever plantings had existed when the house was built had long ago disappeared, with the exception of those few old trees. The yard stood completely and unacceptably open on all four sides.

As my clients loved to cook and entertain, restoration of the front entranceway seemed a top priority, as did creating a space to sit and relax outdoors. They also wanted a small garden area that could be easily maintained yet would provide bountiful flowers and herbs for the house. And besides the parking problem, the owners needed a way to get to the back door easily and dry-shod, without compromising at least some privacy for the backyard. The only outbuilding on the property was a large shed, which, given the absence of a garage for storage, the owners were loath to part with. It was quite ugly, however, and unfortunately sited in the middle of what little space they had to the rear of the house. Finally, there was a dog that needed a fenced run.

Simply by considering these circumstances and writing them down on paper, I was able to see the elements of the property begin to fall into place. The first step to designing a cohesive landscape is to ask yourself: *What spaces are essential and how will people move through them?* In this property, I put the front walk back, and the whole front of the house suddenly made sense. (Houses with no access to their front doors always seem lonely and unloved to me, like the proverbial Cinderella, relegated to the day-to-day drudgery of the back door and never getting the chance to celebrate or put on a party dress.) Designing a more attractive driveway also helped that area come together. (Chapter V explains more about the front walk and drive areas.)

The terrace was another easy feature to locate, as was the garden. Terraces should always be as near to the kitchen as practically possible, and gardens, especially flower and herb gardens, should be in the sunniest areas possible (so should swimming pools, for those who may be interested). That took care of siting the garden, since only one area was sunny enough.

The clients' desire to keep the shed made that a natural utility area. I did, however, move it back and alter its design to make it more similar to the house architecture; I added a small sitting arbor on one side to anchor the structure to the garden. Notice how all these areas line up along two general axes, a primary one parallel to the long dimension of the house and another, shorter one behind it. This positioning is deliberate and is meant to tie the landscape to the house. The layout, like the house, is not exactly symmetrical, as a Colonial landscape might have been, but it is balanced and ordered, with a rectangular, geometric design that echoes the simple lines of the house.

The next step was to define the borders of these spaces and make the overall landscape coherent. There are many different ways to do this, but the method I chose is typical of urban gardens: a mixture of fencing and hedges. Delineating the exterior boundaries was easy—on the drive, south, and rear sides of the lot, where the clients planned to spend their time outside, I wanted a fairly tall fence for immediate privacy; plantings would have worked but would have taken too much time to mature. I chose a 6-foot wooden fence, with solid 4-foot panels and a 2-foot picket top that matched the house details and made the fence seem a natural extension of the architecture. In addition, the continuous line of this fence around the borders of the outdoor living areas helped to link them all together. On the north side of the lot and in front areas of the yard, I used a shorter version of the same simple picket used in the upper portion of the 6-foot fence, which defined the lot line and kept the front from visually falling off into space.

Deciding on the internal divisions was much trickier, because while I wished to define the area inside the property boundary in logical units, I wanted to do so in a way that maximized the internal space and didn't divide the lot into tiny unusable

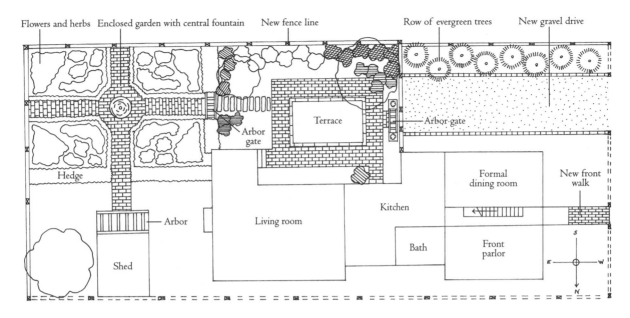

Flowers and herbs   Enclosed garden with central fountain   New fence line   Row of evergreen trees   New gravel drive

Hedge

Arbor gate

Terrace

Arbor·gate

Arbor

Living room

Kitchen

Bath

Formal dining room

Front parlor

New front walk

Shed

The proposed layout answers many of the owners' wants and concerns—for parking, additional garden and seating space, and more privacy—but still maintains the property's period feel.

spaces. This is where those sight lines so common in Victorian landscape plans come in. In this case, there was nothing to see beyond the property lines except the neighbors' wash, so I enclosed the exterior borders fairly tightly. On the inside, however, I tried to maximize the sight lines as much as possible. As you enter from the driveway gate, for instance, you can see all the way across the property into the garden, with its fountain. From the fountain you can look across to the arbor seating area next to the shed. This is possible because the internal dividers are boxwood hedges, which are compact enough to allow you to see over them and which carry the eye forward and beyond into the next area. These hedges give a feeling of spaciousness and continuity to the landscape, without appearing overly confining.

Finally, I repeated similar design elements throughout the garden to unite the various sections. The fence, the boxwood, and the other plantings echo one another throughout the garden. The brick in the front walk is the same as that in the back terrace, although in a different pattern. The cobbles of the garden are repeated in the walk and drive edgings. The shed reflects the house, and the arbors borrow from the same architectural vocabulary. Together, all these elements helped to join the garden sections together and make a pleasing, coherent whole. Lastly, I made sure each area had a defined focal point or center—the front walk, the drive, the terrace, the fountain, and the shed all anchor their respective sections of the yard, and together they form a harmonious whole.

Details

$\mathcal{L}$et's face it: Many modern gardens, even those that were professionally designed, lack the old charm. They aren't romantic, magical places. True, they are filled with flowering trees, shrubs, and flower borders like their predecessors. The lawns are green and flat, the beds are well maintained, everything trimmed and prim. And *boring*. Why? Because old guiding principles are being ignored, and because new gardens lack the wonderful details that gave the great old gardens such personality.

At its best, a garden is never just a collection of beautiful plants. It is an open structure, with man-made elements that give the garden definition, individuality, and something approaching permanence. America's historic gardens contained artfully laid-out walks and drives; well-designed and well-constructed railings, fences, and ornaments—features that were critical to each garden's unique sense of place.

Nowadays, many gardeners shy away from these beautiful items because they can be expensive. But there are two reasons why I believe we should reject this kind of thinking. The first is that we don't hesitate to add expensive items inside the house—giant TVs, intricate stereo systems, granite counters. Why, if we can afford this expenditure inside, have we stopped using detail to decorate our gardens outside? And second, providing interest and appeal to the garden does not always require huge expense or additional elements. Our gardening forebears took the time and effort to make sure that even the most common and utilitarian elements in the landscape had some intrinsic value. We can do the same for little or no added cost. Let's take a look at some common elements of our gardens and see what can be done to improve them.

Fences

Fences are one aspect of American gardens prime for improvement. Instead of the beautiful, carefully crafted fences of old, these days you'll find miles and miles of awful chain link, cheap post and rail, and pencil-like picket fences that add nothing to either the house or the garden. Commonly the fence line itself doesn't even make sense. The homeowner or landscaper simply decides some type of barrier or separation is needed and then plunks down whatever blocks out the offending view or closes off the needed space, without considering how the fence relates to the rest of the landscape. If we think about the original purpose of fencing, we can see why this doesn't work. Fences were initially designed to enclose an area from animals, starting at a logical point and finishing up at an equally logical conclusion. They didn't just arise, like a proverbial Venus from the waves, and run halfway down a front or side yard as they often do today.

In the best of all cases, fence lines should begin attached to some structure, such as the side of a building, and run to some end point, such as another fence, building, or large terminal post. If it is not possible to begin or end a fence against a hard surface, one trick is to use some type of large planting that obscures one end of the fence line and makes it seem as if it continues out of sight. Whatever the specifics of the property, it is important that the fence be logically linked to the garden structure around it.

This relation extends to the design of the fence as well. Given the nature of the fence and house, the fence line is actually an *extension* of the architecture into the garden, so it is extremely important that the fence echo the

WOODEN FENCES

Wooden fences appeared in American gardens with the first settlers. Over the centuries, a wide variety of fence styles, like these historic examples, has arisen to match almost every type of house. (Illustrations from *Fences: Authentic Details for Design & Restoration* by Peter Joel Harrison. Copyright © 1999 John Wiley & Sons, Inc. Reprinted with permission of John Wiley & Sons, Inc.)

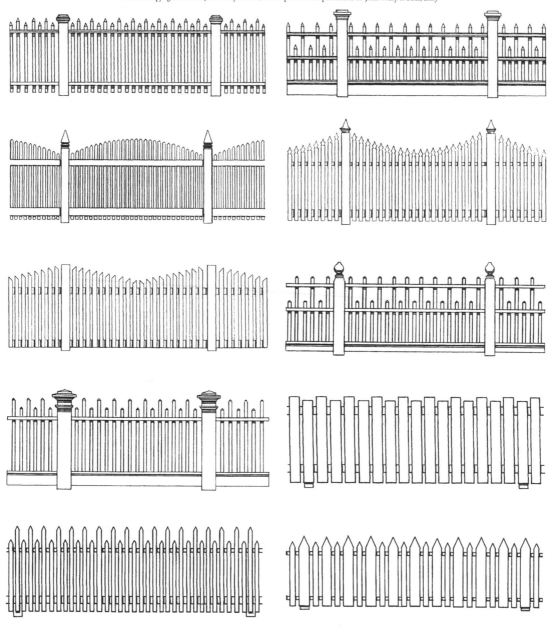

In this wonderful illustration from Scott, the iron cresting on the fence echoes the trim on the porch, giving the impression that the house and fence were designed as one.

house. Fence styles and house architectural styles developed together, each new housing style driving the creation of matching new fence types; for most homes, there is an appropriate fence style to match. The first houses at Plimoth and Jamestown had rough-hewn pales around their gardens. Later, as houses became more sophisticated, so did fences; Federal and Georgian styles produced a wide variety of wooden picket and board-style fences that were appropriate to these houses. Later still, the Victorians created even more elaborate wooden styles, as well as intricate cast- and wrought-iron fences, which became common during the early 1800s.

If a search through the standard options doesn't produce a suitable choice for your house, whatever its style, consider a custom fence. Copy a portion of railing or baluster from your home or one in the neighborhood and have a local carpenter make up the sections for you. There are even firms that can ship fencing sections to you at a very reasonable cost. (See the list of Suppliers in the appendices.) Fences are worth the effort, and they are one of those items that you should be very fussy about, if for no other reason than that they are a highly visible component of the landscape that do more than any other single element to define the style and feeling of a garden. They are also generally one of the most expensive parts of the landscape. This is not an item to scrimp on. Cheap fences are visible from a mile away and generally wind up costing you more in the end. Good fences, on the other hand, last for decades, so care should be taken to make sure your choice of style, height, and material is an apt one.

I learned this the hard way in my own yard. One of the first areas to be built after I moved in was the dooryard garden, which was to be enclosed by a simple white picket fence to match the simple architecture of my 1852 farmhouse. But I was in a rush to finish off this area of the yard, and I disregarded my own advice to be patient. Instead of waiting and installing a good-quality fence when I could afford the time and money to do it properly, I went out and bought a cheap pine picket fence from the local hardware superstore. In this day and age when labor costs as much as or more than the materials, this was an expensive error. The workmen would have charged the same price to install a good-quality fence. As it was, within five years, the nails and screws

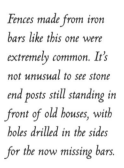

Fences made from iron bars like this one were extremely common. It's not unusual to see stone end posts still standing in front of old houses, with holes drilled in the sides for the now missing bars.

IRON FENCES

Nothing says Victorian like these fences from Stewart Iron Works (see Suppliers), which are all reproduced from period designs. (Courtesy of Stewart Iron Works.)

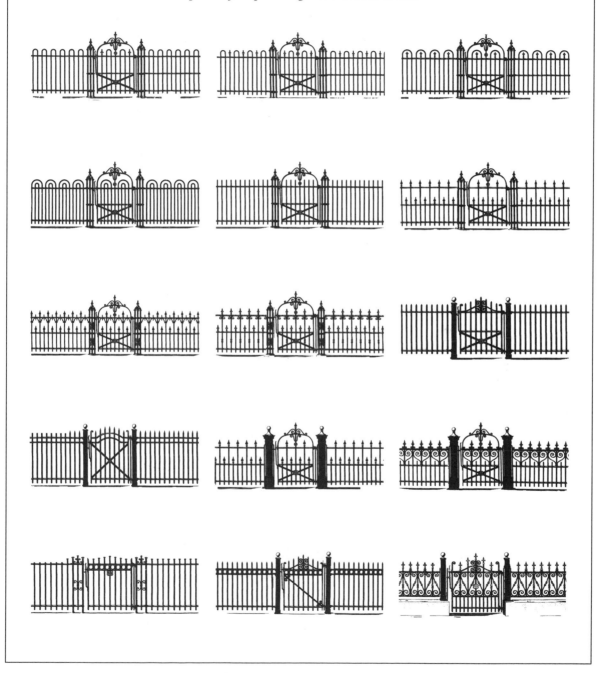

had popped through the wood, and several of the pickets had rotted; now the whole cheap affair needs to be yanked out and replaced.

In a way I wish I could install one of those marvelous Victorian wrought-iron fences that are again offered by various suppliers. For years it was impossible to buy quality iron fences in historic styles, but now several companies are reproducing old patterns (see Suppliers in the appendices). Unfortunately, such an ornate fence would probably be too much for the simple architecture of my house—but if you have an ornate Victorian such as a Gothic Revival, Queen Anne, or Shingle Style house in a fairly urban setting, these fences are ideal!

In fact, if you are a city dweller, chances are your old house may have been originally fronted by an iron fence. Like iron roof cresting and other architectural ornaments common in the Victorian period, these fences were produced in hundreds of different designs, some of which can appear almost gaudy to the modern eye. During World War II, many historic fences were patriotically given over to scrap-iron drives to support the war effort and thus were lost to the modern admirer. These iron fences didn't go quietly, though; you can find hints of their existence wherever they were previously installed—remnants of stone posts with iron bolts and, commonly, a stone coping piece that ran along the base, often to be found buried just under the modern soil level. If you uncover some of these old ghosts, you owe it to your landscape to try to restore the iron fence. It was integral to the original design of both house and yard, and you'll be amazed at what a positive effect its restoration will accomplish.

GO TO JAIL, GO DIRECTLY TO JAIL

Unless you want your house to look like a frontier fort, at all costs avoid the so-called "stockade" fencing so often found in landscapes today. This ugly fence with its sharp, pointed, pale tops screams "go away!" and really has no place in a domestic setting. While stockade fencing is often slightly cheaper than other more appropriate styles, the nominal cost savings don't justify the aesthetic detriment to your garden.

Garden Structures

Freestanding pergolas, arbors, or summerhouses (also called gazebos) used to be ubiquitous in our gardens. To me, they represent the best and most romantic part of our gardening past. If you've ever had a chance to sit under an arbor in a place such as Williamsburg, with the grapevines providing cool shade overhead and the warm air redolent with the smell of grapes, you know what I am talking about. So why aren't they commonplace in our gardens? The answer is partly their cost, but there is another reason, too. Many of these structures, installed in the 19th century, started to need repair during the 1940s and '50s, just when they were the least valued aesthetically. Rather than undertaking the cost of repair, people simply took them down or let them fall down. This practice was extremely common with exterior architectural ornaments as well, which is the reason why so many of our houses lack the beautiful detailing that they possessed at the time they were built.

To some degree, the original builders were at fault. A lot of this stuff, although lovely, was not designed with maintenance in mind and proved overwhelmingly costly or even impossible to keep up. I believe, however, that we have an obligation to ourselves and to our children to preserve, replace, and repair whatever we can, both in our houses and in our gardens, so that future generations can share in our rich inheritance. And we really have no excuse not to, as technological advances in preventing rust, rot, and decay now allow us to enjoy these garden structures at much lower cost and with much less maintenance.

Arbors, pergolas, and summerhouses have a myriad of functions in the garden. They are especially suitable as spectacular focal points—at the intersection of two paths, for example, or at the end of a long vista. Two things to keep in mind, however: Like fences, their positioning must make sense to the overall design of the landscape, and the style of the structure should closely parallel, even echo, that of the house. Fortunately, we still have the original patterns for many of these wonderful garden additions, and it shouldn't be too difficult to choose one, or several, to complement whatever style of house you own.

Garden structures like these add grace, charm, and, most important, focus to important areas of the garden.

Decks

While we are on the subject of garden structures, I suppose a few words should be said about the modern mania for decks in the American landscape. When decks first started to appear in the 1970s, they were fairly modest affairs, built low to the ground—simply extensions of the house that were not too dissimilar from the wonderful Victorian porches that had preceded them. Then suddenly, decks started to appear hanging off the sides of homes 5, 10, 15 feet above the level of the land below, like some giant stilt-legged spider trying to envelop the back of the house. Not only are these monstrosities ugly, but the dry, shaded, barren earth below them is absolutely useless, except as an unsightly storage area, and they are impossible to integrate into the overall landscape. What's more, with the deck hanging off the back of your house at 15 feet above the ground, you are subject to every burning ray of sun, cold gust of wind, and prying stare from your neighbors. Decks such as these are truly abominations, being neither of the garden nor of the house, and should be avoided at all cost (which conversely should save you a lot of money, because they are also extremely expensive!).

There is an undeniable appeal to a porch. It's at once romantic and welcoming, and says "Set awhile and take a load off your feet" in a way that no deck ever will.

In fact, I would go so far as to say that decks really have no place on old houses, and with newer house styles, you should proceed cautiously and keep several things in mind. The first: Decks should be low to the ground—no more than several feet above the surface of the land below. Don't try to use decks as a means to make a transition of a story or more from the back of the house to the yard level—it just won't work. Instead, in new construction, design the house itself so that you have access from the kitchen or back levels as directly as possible onto a terrace or deck more or less at ground level. In already built houses, where this may be impossible, call a spade a spade and construct a well-built *porch* or *balcony* that is consistent with the architecture of the house.

This leads to my second point. Whatever type of deck you choose, make sure the detailing on the deck matches that of the house. Work like this is expensive, and there is always a tendency to cut corners and skimp on what may seem at first glance to be nonessentials. This is a big mistake, as it's these little finishing touches that often determine how successful a structure is. I've known people to spend $20,000 constructing a huge, elaborate deck and then decide to forgo spending the few extra dollars required to install well-crafted spindles, railings, and other details that make the structure actually *look* like something and unite it to the house. If money is an issue, wait until you are comfortable with the expenditure and build what you *really* want; don't compromise and build something less. You'll never be satisfied with the compromise, and it will only wind up costing more in the end. Patience is definitely a virtue in the garden, and there is nothing wrong with waiting to achieve the effect you want. Most people have only one chance in life to build a truly wonderful garden—it's a privilege and a pleasure, and you should take your time and do it right.

Ornaments

Over three hundred years of gardening history have given us examples of almost every type of ornament imaginable, from classical statuary to Victorian rockeries. Choosing garden ornaments can sometimes be a tricky business—witness those thousands of plastic pink flamingos that dot front yards from Oregon to Florida. With so many possibilities, it's hard to give specific advice—each yard will have a different set of requirements. In general, though, I can recommend that you make conservative choices that you are fairly sure match the style and materials used in your gardens.

Also, avoid inexpensive imitations. If you feel a lead birdbath will make the perfect focal point, then wait and buy exactly the one you want—that plastic counterfeit made to look like metal will be seen a mile off for exactly what it is. Garden ornaments should appear to be happy with themselves and not attempt to be something they are not. There is nothing inherently wrong with plastic in the garden—as long as it looks like plastic, not fake wood, stone, or metal, and is appropriate for its site. Craftsmanship in garden ornaments is another issue to watch out for, especially in statuary—make sure that whatever you buy is well made, with finely delineated line and form. Even badly made garden ornaments are often quite expensive, so it pays to keep an eye out for quality and buy the best you can afford.

One of my favorite garden ornaments for the traditional garden—the sundial—dates at least to ancient Greece and, until recently, was not really an ornament but an essential timepiece. A great amount of science and engineering went into producing the most accurate dial possible, so much so that some modern dials are correct to a fraction of a second. (While most people could tell time only by the sun, others used moonlight and could accurately predict the rising and setting of various stars and planets.)

Sundials make wonderful garden focal points, all the more so because they often bear poignant mottoes. The themes vary from morbid to cheery, although almost all have to do with the passage of time in some way. Latin has traditionally been the preferred language for dials in the West, although many other languages are found as well. Here are some of the more interest-

SUNDIALS

Created in almost every style imaginable, sundials personify the perfect amalgam of grace and utility.

ing mottoes I have noted, with translations by me. All are taken from dials before 1900.

NON NUMERO NISI SERENAS (or AUREAS) and variations ("Let others tell of storms and showers, I count only sunny hours")

TEMPUS FUGIT and variations ("Time flies")

BEHOLD AND BE GONE ABOUT YOUR BUSINESS

CARPE DIEM ("Seize the day")

DEPRESSA RESURGO ("I set to rise")

DISCE TUOS NUMERARE DIES ("Learn to number thy days")

EHEU FUGACES LABUNTUR ANNI ("Alas the fleeting years slip by")

TRIFLE NOT, YOUR TIME IS SHORT

L'HEURE PASSE, L'AMITIE RESTE ("Time passes, friendship remains")

FESTINAT SUPREMA ("The last hour approaches")

FUMUS ET UMBRA SUMUS ("We are naught but smoke and shadow")

HOC TUUM EST ("The present is all you may claim as yours")

HODIE MIHI, CRAS TIBI ("Today is mine, tomorrow may be yours")

THE IDLE WHO WOULD BE COUNTED WISE
THINK ALL DELIGHT IN PASTIME LIES
NOR HEED THEY WHAT THE WISE CONDEMN:
AS THEY PASS TIME, TIME PASSES THEM

I NOTE THE TIME THAT YOU WASTE

NOW IS YESTERDAY'S TOMORROW

MORA TRAHIT PERICULUM ("Delay is dangerous")

MORS OMNIA VINCIT ("Death conquers all")

NIL DAT QUOD NON HABET ("Nothing comes of nothing")

A CLOCK THE TIME MAY WRONGLY TELL, I NEVER IF THE SUN SHINES WELL

NEQUE LUX SINE UMBRA ("There is no light without shade")

NIHIL VELOCIUS ANNIS ("Nothing is swifter than time")

C'EST L'HEURE DE BOIRE (or VIVRE) ("It's time to drink [or live]")

WITH MY SHADOW MOVES THE WORLD

SOL SPLENDIT OMNIBUS ("The sun shines for all")

LAS KLEIN STUND FURUBER GHAN
DU HABST DEN ETWAS GUT GETHAN
("Of the hours let there be none in which by you no good is done")

WE BOTH HASTEN TOWARDS SUNSET

SILENS LOQUOR ("Though silent, I speak")

LEAD KINDLY LIGHT

If you want your sundail to keep accurate time, you need to position it very carefully. The gnomon, the part that sticks up off the face, must point directly north and be set precisely level, not even one degree off. This much is pretty straightforward, but there's a bit more to positioning a sundial correctly. Sundials are place-specific, in that the angle of the gnomon must be parallel to the North Pole and therefore varies by latitude. Thus if you move a sundial north or south of the latitude for which it was constructed, it won't tell time correctly. What you need to do, then, is tilt the dial slightly off level to make up for the difference in latitude. Any of the books on sundials that are mentioned in the Bibliography will help you determine what latitude your dial was constructed for, and you can adjust it in a matter of minutes. Of course, if you don't care about telling time, you don't have to worry about precise positioning, although it seems a shame not to share in the age-old ritual of sun time.

Topiary

The art of topiary—sculpting fantastic shapes from growing plants—dates at least to the Roman Empire. Pliny the Elder describes topiary of "hunting scenes, fleets of ships, and all sorts of shapes," attributing the art's invention to a friend of Julius Caesar's, Gnaius Matius, although other sources mention topiary much earlier, in ancient Egypt. Whatever its exact origin, topiary was found throughout the Roman world and, to a large degree, almost disappeared with it. With the end of the age of cities and large country villas, the urbane practice of making topiaries was forgotten, not to be revived until well into the late Middle Ages, when the confined spaces of cloister and castle gardens necessitated the growing of

Topiary allows practiced gardeners to echo architectural shapes in the landscape. This Goreyesque illustration comes from a late-Victorian landscape manual.

various trees and shrubs in tight surroundings. Fruit trees were pruned flat against walls in a form of topiary known now as espalier, and as time progressed, various other trained shapes were devised or rediscovered. Renaissance and Baroque gardens were filled with topiary in every imaginable shape, both geometric and realistic. Wild animals, historical figures, even entire fox hunts have been created in topiary—living sculptures in green.

According to Barbara Gallup's *Topiary* (one of the best books on the subject), the first topiary on our shores was found in Williamsburg during the 1690s. From there, the art form soon spread throughout the colonies. Spared the dramatic decline that the English landscape movement caused to European topiary gardens, American topiary continued to be created throughout the early 19th century and experienced a mini-renaissance during the Victorian period, when all sorts of interesting shapes and patterns were attempted. The Victorians were particularly fond of training trees and shrubs into architectural shapes, thereby tightening the connection between natural and artificial elements in the garden. In fact, Frank J. Scott devotes an entire chapter in his *The Art of Beautifying Suburban Home Grounds* to the "artificial adaptations" of trees and shrubs, noting that where "less costly construction" is wanted, topiaries make charming, verdant arches, bowers, and pavilions.

Topiary is fashioned in one of three ways: by patiently carving the shape out of a large plant or shrub, by training the shape to follow some type of framework, or by shaping and pruning. Framework topiaries are really pretty easy. (The figures at right show several common Victorian

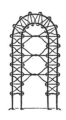

Above: Commercial Victorian wire topiary forms. Left: Victorians were ever practical. This simple form is made from three willow branches bent and tied with a string, to train vine topiaries.

shapes.) All that's required is enough patience to allow the plant to slowly climb over the shape (an ivy-clad heart, for instance) and a certain amount of diligence in keeping the vines or branches trimmed and bound to the framework. The other two forms require a certain amount of knowledge and finesse. Essentially, it's a process of diligently molding the plant through a combination of pruning and shaping the supple new growth into the form you want. It does take a number of years to achieve the full effect, but given the high prices topiaries command, and the terrific interest they generate in the garden, the effort's well worth it.

Many types of plants are ideal for topiaries. Boxwood and yew, among the shrubs, and ivy, among the vines, are classics. Many other plants are commonly used, too—dwarf junipers, rosemary, myrtle, roses, fuchsias, and numerous members of the ficus and citrus families, to name just a few of the possible candidates.

A topiary archway, made from two trees tied together seen at the beginning of its training period, and later, fully grown. Here, a weeping tree has been used.

Historic Garden

In Glorious Detail: The Longfellow House

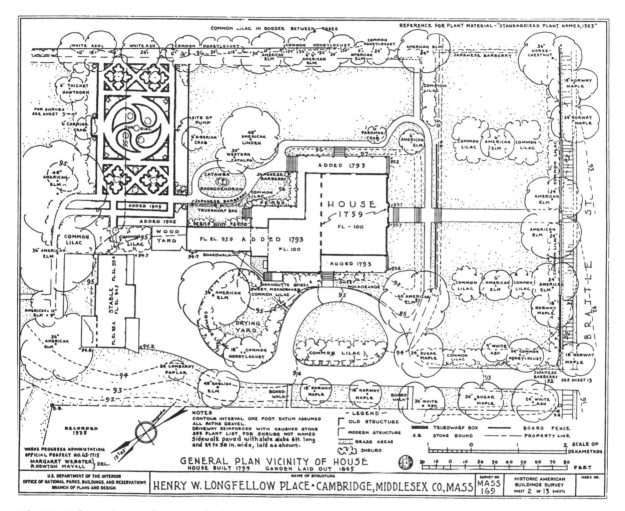

This 1935 plan of the Longfellow House landscape fortunately documented many features of the garden before neglect, decay, and the Great Hurricane of 1938 took their toll. (Illustration provided courtesy of National Park Service, Longfellow National Historic Site.)

It is rare to have an extant home, grounds, and a landscape plan dating to *before* the Revolution, but the Longfellow House in Cambridge, Massachusetts, has all three. Built in 1759 by Maj. John Vassall along a part of Brattle Street known as Tory Row, the house originally was part of a 100-acre country estate, with numerous outbuildings, gardens, fields, copses, orchards, and a series of wide-sweeping vistas over the marshes to the Charles River. The major spared no expense on house or garden: in front ran an elaborate brick wall (somewhat rare for the North, but not so for Cambridge, owing to the proximity of good clay) flanking the wide entrance walk and a symmetrically planted forecourt of American elms. In the rear, there was a paved service court, another rarity, and just beyond, two large elms stood guard over the entrance to the large formal garden.

Vassal, who was loyal to the Crown, hastily decamped at the start of hostilities in 1775, and the house was occupied by George Washington for ten months as his headquarters early in the Revolution. Emerging from the conflict relatively unscathed, the home was substantially enlarged by Andrew Craigie in 1793. He added two greenhouses and a classical temple and replanted the orchards, which had been cut down for firewood during the war. He also replaced a portion of the front brick wall with the latest fashion from Europe: a chinoiserie-patterned wooden fence. Unfortunately, Craigie's wallet didn't match his wonts (a fault common to old-house owners), and he died heavily in debt in 1819. His widow carried on for thirty years by renting rooms to Harvard students and professors, one of whom was Henry Wadsworth Longfellow.

In 1843 Longfellow and his new wife, Fanny, purchased the house and 5 acres of the original estate and set about restoring some of the former grandeur to the place, updating the house and outbuildings and adapting the neglected grounds to their tastes. Neither Longfellow nor his wife was an avid gardener, but they enjoyed flowers and the beauties of nature. They added shade trees, fruit trees, rustic seats, arbors, and an extensive formal flower garden patterned on one that Longfellow had seen in Italy. This garden, laid out in an elaborate "lyre pattern," was edged in boxwood and planted with a "variety of flowers." It contained a sundial with one of Longfellow's favorite lines from Dante: *Pensa che questo di mai non raggiorna* ("Remember that this day will never dawn again"). The many details—the edged, sinuous paths; the colorful flower gardens; the garden seats, benches, trellis, even a tree house—combined to provide the Victorian ideal of the garden.

After Longfellow's death in 1881, his daughter Alice inherited the house and land, and she made considerable alterations to the grounds in 1905 and 1925 with the help of two famous landscape designers: Martha Brookes Brown Hutcheson and Ellen Shipman. While the changes wrought by these two women were not historically accurate (in keeping with the Revivalist feeling of the teens and twenties, they were meant to furnish more "Colonial flavor" to the gardens), they most certainly further enhanced the beauty of the former design. Additional garden and shrubbery beds, intricate arbor seats, a large pergola, a woodland walk—all these allowed the garden to reach heights of splendor and beauty not seen since the Revolution.

Chinoiserie patterned fence

The beauty of a garden is ethereal, however, and changes wrought after the 1930s have not been kind to the Longfellow House landscape. While the house itself has been well preserved, the gardens suffered greatly during the famous hurricane of 1938, which destroyed vast numbers of the old trees and plantings. Land sell-offs before the National Park Service took over the site further diminished what remained. Subsequent funding shortages have meant that the garden focus to date has been on preserving existing features rather than on restoring what has been lost. Fortunately, the gardens were well documented in the early 1930s, and current plans call for the restoration of this marvelously detailed garden to its former glory.

The Rustic Style

Rustic-style pieces—essentially anything made to look as if it was constructed from natural logs—have been pretty much absent from the American garden scene for almost a hundred years, so it's hard to believe that rustic furniture and garden ornaments were all the rage from the middle of the 1800s to the turn of the century. Now, though, the style is becoming popular again, and it deserves a second look for modern gardens, especially ones where historical accuracy or a relaxed, country feel is important. Rustic-style pieces blend easily with all but the most formal garden elements.

The rustic style arose from necessity. Faced with limited means of transportation and the lack of milled lumber, many early gardeners of the 1800s simply created their own furniture, fences, and later even elaborate bridges and gazebos from rough-hewn limbs of whatever type tree was available. These homemade creations appealed to members of the early Romantic and, later, the Arts and Crafts movements, who recoiled from

The Rustic style even spread to house trim. Here, rustic porches, arbors, and railings adorn this cottage.

the harshness of the Industrial Revolution and sought solace in simpler, homemade products. The irony was that the extreme popularity of these objects created such a demand from urban and suburban gardeners that soon they could buy mass-manufactured rustic-style ornaments and furniture from many large firms, delivered right to their garden for easy assembly.

By the late Victorian era, rustic-style furniture was even being made in iron, uniting the two conflicting passions of the age—rusticity and industry. Even as a lover of Victoriana, I think that the crudely wrought iron limbs and boughs of some of these later, mass-produced pieces are rather ugly, and it was just this gaudy overexuberance that finally killed the demand for pieces in this style. On the other hand, the natural wooden product, especially when well and cleverly made, is quite appealing in a relaxed garden setting. Several sources are now making rustic pieces again, and if you are handy, you can even make your own, and re-create one of the great garden passions of the 19th century.

THE RUSTIC STYLE

Rustic-style wooden craftsmanship was applied to the classic structures and ornaments in the Victorian garden.

Stair rail

Gazebo near a lake

Table

Flower box holder

Tea house

Roofed bench

A Driveway Makeover

Driveways are one of the most common challenges I face as a landscape designer and restorer. They are ubiquitous in the modern landscape, setting the tone of the house and garden for every person who enters the property, so they deserve considerable attention. Yet in today's gardens, they are the element most often overlooked. Even gardeners who go through considerable trouble with the rest of their yards often neglect their drive. This house was a perfect example: although we had constructed a magical garden in what was once just a plain grass backyard, our efforts to create a more appropriate tone and mood for the property were in vain until we tackled the front approach.

The house, built in 1923, was designed by Royal Barry Wills, whose name later became synonymous with the Cape-style house he helped to popularize. Although the design subsequently became bastardized and degraded, the first Cape houses had truly elegant layouts and lines. This was one of those, designed and built by the master himself. The owner was an avid gardener and hostess, and it was important to find an approach to the house that matched the elegant gardens in the back.

Taking my cue from the classical lines of the architecture, I replaced the beat-up asphalt drive with one of river-washed pea stone. (Old-fashioned macadam, in which the stones are pressed into a hot tar mix and then rolled, would have achieved the

A Driveway: Before

same effect, and it would be a better choice for any type of site with a slope, as gravel always has a tendency to move downhill.) To give some idea of focus to the space and to break up the expanse of gravel, a simple circular medallion made of cobbles and granite was installed, which invites the eye to roam in all directions. Note the edging—aggregate materials such as gravel must be edged, or they will begin to spread into surrounding areas. For this drive, we decided on cobbles, which matched the medallion and echoed those used as border edging in the backyard.

The finishing touch to this driveway is the fence and the boxwoods in their Versailles planters. The classical lines of the fence shield the private garden behind, while at the same time exactly echoing the lines of the house, extending the architecture into the garden. Once again, note the fence line and how it begins and ends with crisp, visual logic. Even though there is no building or structure to terminate the fence on the right side, the fence is able to successfully end at this point because the carefully placed plantings hide the corner and fool the eye. This trick, of letting the fence "die" into a dense planting, often comes in very handy. The key is that the termination must be out of common sight—merely running the fence into a planting in the middle of the yard won't work. The planters, made of the same cedar as the fence, also complement the house and work to soften the overall space, their greenery suggesting the idea of a planted courtyard in an otherwise empty space. All in all the ensemble sets a quietly elegant, period tone for the home, welcoming visitors to both house and garden.

A Driveway: After (Driveway illustrations by Penny Delany.)

How-to: Laying Out Traditional Walks and Drives

With a little planning and forethought, it's not too difficult to build attractive, hard-surface walks and drives that can meet the demands of modern convenience, while at the same time adding to the overall beauty of the grounds.

The first step in this process is to assess the current state of your walks and drives. If you are lucky enough to have an existing surface that meets your needs but is in need of redoing, you need only to decide what type of new paving will serve you best. Unfortunately, in most cases, the issue is not so simple, because the original walks and drives have all but disappeared or have been severely modified, typically stranding an unused front door or side porch without means of egress. So in old property, I like to begin with a thorough search for "ghosts" of the former landscape that I might have missed initially. Often a depression in the lawn, a piece of broken pavement, or the placement of large trees will indicate the former approach to the house.

If no clues remain, if the original scheme is no longer practical, or if the house is brand-new, a layout must be drawn from scratch. The first step is to chart the scheme on paper, preferably to scale, with much more precision than you did on the larger-scale plan of the entire garden. There, a matter of inches was of relative unimportance. Here, precision really counts, and it will be amply rewarded by time and money saved.

There are essentially two general categories of walks and drives: those required on a daily basis for practical purposes, such as getting to the front door, and those whose function is purely recreational. Recreational walks and drives are

One of the most common mistakes in creating front walks is to make them too small. Large houses should have large walks to balance the facade. Here, the walk is at least 6 feet wide. Even for smaller homes, 4 feet is the minimum for front walkways.

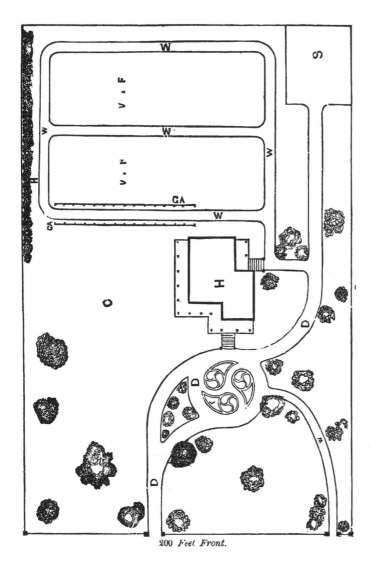

In this Victorian plan, the importance of the drive is clear—it is the central, decorative feature of the front landscape. While the elaborate bedding pattern in the center of the driveway would be appropriate only for a fairly grand house, a single shade tree could be substituted for a simpler effect.

fairly easy to design; their path and form have only the dictates of aesthetics to answer to—curved or straight, wide or narrow, paved or not, depending on the requirements of the site. Service walks and drives, however, are a different story. They are a required element of the landscape, and they need to be practical and easy to use as well as visually pleasing.

Choosing a new route is sometimes easy: that muddy rut in the grass worn down by the kids, the dog, the mail carrier, or visiting cars is a good indication of the current traffic pattern! In the absence of a muddy rut, think about where you will

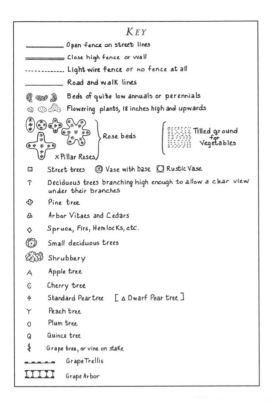

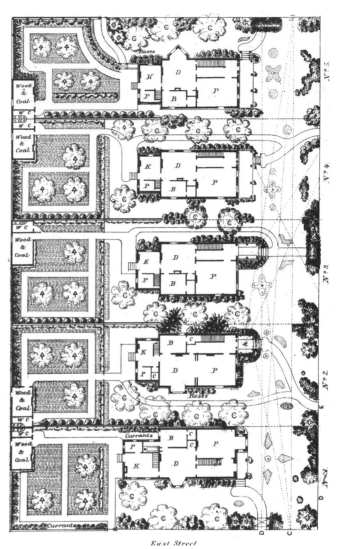

This illustration shows several options for driveways and walkways in small city properties of the Victorian period.

need to go in your yard and how often you will need to get there. If the answer is more than twice a week, you will probably need a path.

Should the service walk or drive be straight or curved? It depends on the length to be covered. If the distance is less than 50 feet, the most direct route is probably best. However, if the site is large enough and a curved walk or drive does seem to fit the bill, by all means use it, but be gentle with the curves. "Nearly all amateur landscape gardeners will blunder in their first attempts to lay out roads or walks, by making their curves too decided," wrote Frank J. Scott in *Suburban Home Grounds*. "If the grounds were seen from a balloon, the effect would be the same as upon your plan;

WALKWAYS

Walkways are one of the most common features of the landscape and, due to unimaginative design, also often one of the most prosaic. Yet this wasn't always the case, as these period designs from historic sites across the country show.

(Illustrations courtesy of Peter Joel Harrison.)

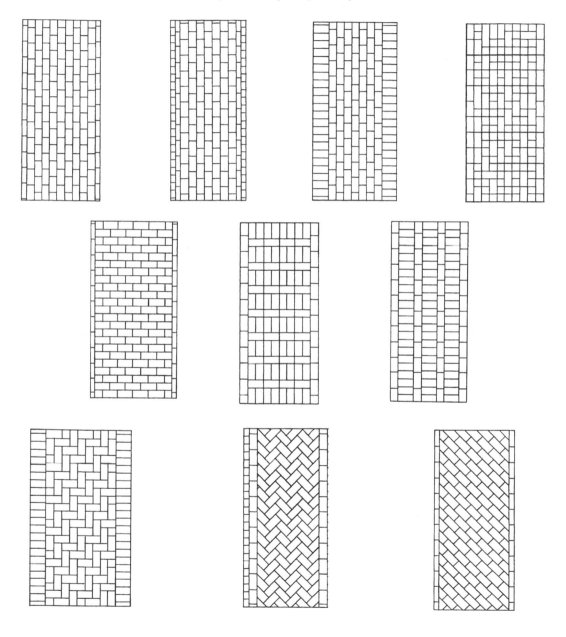

One of the easiest ways to test the route of a proposed path or drive is to lay it out with a piece of hose. Just let the hose warm up in the sun first to become more supple.

After you lay out the path with a garden hose, use a line of stakes to mark both sides. This will give you a good idea of how the finished product will look, and whether it will be wide enough for your needs.

but as we are all destined to look along the ground instead of vertically down upon it, it will be seen why curves that look graceful on paper are likely to be too abrupt and crooked in perspective."

I like to lay out the prospective walks with a section of garden hose, which I leave in the sun for an hour or so to warm and become suppler. In this manner I can walk along the proposed path and play with various degrees of curvature and straight runs to see which looks best on a particular site.

Be sure to consider the issue of walkway width. For a Colonial or Colonial Revival house, aim for 4 feet or so. For a Victorian, rear walks can be 3 feet wide and principal walks 4 to 6 feet, flaring out near the house. The common width for drives was 12 to 14 feet, which is generally sufficient for *one-way* passage of modern vehicles as well. But for convenience, leave a little additional space for a car to pass and turn around, if possible. If you are unsure of the minimum amount of space required for this, consult a good landscape guide such as the *Reader's Digest Practical Guide to Home Landscaping* (see the Bibliography), which lists many commonly required turnaround distances. Or find a competent designer to help you.

Paving Materials

Brick

Brick is not, nor has it ever been, inexpensive. Yet time and time again, we take this costly material and lay it down in the most common and uninteresting way imaginable—straight running bond—when for practically the same effort and cost, a whole slew of fascinating pattern variations are possible that add visual interest and excitement to otherwise mundane structures. These possibilities were certainly recognized and valued historically, as you can see from the many patterns and combinations in the illustrations on pages 127 and 129. Each design gives a slightly different feel to the very same walk or drive.

Modern paving bricks fall into two general types: extruded and molded. (Handmade bricks are also still available, by the way. See Suppliers in the appendices.) Extruded bricks are rather modern-looking and have a coarse texture that I find distasteful. Molded bricks, on the other hand, are made in a traditional way and have a smoother, more handcrafted look. The color range available in molded bricks also tends to be greater, and this can be very important, especially in a small area. Darker colors contract a space, lighter ones expand it.

Before you lay down a single brick in your garden, experiment with different pattern types and layouts. You'll be amazed at how a relatively small change in pattern

TERRACES

What could be more restful than whiling away a few lazy hours on one of these terraces? Both decorative and useful, these historic patterns from sites across the country will enliven almost any landscape. (Illustrations courtesy of Peter Joel Harrison.)

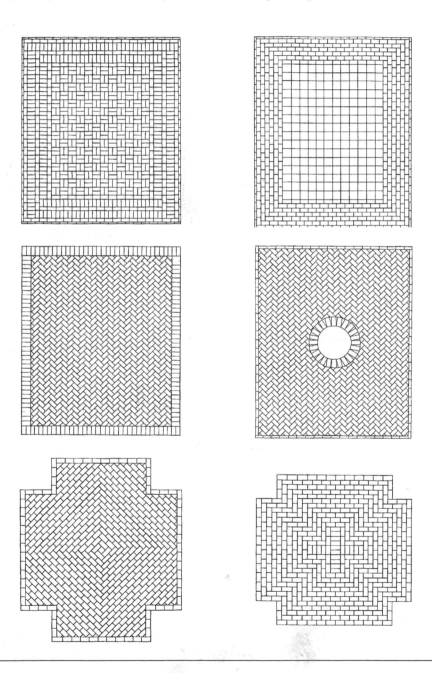

can completely alter the feel of the space. One of my favorite designs for a brick terrace or patio is an "Oriental rug" pattern. The idea first occurred to me when I was visiting a Victorian house museum, where the small brightly patterned Oriental rugs were laid over larger, solid-colored carpets, a common practice at the time. Instead of laying out a terrace using a single boring pattern from end to end, choose a more complicated design, such as herringbone, for the inner section and a simpler pattern for the outer, separating the two with a band of flat stone, such as bluestone, cobbles, or sawn granite. Another possibility is to insert a design or medallion made of contrasting stones in the central field as a permanent decoration. For my own garden in Southborough I built a back terrace with a wonderful compass design in the center that never fails to delight, whether viewed from ground level or from the kitchen windows above.

Gravel

Gravel has a long history in courtyards and, later, in suburban drives. I also like to use gravel for walks that are not to be the main entrance and egress to the house.

There are many different grades and sizes of gravel available, but my favorite for landscape use, and the most historically correct, is river-washed pea gravel, with the modern addition of 10 percent crushed stone as a binder. Pure pea stone is very pretty but has a tendency to move around too much, and crushed stone alone, while very stable, has a very harsh, modern appearance. The 90/10 mix is the perfect blend of the two.

I am inevitably asked when I propose gravel drives about maintenance and winter plowing. It is true that there is some maintenance involved, mainly a yearly raking and a bit of weeding or controlled spraying in the less trafficked areas. But the natural look of gravel far outweighs the little work involved. And plowing is not a problem as long as the plow is set an inch or so higher than normal. It is imperative that gravel walks and drives be edged to contain the aggregate and to provide a crisp definition between drive and garden.

Cobble/Stone

Cobbles make fine, but costly, drives, though they are much too uneven for walkways. I particularly like cobble as edging material for gravel drives. Paving stone, such as

---

THE GRACEFUL CURVE

From the street to the house door—from the kitchen to the well, or the stable—the communication should be as direct as possible. Over paths that must be traversed many times a day, and often, perhaps, in hot haste, no one wishes to be compelled to describe the lines of beauty, though Hogarth himself had drawn the graceful curve. In gardens and pleasure walks the case is different, and we enjoy as a lawful luxury their easy windings and purposed prolongation. Yet even these should not be wholly capricious. Let there be at least some reason for every turn—some compensatory attraction for every delay.

—Henry Cleaveland and the two Backus brothers, William and Samuel: *Village and Farm Cottages (1856)*

bluestone or other locally available flagstone, was and is another favorite and expensive material for walks. Except in the warmest climates, where heavy frost is not a problem, avoid using small, irregularly shaped paving stones, such as multicolored pieces of slate, especially if set in a mortar base. Frost will inevitably buckle this type of path and break the stones out of the mortar, requiring that the walk be reset—at great cost. Instead, follow the traditional formula and use larger, much heavier, regular stones (at least 1½ inches thick). Gravity will keep these heavier pieces in place even when they are set in a bed of stone dust or sand.

Asphalt

Personally, I don't much care for asphalt walks, but for urban driveways, asphalt can be quite attractive, especially when it is made by the "hot tar," "liquid asphalt," or "macadam" process, where pea stone is pressed into the surface of the tar, leaving a loose stone layer on top that resembles a gravel drive. Although it may take a while to search down a contractor in your area who offers this process, it's worth the effort to try to find one.

Concrete

The first concrete paving was laid in this country in Bellefontaine, Ohio, in 1894, and its use spread widely after that time. To my eyes, concrete is not much of an aesthetic option in the garden, although there is a process called brushed aggregate in which gravel is added to the concrete before it's poured and, once partially set, the concrete is brushed, resulting in a rather pleasing, pebbly surface that is extremely durable.

Wood

Wood should be given more consideration for walkways these days. It is relatively inexpensive and can be easily shaped and contoured. Wooden pathways are particularly appropriate in Colonial settings or where a rural look is desired. The one drawback is that wood can be quite slippery when wet.

It's hard to imagine a more appropriate surface than wood for the front walk of a 1700s Cape Cod house. (Photo courtesy of Barbara Reese.)

Wide pieces of stone are often perfect for walkways for period homes. Try to use fewer, larger pieces, as in this illustration, to avoid the more modern "random pattern" look.

Stone curbs were de rigueur *for Victorian walks and stairs. While expensive to duplicate these days, they have sometimes been found buried on a property or stored in a basement or barn, still in usable shape.*

Edging

The Victorians were fond of well-defined boundaries in the garden, and this love of the precise extended to their walks and drives. Even the humblest of surfaces made use of various edging materials to keep their edges visually crisp. Gardeners used bricks (whole or pieces of), cobbles, rough stones, cut stones, shells, steel strips, and even specially made clay garden tiles. Not only did these materials provide visual clarity, they also saved their owners the considerable labor of edging several times a year by hand—a fact that today's time- and budget-stressed homeowners should keep in mind.

For a traditional look and feel, nothing can beat these clay edging tiles, now being manufactured again in period patterns. (See Suppliers.)

Follow the advice of Edward Kemp in his 1850 treatise *Landscape Gardening:*

[Edgings] should be quite smooth, thoroughly flat along the margins, and for some of their width at least, precisely on the same level at both sides and very well defined, though not more than a half an inch above the level of the side of the walk. . . . Walks that are not carefully formed in accordance with all these conditions will appear more or less slovenly, deficient in the expression of art, and indicative of unrefined taste.

Edgings may be combined in many different ways with different paving materials. Just make sure that the edgers and the pavers are sympathetic in color, texture, and degree of formality; rough-hewn landscape timbers with a formal herringbone walk would probably not make the best combination, for example.

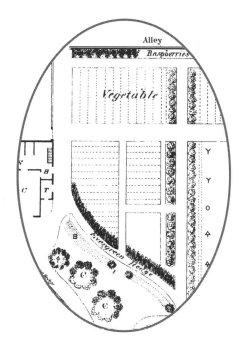

℘racticality

The earliest Americans were practical, almost above all else. And so were their gardens. Our forebears looked around their new continent, took the best of the European gardening traditions—ones that met their needs and could be adapted to a new climate and lifestyle—and jettisoned the rest. And they searched with almost religious zeal for new and unknown plants that would improve their gardens. These gardeners worked with nature, importing, hybridizing, borrowing, and bartering their

This boy has reason to be glum—the mechanized lawn mower, shown here in one of its earliest versions, forever doomed generations of youth to the dreaded Saturday morning cry of "mow the lawn before you go play!"

way to a distinctly American sense of garden style, a practical one adapted to their homes and climate.

Somewhere along the way, however, we abandoned this approach, and now we are simply content to throw money at our gardens—more-potent fertilizers, more-lethal pesticides, better herbicides, anything and everything that will make our landscapes bigger, greener, faster, easier. Are our gardens any better than gardens were a hundred years ago? Decidedly not, because this gardening approach is not sustainable. In the end, nature always wins, and we should play on her side, as our ancestors did.

The current American obsession with the flawless, weed-free lawn is a good example of how impractical modern gardening has become. This passion for wide expanses of unblemished grass is a disease that strikes people (especially men!) of all ages and stations and causes them to spend huge amounts of time, money, and resources attempting to create the perfect lawn. The only way to accomplish this, of course (and then only for a while), is to load the turf with massive quantities of fertilizers, herbicides, and pesticides. It's all just modern madness.

To the American colonists, the term *lawn* meant a flat, green ornamental area specifically for outdoor pastimes, such as bowls. After 1850, the game of choice became croquet, but the basic use of the lawn was unchanged. Larger manicured lawn areas were quite rare and were the exclusive

The Victorian quest for the perfect lawn, like this one from an 1890s seed catalog, has become an American institution, long after the original reasons behind the craze have disappeared.

province of the very wealthy, since maintaining a lawn required full-time gardening help to meticulously scythe and roll the grass flat. Then along came Edwin Budding and James Ferrabee, who adapted the large-bladed machines used in cloth mills to remove excess nap and created, in 1830, the very first automatic lawn mower. Suddenly everyone from maid to minister could have their own miniature green sward with minimal labor, and lawns sprang up everywhere as the ultimate status symbol of the Victorian garden.

The earliest American lawns were just cut (or cropped) pasture; whatever flowers or "weeds" existed on the property were left alone. Later, in the 1800s, nurseries began to sell specialized seed mixtures, although these were very unlike those found at your local hardware store today. The lovers of the monotone modern lawn would wince at Frank Scott's seed mixture for the perfect lawn, circa 1876:

12 quarts Rhode Island bent grass
4 quarts creeping bent grass
10 quarts red top
3 quarts sweet vernal grass
2 quarts Kentucky bluegrass
1 quart white clover

Some lawns were not even made of grass at all: clover, rye, crabgrass, and dandelions *(quelles horreurs!)* were considered by many to be perfectly acceptable. The only thing that mattered was that the lawn be *flat* and *green*. Much care was taken to cut and roll the lawn every other week or so. This happy state of affairs was to change forever early in the 20th century with the rise of the use of fertilizers, "clean" (all-grass) seed mixtures, and that boon to time-pressed homeowners, weed-and-feed mixes. And although the perfect lawn has long since ceased to be a symbol of wealth, like lemmings to the sea we continue to follow the path our Victorian forebears forged, to the point where the lawn has come to dominate the collective American landscape, not harmonize with it as one part of the greater whole.

Colonial landscapes had very little grass that wasn't part of some pasture: it was too costly and impractical. Instead, areas surfaced with brick, cobble, or fieldstone were common where outdoor activities occurred, and beds of flowers, vegetables, and

With the rise of the American lawn came a legion of required tools: here is an early Victorian edger.

Sod cutters like this one from 1891 meant that people could now have a perfect, instant lawn, without waiting for seeds to sprout.

Sprinklers were the rage when they first became common in the late 1800s. Called "lawn fountains," their use meant that a household was sophisticated and modern enough to have internal plumbing and town water.

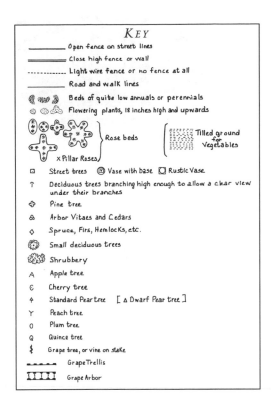

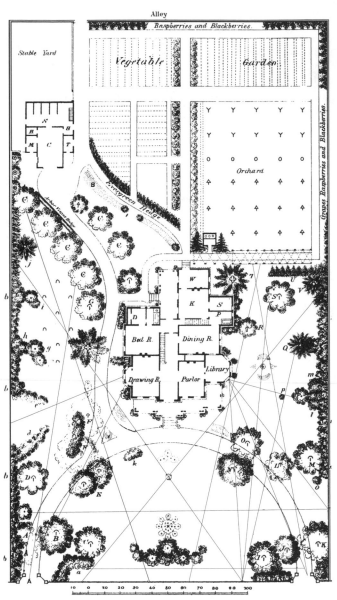

Lawn for lawn's sake was not a traditional dictum. In this illustration, the lawn was broken into practical areas to frame and enhance various features of the landscape.

useful ground covers filled most of the other property near the house. Woods, meadows, and other wilder areas completed the landscape.

Lawn size increased as the 1800s wore on, but the Victorians used expanses of lawn to showcase specimen trees, flowering shrubs, and beds of annuals and perennials. And notice, too, the many paved areas for paths and outdoor seating (see figure above). Even by the early 1900s, the beginning of the heyday of the Great American Lawn, lawns were only *part* of the overall design of a yard, not the focal point. After all, lawns were meant to complement the house and other areas of general landscape and to link the various parts of the whole into a single unit. This should be the focus of your lawn today as well.

Another area currently ripe for reform is the bizarre American habit of burying our houses behind masses of monotonous, overpruned evergreens, so much so that the house sometimes disappears. This practice is a late-20th-century creation, and it has become so common that we no longer step back and consider exactly how *ugly* this really is and how much our houses suffer because of it. Contrary to popular thought, this is not a historical treatment. Until relatively recently, most houses were kept in a state that would seem almost naked of vegetation to modern eyes.

The desire for a bare foundation is perhaps not too difficult to understand. The first European settlers found a continent of dense, dark forests. The last thing the inhabitants of newly cleared countryside wanted was a house surrounded by "gloomy vegetation," to quote a period guidebook. Heavy planting near the house, it was felt, "shuts out the light of the day and the wholesome warmth of the sun.... The shade and humidity ... is unfavorable to the health." This belief was further supported by physicians, who warned against the dangers of consumption and other contagions thought to be born in and to thrive in dark and damp places. Other practical considerations were noted as well. Planting large trees and shrubs close to the dwelling "sometimes fill[s] the house with insects," and wooden roofs, "when overhung by branches, rapidly decay."

Finally, there was an important aesthetic objection:

If a house be well designed, it should make a picture of itself and only require the aid of vegetable forms, at a little distance from it, as supports and accompaniments. An occasional tree or plant may be valuable to balance the several parts, to soften the abrupt transitions of outline, to sober and break a glare of color, or to impart an air of finish in some cases; and even a mass of trees or shrubs would often be effective in blinding inferior parts of the building, or covering defect in symmetry or enrich-

Even in this Edwardian example, where the yard layout had been considerably simplified from its Victorian predecessors, lawn areas occurred only to provide practical gaming space or to complement planting areas.

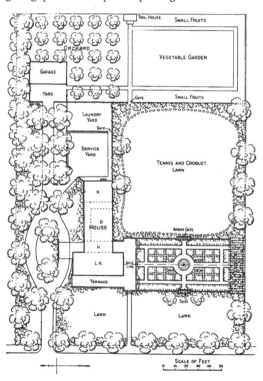

ment. But where the architect has thoroughly studied his subject and treated it as a picture, aids of this sort will be but little wanted and should be adopted with the utmost care. There is probably no point in landscape gardening wherein less of the true feeling or art is exhibited than in the choice of accompaniments to a building.

—Edward Kemp
Landscape Gardening (1850)

Given all this, what if anything should be planted near the house, whether it's antique or modern? It depends entirely on the architecture. Colonial houses were designed with clapboards almost down to the ground and thus should remain almost completely bare of vegetation near the foundation to prevent decay and rot, something many modern owners of these old houses have discovered to their chagrin. Nineteenth-century homes were treated differently. Engravings, plans, and early photos show a decided fondness for vines climbing up walls and twining around verandas, with low plantings of flowers and deciduous materials against the foundation, and the occasional evergreen tree or shrub as an accent. Taller material was especially favored off the four corners of the building or between odd angles or nooks in the architecture. As the Victorian era wore on, more and more material was added around the foundations, principally because the houses of that period had higher exposed brick or stone foundations, which were thought appropriate backdrops for planting. However, it is important to note that other than an occasional accent plant or vine, *the general plantings were never meant to rise much above the height of this exposed foundation, that is to say, 3 to 4 feet.* In a typical late Victorian plan by Scott (see figure on page 68), two junipers flank the walk, while near the house are low plantings of lilies, "choice perennials," and annuals, set off by boxwood, *dwarf* azaleas and rhododendrons, and low decid-

uous shrubs such as weigela, deutzia, and roses. Scott's theory was to "nest the house . . . with plantings that seem to spring out of the nooks and corners with something of the freedom that characterizes similar vegetation springing naturally along stone walls and fences."

Obviously, though, even Victorian homeowners had trouble interpreting this advice with appropriate plant material, because there are constant warnings in the gardening books of the time about planting overly large specimens too close to the house. In fact, I believe that the disregard of these instructions has led us to our current sorry state. As it became the fashion to plant the foundation, rather than to select slow-growing varieties that would mature to the proper height and give the effect of "springing vegetation,"

Those little trees may be cute now, but unless you choose your plant materials wisely, your house and garden may soon be overwhelmed, as this Victorian illustration shows.

When you see a mature yew like this magnificent specimen, you begin to understand why these shrubs should not be crammed against a house's foundation.

people unwittingly selected plants that grew far too large. So many foundations were planted and let go that soon, despite the warnings of the experts, front facades completely covered in shrubs became the norm, rather than the exception.

Actually, it's very easy to fall into this trap even today: it's so tempting to place that cute little tree near the house—how big could it possibly get? Ha! Just wait and see. Few gardeners seem to heed those cautionary words found on so many plant labels: "Grows to 40 feet." The poor yew is a common victim of our misplaced optimism. It is one of my favorite garden plants, but it has been horrendously overused. The dark green color foliage and bright red berries make yews ideal for a number of landscape purposes, but, except for one or two of the rarer dwarf varieties, *foundation planting is not one of these.* I say this emphatically because every year thousands of beautiful yews are doomed to a miserable fate. These lovely trees (that is what they really are—they often grow to 35 feet) are placed in locations where they will look ridiculous, either dwarfing and darkening the house or crushed into tiny spaces and mercilessly pruned into a series of ludicrous shapes that are both time-consuming and costly to maintain. Rhododendrons, hemlocks, and other large-scale evergreens are often similarly abused.

With very few exceptions, only those houses with 3- to 4-foot-high, bare concrete or stone foundations can or should have a lot of material massed around them. In fact, while health considerations are no longer a concern, it is certainly still true that masses of vegetation near wooden siding encourages rot, decay, and a host of other problems, including carpenter ants. (Carpenter ants trouble only wood that is constantly soaked and moist. If you remove the moisture, you remove the ants—no spraying required.) Finally, most houses look better without so much solid, heavy front planting, especially single-story homes, where dense shrubbery overwhelms the facade and makes the structure look like a doll's house.

The same caveat holds true for placing trees and shrubs in the landscape: *Read the label* when choosing and placing plantings. It seems truly impossible that that little stick of a plant will be 20 feet high in seven years and 50 feet high in twenty, but it's true, and you will rue the day you planted that shrub or tree when it requires tough and expensive pruning several times a season just to fit it into the garden space you mistakenly placed it in. I don't believe in planting anything that needs constant pruning, other than topiaries or special ornamental shrubs, simply because I despise pruning. I hate finding and sharpening the shears, I hate cutting the branches, and I especially hate the cleanup.

I prefer to take the approach our Colonial ancestors did. They had many more important things to do than worry about whether a tree would get too big, and they practiced that admirable quality of *patience*. Patience is the most practical of virtues: not only does it save the unneeded expenditure of both effort and funds, but it also produces a better overall effect. Unfortunately, patience is also the one quality almost totally lacking in our approach to gardens today, where everything has to be instantaneous—instant trees, instant bushes, instant flowers. Garden suppliers have catered to and fed this desire by growing larger and larger trees and shrubs, with the result that the average buyer now pays a fortune for plants that are far too large and then crams them together in a space far too small for their eventual size.

The result is always less than expected because, with very few exceptions, you are much better off buying smaller trees and shrubs, spacing them correctly, and letting them grow and mature into their location. They may look silly in the beginning, but wait just a few years. Most people don't realize that when big plants are moved, they suffer from extensive shock. For these plants, it's like recovering from surgery—the transplanted root balls need considerable recuperation time and often remain almost in stasis for a few years, with little or no growth. Take, for instance, that great garden favorite, the white pine, which is commonly used in the Northeast for quick screening, because of its rapid growth rate. If a 5-foot specimen for $63 and a 9-foot specimen for $240 are planted together and given identical care, which is bigger in seven years? If you guessed the 9-foot specimen, you're wrong. After a few years, both trees are about the *same* size, because the larger tree remained almost inactive for several seasons, while the little one was growing merrily, having recovered from its transplant shock much faster.

In addition, smaller specimens grow *together* better. If you have ever seen a beautiful shrub border that you admire, where different colored foliage and leaf textures seem to blend together seamlessly, I'll bet that that border was planted as young shrubs and allowed to mature. You simply can't buy that luscious patina of age, so don't waste your money trying.

Here's a summary of some foundation planting dos and don'ts.

- Learn from history. The older your house is, the less vegetation would have been planted next to it.
- Even when heavily massed, each member or grouping of the foundation planting should be considered a separate unit, to be viewed and appreciated individually.
- Avoid overuse of evergreens, especially those tall, upright varieties that will almost certainly grow too large and hide the house.
- Use flowering and deciduous material, especially plants that are interesting in more than one season. Pay attention to attractive contrasts in leaf shape and form; the Victorians especially used plants with colored, variegated, weeping foliage.
- If you are interested in exactly re-creating a period landscape, use the Historic Plant List in the back of this book to insure that the plant varieties you choose were in cultivation during the period you want to re-create. If your aim is less strict and you merely want to evoke the feeling of a certain period, consider using some of the more recently introduced cultivars of plants commonly found in the 19th century. These newer varieties of old favorites may have improved features (such as greater range in size or color or better disease resistance) and still reflect the spirit of the era.
- Design the planting to be seen and appreciated from both the outside and the inside of the house.
- Use vining materials where possible; they will be appropriate for any historical period.
- Whatever plant material you choose, remember to keep in mind the plant's *eventual size, not its current one.* Carry as your caveat the words of Cleaveland and Backus: "If you are not ashamed of your house, pray let it be seen!"

Historic Garden

Models of Practicality: Old Salem, North Carolina

A view of Old Salem from the northwest, from a 1790 watercolor, artist unknown. (Courtesy of the Archives of the Moravian Church, Winston-Salem, N.C.)

The gardens of Old Salem are an amazing resource for anyone interested in a true representation of how small town gardens appeared in 18th-century America. The town was founded in 1766 by a group of German immigrants, the Moravians, who sought a land in which they could freely practice their religion. It was a planned, congregation town: all land was owned by the Moravian Church and leased by the settlers. Nor did the church's authority stop there. The day-to-day lives of the members (called Brothers and Sisters) were carefully controlled by the church, right down to what the settlers planted in their gardens. Meticulous records were kept as well, which has provided modern garden historians with a wealth of information about exactly what was grown during the period of church control, 1768–1856.

Above all else, the gardens of Old Salem were models of practicality. They had to be. Much like the harried modern commuter, all members of the community tended their own gardens in whatever free time they had after their full-time occupation (which was also decided by the church). To simplify matters, the church fathers had laid out Old Salem in a rigorous grid pattern in which the residential lots were all more or less the same size, 67 by 197 feet, with the house at the front facing directly onto the street.

The Miksch House is a typical example. A service yard of packed, swept dirt was located immediately around and behind the structure, connecting the various outbuildings in back with the house. No plantings were made in

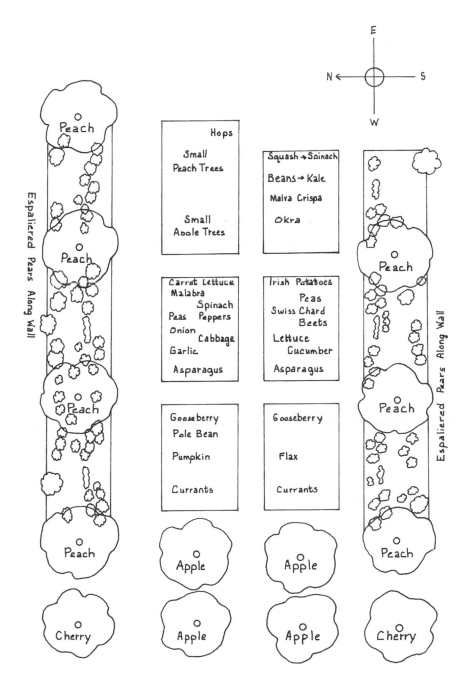

Peach

Hops

Small
Peach Trees

Small
Apple Trees

Squash → Spinach

Beans → Kale

Malva Crispa

Okra

Peach

Espaliered Pears Along Wall

Peach

Carrot Lettuce
Malabra
          Spinach
Peas Peppers
Onion
          Cabbage
Garlic

Asparagus

Irish Potatoes
        Peas
Swiss Chard
        Beets
Lettuce
        Cucumber
Asparagus

Peach

Espaliered Pears Along Wall

Peach

Gooseberry

Pole Bean

Pumpkin

Currants

Gooseberry

Flax

Currants

Peach

E
N ← → S
W

Peach

Cherry

Apple

Apple

Apple

Apple

Cherry

The modern planting plan of the Miksch House garden reflects how the landscape may have appeared in the early 1800s. Notice how every bit of space in this garden is utilized—even to the point of growing espaliered pears on the fence. (Illustration by Penny Delany.)

The restored Miksch garden. (Photograph by Virginia R. Weiler.)

this area, and although spartan, the utilitarian yard perfectly accommodated necessary tasks such as washing, soap making, and baking. Behind the out-buildings, the rear of the lot was fenced and contained a large garden. In this plot, supplemented by other larger parcels outside the town limits where field crops were farmed communally, the Brothers and Sisters were expected to grow enough of their own food to maintain their immediate households.

The gardens of Old Salem were very much like those in Plimoth Planta-tion. Both were laid out by the settlers on leased land, in large, easy-to-work rectangles. They were completely practical, dedicated to the production of herbs, fruits, and vegetables for the table. But what a difference a hundred years or so made. While the Plimoth gardens were almost gritty in their de-termination to provide, the Old Salem gardens, while still utilitarian, made a nod or two to ornament and easier living: flowers were tucked in here and there for their own sake, espaliered pears grew along the fence, even a hops vine appeared for that all-important German essential—beer. In many ways the gardens of Old Salem were the quintessential blend of practicality and beauty, and they would make a perfect model for a small town garden even today.

And, fortunately, these gardens have been preserved and restored for you to visit. After the hold of the church community on Salem began to dissolve in the 1850s, the old town was gradually swallowed up by its growing industrial neighbor, Winston, with which it merged in 1913. Saved from decay and de-struction in the 1950s by a group of concerned citizens, today the town of Old Salem is one of the most fascinating and beautiful living museums in the United States.

Croquet, Anyone?

Practicality takes many forms, and one is to think of innovative ways to make the most of landscape areas you already have. If you have been gazing out at an unused patch of lawn, why not take a page out of the Victorians' book and consider a croquet court? All it takes is a fairly level stretch of decent grass, a good croquet set, and a group of fun-seeking guests.

The exact origins of croquet are obscure, but a version similar to the modern game was called *paille maille* and was played in France as early as the 14th century. Somehow or other, croquet was exported to Ireland in the early 1800s, and it had arrived in England by 1852 or 1853, where it quickly became all the rage. Croquet was introduced in this country in the early 1860s, soaring in popularity just after the Civil War. In crossing the Atlantic, however, the game was changed to better match our more "savage" climate. As America lacked the pristine flat lawns of the British Isles, croquet manufacturers popularized a version of the sport that could be played on rough turf with lightweight, inexpensive equipment. It is this scaled-down version of croquet that most Americans are familiar with.

The popularity of croquet was such that hardly a landscape of distinction was designed during the last half of the century that didn't prominently feature a croquet lawn. Public croquet teams and tournaments were formed all over the country, and results were followed with

The all-American pastime, at least until the rise of baseball, was croquet. Rare was the Victorian landscape that didn't set aside a flat patch of lawn for the game.

as much zeal as professional baseball or hockey is today. Such enthusiastic participation led to problems, however: in 1890s Boston, where the game was avidly played on Boston Common, the clergy felt the need to speak out against the drinking, gambling, and licentious behavior associated with croquet meets.

By the early 20th century, the rise of baseball and other national sports led to a precipitous decline in croquet's popularity. Thereafter, team croquet, like polo, became the province of the wealthy. Today there is a new enthusiasm for public croquet—often the more complicated British version—and now a nationwide network of clubs play organized tournaments and competitions. (If you'd like to learn more, check the United States Croquet Association's Web site at http://www.ontheweb.com/usca/home.html, which includes a complete set of rules.) The home version of the lawn game is also alive and well, judging from the number of croquet sets sold each year.

If you're interested in playing croquet in your yard, the first thing you'll need is a good lawn surface. Traditionally the court measured 50 by 100 feet; however, the dimensions may be reduced to fit the size and shape of the space available. (If you reduce the court, try to maintain a 6-foot separation between the starting/turning stake and the adjacent wickets; a shorter distance constricts the playing space and affects game tactics.)

A flat lawn surface of closely mowed grass is best. The type of grass is relatively unimportant at the amateur level, although tradition dictates one of the several varieties of bent grass, the type found on golf greens. These include Colonial bent *(Agrostis tenuis)* varieties 'Astoria', 'Highland', and 'Exeter'; creeping bent *(Agrostis palustris)* is also used. Just make sure you avoid common bent *(Agrostis alba)*, which is often seen in cheap mixes; it becomes bumpy, brown, and coarse with age. Although the croquet yard should appear flat to the eye, some slight pitch is necessary for good water runoff; a gentle slope of ½ inch every 10 feet should suffice. And be sure to use a lawn roller often: that is what produces that perfectly smooth surface.

How-to: The Practical Lawn

Now, don't get me wrong. I love lawns (at least ones that are not loaded with pesticides, as many are today). Their soothing green is a perfect foil for many garden features and introduces a pleasing, pacifying tone into the landscape as a whole. And for kids, nothing can beat the lawn as a prime play area. It's just a question of how and where to use lawns.

The first step toward a more practical lawn is to assess your entire property and justify your areas of grass. This is especially true for historical landscapes, since large expanses of manicured lawn around a house built before the late 1800s are an anachronism, as we've already seen. Remember, on a per-square-foot basis, grass is one of the most expensive means you can employ to cover ground in your garden (much more costly annually than trees, shrubbery, or perennials, for example). Therefore each and every lawn area should have a very good reason for its existence.

Once you have made sure that what you have is what you need, the next order of business is to fire those lawn-care people who insist on spreading tons of toxic chemicals on your grass and charging you a fortune for the very dubious privilege of having a weed-free lawn. Here's what we have forgotten over the course of the last two hundred or so years: Lawns were once a heterogeneous mixture of grasses and other ground covers, which were much better adapted to our American climate than are today's seed mixes, which consist of highly demanding imported grasses such as bluegrass and Bermuda grass. These old-fashioned lawn blends stayed green by themselves much more easily during even the hottest summer, and they had superior durability and character. Is there really anything wrong with a few flashes of color (from dandelions, clover, or some other plant) dotting the lawn? Quite frankly, they are often quite pretty, and any that get too enthusiastic can be controlled by mowing. Remember, it's the green color and smooth expanse of the lawn *from afar* that make it such an important part of the garden. And for that, clover works as well as bluegrass.

And speaking of clover, gardeners in drier climates should know that certain types of ground-cover plants, such as clover, help keep the lawn area green during periods of scant water. Here at my home in Southborough, there is an area that was always out of reach of the hose and therefore browned out every summer in July and August. Refusing to install a watering system (mostly because I was too cheap to spend money on the lawn), I instead topseeded white clover into the existing grass. Now that the lawn is established, not only does it stay green all summer with minimal watering, but in early June, my bees have the benefit of all those clover blossoms for honey production. And don't forget that lovely scent that fills the house when the evening breeze kicks up.

So the next time it's 90 degrees outside and you are contemplating once again having to satiate that useless half-acre of manicured lawn's constant addiction to mowing, water, and fertilizer, do yourself a favor. Sit down in the shade and think about ways to make your lawn areas more practical. You (and your checkbook) will be glad you did.

A FLOWERING MEAD

One of the simplest ways to utilize your lawn and delight your senses is to set tiny spring bulbs in the ground underneath the grass. This lovely idea, known as a *flowering mead*, dates to the Middle Ages. Crocuses, snowdrops, even some of the dwarf daffodils and very early miniature-species tulips look absolutely charming against the dark green background of the first blades of grass.

It's easiest to plant spring bulbs before the lawn is installed or in areas where some disruption will necessitate replacing the grass anyway. Before the grass is laid or seeded, remove the soil over an area of several square feet to the depth required for whatever bulb you're using, and then plant the bulbs en masse, every few inches. Replace the soil over the bulbs and either seed the grass or lay sod.

Don't underestimate the number of bulbs required, though—multiples of 500 of these tiny gems are required to make any sort of effect. Once the bulbs are installed, all you have to do is sit back and enjoy; planted correctly, the bulbs will naturalize and spread throughout the lawn. Just remember to hold off your first mowing until the bulb foliage has died back, which generally takes two to three weeks. If you cut the foliage off before it dies down, the bulb will be robbed of the energy it needs from photosynthesis and will not flower next year.

CHAPTER VII

Unlike the search for other qualities of American gardens, the quest for beauty is one that has remained more or less a constant since our Colonial ancestors became established enough to begin enhancing the aesthetics of their lives. But what is considered beautiful in the garden has changed radically over the course of our 300-odd-year history. This is especially apparent in the use of flowers in the landscape.

The first American gardeners were far too concerned about survival to worry overly about the flowers in their gardens. That's not to say that they didn't care about blooms. Flowers were necessary to set fruit, and if in the process they added beauty to the garden, all the better. As time passed and situations improved, however, the colonists started cultivating flowers for their own sake. By the latter part of the 18th century, a multitude of gardening enthusiasts, many of them the founding fathers of this country, were actively building purely ornamental landscapes and were aggressively collecting new and interesting plant materials from all over the globe for their new gardens.

We have a pretty good idea from existing plant lists and nursery catalogs of what was grown in the 18th and early 19th centuries, and we know that, like the landscapes in general, the shape of the borders was generally geometric and maintained a strict alignment to the house and outbuildings. What happened *inside* these beds—how the gardens were laid out—is much less clear. Chances are, though, Colonial American flower gardens were very similar to what we would today call the "cottage" style, which had its origins in the English cottagers' plots of the 16th and 17th centuries.

Although normally not the owners of the little houses in which they lived, workers on the great English estates often tended their own small, profuse gardens, containing bits and pieces of what was admired or required. These gardens typically were just large square beds, separated by paths for easy maintenance. Segregated vegetable and herb gardens did exist, but it was not at all uncommon to find favorite herbs, vegetables, and flowers growing side by side in a relaxed, casual manner. The same plants were given a much more formal treatment in the estate gardens. When these "cottagers" left for America, they brought this style with them, and here it flourished until the early 1800s. By then, the very strict geometry of the early Colonial flowerbed layout began giving way to a looser, more relaxed outline, a trend similar to that followed in the overall landscape. The mixture of plants, however, was essentially unaltered. It was not until after the Civil War that things really started to change markedly. The shift again came from England, where that entire country was in the grip of the "bedding" craze. Suddenly mixed borders in the cottage-garden style were out of fashion, and large, exceedingly complex designs for beds composed solely of annuals were all the rage.

This sea change stemmed from several unrelated events. First of all, the English glass tax, which had made large panes of glass a great luxury, had been lifted, and almost overnight the greenhouse or conservatory became affordable to the middle class. Second, the increased ease of travel and commerce in the early part of the 1800s had brought a large number of previously unknown, nonhardy plants to the market, which breeders soon hybridized into a wide array of never-before-seen colors and sizes. Today, with our nurseries literally stuffed to the gills with tender plants from all over the globe, it's hard to realize what an impact these novelties made on the gardening world at the time. Gardeners were simply agog at these new plants and rushed to find ways to grow them. Of course, a place had to be created for these beauties in the garden, and thus a whole new landscape movement was born—annual bedding out. This trend of filling a bed with fast-growing annuals to create a mass display reached our shores after the Civil War, and our gardening habits changed forever. In fact, when you scurry out to the nursery each spring to buy the latest petunia, you follow in the footsteps of your Victorian garden predecessors.

To keep these Victorian carpet beds (so called because the patterns resembled a decorative carpet) always at their best, the plants were often changed *three or four times a season*. Commonly, the show started with a large display of spring bulbs, which were removed immediately after flowering and replaced with early-spring annuals such as pansies. The Victorians adored pansies, but when these velvety flowers faded in the summer heat, the plants were ruthlessly removed and replaced with heat-loving summer annuals, which in turn were replaced in late fall with a final show of cold-tolerant plants.

The placement and shape of these Victorian flower gardens were also

With never-before-seen flowers like these asters, it's easy to see why the Victorians went crazy over annuals.

unique. Cut out of the turf and edged with beautifully worked iron surrounds or clay tiles, these beds were created in a wide assortment of shapes—circles, squares, diamonds, crosses, teardrops, and other variations—all intricately subdivided into masses of annual flowers.

Although they appeared in plan view as if they were flat and everything was of uniform height, in reality these beds were three-dimensional. They were almost always raised in the center, which was accomplished either by mounding the ground or by using the tallest material in the center and gradually lowering the plant height toward the outer edges.

Both then and now, the only difficulty with carpet beds (aside from the cost of all the plants, which is considerable) is in their maintenance. Any spent flowers and dead leaves must be rigorously removed in order to keep the beds looking presentable, which in the heat of summer can amount to quite a

BEDDING PATTERNS

With the advent of so many new and exciting annuals to the 19th-century garden scene, special bedding schemes were developed to highlight the special effects that contrasts of form and color could achieve.

lot of work. Also, depending on what material is chosen, sections may need to be replanted as the plants fall out of flower. (Today, you can avoid this chore by choosing modern everblooming flower varieties.) When well done, the Victorian annual bed is truly something to behold. You can understand why these opulent beds could be found, at one skill level or another, in most American landscapes between 1865 and 1900.

Like most fads, however, carpet bedding eventually passed out of fashion after the turn of the century, killed off partly by the number of bad examples of the form. (Carpet bedding is easy to do poorly, given the loud and often glaring color combinations possible with annuals.) But another factor had a great impact on its decline: the cottage-gardening style had been "rediscovered" and readapted in England by Gertrude Jekyll and William Robinson, and soon a host of American imitators took up the chorus as well.

The "new style" of garden emphasized perennials and natural planting, discarding the whole carpet-bedding approach. This is actually a bit of an oversimplification, because within the revolt against the status quo, there were two distinct factions, both united in their dislike of annual bedding. One, headed by Reginald Blomfield, was dedicated to a more formal, geometric approach to landscape design. The other, with William Robinson at the fore, advocated a looser, more naturalistic style. Really two sides of the same coin, these movements were unified by Jekyll and her subsequent imitators, who were less concerned about the labels "formal" or "informal" and instead concentrated on designing good gardens, more or less structured, as the house and site seemed to demand.

Patterned annual beds were often raised to give passersby a better perspective, and to add a much-needed vertical element to the landscape.

Late Victorian and Edwardian gardens were in many ways similar to gardens of two centuries previous—although more urbane and ornamental. Essentially Jekyll and her followers reflected the same societal angst that motivated the Arts and Crafts movement of interior design. They turned away from modern society's industrialization and mass-production mind-set (so well evidenced by the "fake" and "common" carpet beds) and instead embraced a simpler, more old-fashioned, handcrafted style of gardening. Interestingly, in this country, the old cottage style had not diminished to the point of disappearance as it had in England. We Americans are by nature a fairly conservative and frugal lot, and while carpet bedding had real appeal, we could never bring ourselves to throw out the old ways entirely, just as we had earlier resisted the complete changeover from the more formal to the looser, parklike landscape that had so dominated popular taste in England. Ever practical, we kept what we liked and ignored what we didn't, and so during the long Victorian/Edwardian twilight (1870–1920), Americans showed a considerable "mix and match" approach to gardening. A typical turn-of-the-century house might have had, concurrently, a naturalistic, Victorian landscape with a formal,

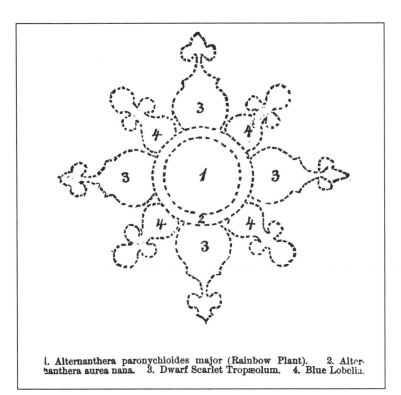

1. Alternanthera paronychioides major (Rainbow Plant). 2. Alternanthera aurea nana. 3. Dwarf Scarlet Tropæolum. 4. Blue Lobelia.

Victorian patterned beds were very carefully planned in advance. Plants were chosen not only for bloom, but for leaf color and texture as well. The scheme above features multi-colored variegated foliage, along with yellow, scarlet, and blue flowers.

geometric kitchen garden in a style popular two centuries before, and a "modern" Jekyllesque perennial border flanked by several carpet beds.

Overall, though, plantings of strictly annuals became less common, and mixtures of perennials and biennials again were the main feature of flower gardens. From a plant perspective, there was not all that much difference between a Colonial garden and an Edwardian garden. Both relied heavily on perennials and small woody shrubs to carry most of the burden of flowering. But Colonial gardens had stressed practicality—vegetables and herbs were mixed in with the flowers, and the garden was designed around what grew best in a particular location. The gardens from Jekyll's time onward concentrated on appearance—a great deal was made of coordinating colors and shades and extending the period of bloom. Vegetables and herbs were banished to the back corners of the yard, where they languished until fairly recently. Also, many Victorian/Edwardian gardens were much freer in terms of their layout and symmetry than were their Colonial predecessors, especially those created by gardeners who promoted a more natural, informal feeling to the garden.

Large Jekyll-style borders (see Glebe House, p. 164) persisted as a main feature of the ornamental landscape in this country right up to the time of World War II. Very quickly, however, fashions changed yet again. But this time flowers themselves fell out of fashion and were simply replaced by lawn and mulch. To a large degree, people abandoned large floral displays because these required either expensive skilled labor or constant work on the owner's part. Flower gardening during the 19th and early 20th centuries had relied on an economy that provided relatively cheap, highly skilled labor. As soon as this labor supply disappeared after the war, large-scale flower gardening, especially large herbaceous borders, went into eclipse. Granted, people still grew flowers between 1945 and 1980; wherever the owner was interested, and the pocketbook ample enough,

large borders appeared, and many people grew and raised flowers on a smaller scale. But flower gardens as a general part of the average landscape were rarer than the proverbial hen's tooth. Most people thought flower gardening was just too much work.

In the 1980s this trend was reversed. Suddenly home and hearth were popular again, and flowers rebounded into the American garden. Today there is widespread interest in gardening among people who had never lifted a spade before, especially if flowers are involved. Theorists have proposed several reasons behind this groundswell of passion for gardening—a desire by the baby boomers to return to nature, end-of-millennium angst, a growing concern for the environment. My personal belief, especially in the case of flower growing, is that we all need beauty around us, and flowers are one way to fight against the general aesthetic degradation of the world.

So given all this interest and money, why don't we have better flower gardens than we do? Flowers are no longer in exile, but their position in the garden seems unsure and haphazard. You may find in the average yard a few blooms tucked here and there or a border clinging tentatively to the side of a lawn, instead of being the focal point it is meant to be, but that's about it. Part of this hesitancy in using flowers is that we no longer have a completely satisfying model to follow. We do not need to feed ourselves from our gardens, so a purely Colonial approach often doesn't satisfy. We are not impressed by masses of vibrantly colored exotics and ribbon beds of annuals, as were the Victorians. Nor does the modern lifestyle allow us the time to prepare and grow the huge herbaceous borders of yesteryear.

But history is still the most reliable teacher. You need to take the best elements of the past and adapt them for today. From the Colonial garden, remember the practical aspect; don't be afraid to add utilitarian elements such as vegetables and herbs to the "ornamental" garden. From the early Victorians, take the love of the wild and unusual, and add bold color, both from flowers *and* from foliage, to your garden. And from the late Victorian and early-20th-century gardens, adapt the skillful blending of color and texture to a more workable scale. You don't need 200-foot-long borders and beds tucked into every corner of the landscape to appreciate the pleasures of the herbaceous border.

Finally, keep in mind the balance, symmetry, and cohesion necessary in all good design, and make sure your borders relate logically to the landscape as a whole. Plant flowers in those often-neglected spots where you know you will be able to see and enjoy them—along walkways, near the front door, as a focal point beside the pool. In that way you will be able to appreciate the incredible delights of sight and fragrance that flowers can offer in the landscape on a daily basis, and even pluck a weed or two as you pass, keeping those long hours of dedicated labor to a minimum. And while you are planting, don't forget to use some of the wonderful antique and heirloom varieties now available; it's like owning a piece of history—right in your own backyard. Gardens are all about *beauty*, after all, and there is no easier way to achieve beauty than to incorporate flowers into the landscape.

Iris

A Rose by Any Other Name

It's hard to pick up a magazine or watch a program on gardening without hearing something about "old roses," but judging from the small number of these beauties I actually see in the general landscape, the word is not getting around sufficiently. Take note: For once the media hype is actually true. These magnificent flowers make a perfect addition to almost any garden.

Today's roses are the product of numerous crosses—many accidental—between the various original roses (called Species roses) that were native to Europe, the Near East, and the Far East. Growth characteristics, color range, and hardiness are often similar within a rose family, so learning about rose families makes the job of choosing roses for your own site much easier. (A word to the wise, though: Occasionally you will find a variety that is not like the rest of its kin. Be sure to check the individual varietal characteristics before purchase.)

Cabbage rose (Rosa centifolia)

What makes a rose "old"? Well, the exact definition is open to debate, but a rose is generally considered old or antique if it was introduced before 1867, the year the first Hybrid Tea rose was developed. This rule is flexible, however, and certain roses introduced as late as the 1920s (like some rugosas) are often called old because their characteristics are similar to pre-1867 roses. In general, modern roses, such as the Hybrid Teas, are small, perennial-sized plants that are fussy about their growing conditions, require much pruning (because they bloom from new wood, that is, growth produced during the current season) and spraying, are not terrifically hardy, and are often scentless. In contrast, old roses *generally*

- require minimal care once established
- bloom first on old wood (that is, growth produced during the previous season) and thus require little or no pruning
- are resistant to many common rose maladies and recover well from damage
- are quite hardy, often to Zone 4
- have highly scented flowers, and may or may not rebloom

- are usually fairly compact shrubs, although some may grow to 7 feet or more and some are climbers
- have been used in gardens for centuries and make terrific, carefree additions to any landscape

Here's a description of some of my favorite hardy varieties, with some dates of introduction along with sizes and colors.

Species roses evolved naturally and are the only roses that will come true from seed. All other roses are the work of hybridizers and must be propagated vegetatively (from cuttings).

  Rosa eglanteria, the sweetbrier rose of Chaucer and Shakespeare, 7′×6′ (higher in shade), pink

  R. glauca, the "red leaf" rose of Europe, 6′×6′, dark pink

Gallicas, native to western Europe, first appeared in gardens over three thousand years ago. Extremely hardy and tolerant of most soils, they bloom once a year, in colors from pink to purple (and sometimes with stripes), on compact shrubs.

  'Duchesse de Montebello' (1829), 5′×4′, blush pink

  'Nestor' (1840), 3′×3′, medium pink

  R. gallica officinalis (1200), 4′×3′, scarlet

  'Rosa Mundi' (1200), 4′×3′, striped and blush pink

Rugosa (from the Latin *rugose*, which means "wrinkled" or "ridged," referring to the leaves) roses are known for their almost indestructible nature—they can even tolerate the extreme conditions of the seashore. Native to the northern Far East coasts, they produce lovely flowers in colors from white to pink with very showy hips (the red seeds). Most Rugosas repeat-bloom (they are "remontant"), although the first show is definitely the most spectacular.

  'Belle Poitevine' (1894), 5′×5′, medium pink with red veins

  'Blanc Double de Coubert' (1892), 5′×4′, pure white

  'Conrad Ferdinand Meyer' (1899), 6′×4′, silky pink

Damask roses are named after the city of Damascus in Syria, where they were noted by the Crusaders. (They may in fact date back two thousand years or more.) Their popularity in the garden soon spread throughout Europe and to the Americas, where they were brought as early as the 1500s. The Damasks bloom once a year, in colors from white to red. Although sometimes listed separately, the Portlands can be considered a subgroup of this category, as they were derived from Damasks and share many of the same characteristics.

'Duchess of Portland' (1780), 3'×2', scarlet
'Madame Hardy' (1832), 5'×4', white
R. damascena bifera (pre-Roman), 4'×3', scarlet
'Sidonie' (1847), 3½'×3', medium pink, double

Albas take their name from the Latin *alba*, meaning "white," and this aptly describes these white or pale pink roses, which first appeared in the Middle Ages, likely as a series of crosses between the wild *R. canina* (itself varying from white to pink) and the Damask roses brought back by the Crusaders. Albas form fairly large shrubs and bloom once a year. They are known for their cold-hardiness, their great fragrance, a bluish cast to the foliage, and their ability to perform with as little as five hours of sun per day, a relative rarity in roses.

'Félicité Parmentier' (1843), 4'×4', fresh
pink
'Königen von Dänemark' (1826), 5'×4',
deep rose
'Maiden's Blush' (1500), 5'×4', blush pink
R. alba semi-plena (1600), 8'×5', creamy white

The **Centifolias** (whose name means "one hundred petals") are lush, full-blossomed roses favored by and developed by the Dutch some three hundred years ago. They bloom in shades of pink once a year and form large, arching bushes.

'Chapeau de Napoléon' (1820), 5'×4', deep
pink
'De Meaux' (1789), 2'×2', dark pink
'Robert le Diable' (1837), 4'×4', crimson
red with undertones

A Damask rose (Rosa damascena)

Moss roses have perhaps the most interesting foliage of all the roses. They take their name from the mosslike growth that forms on the unopened buds and the flower stems. Direct descendants of the Centifolias, they form large shrubs that bloom once a year, occasionally twice, in shades of white to pink. They were a great Victorian favorite, and many lovely varieties remain in cultivation today. Some are repeaters.

'Alfred de Dalmas' (1855), 3'×2', pale pink
'Salet' (1854), 4'×3', rose-pink
'Soupert et Notting' (1874), 3'×2', lavender

The **Bourbons** first appeared about 1817 on the French island colony of Bourbon (now Réunion) in the Indian Ocean, where they were thought to be a chance cross between an Autumn Damask and the China rose 'Old Blush'. They, too, caused a sensation upon their introduction, which immediately resulted in many new hybrids. Bourbons are another rebloomer, and their pink flowers have one of the strongest scents among the old roses.

'Boule de Neige' (1867), 3½'×2½', white

'La Reine Victoria' (1872), 5'×3', lilac-pink

'Louise Odier' (1851), 7'×5', bright pink

Hybrid Perpetuals have been called the "quintessential Victorian rose," and with good reason. Immensely popular during the 1800s, these repeat bloomers flower in colors from white to red. (However, "perpetual" is a bit of an exaggeration. As with the Rugosas, the first burst of bloom is spectacular and is followed by occasional spurts of flowers throughout the season.)

'Baroness Rothschild' (1868), 4'×3', deep rose-pink

'Paul Neyron' (1869), 6'×4', rich pink

Ten Favorite Perennials for the Period Border

Late summer is the ideal time to take a close, critical look at your flower border. By now, the sections of the bed that succeeded well are in glorious flower, amply rewarding your time and effort. As for those sections that didn't pull their weight, now's the time to think about adding some plants that will bring those problem places up to snuff. Here are ten of my favorites for the period border.

FOXGLOVE

Introduced to America in the mid-18th century, the purple or common foxglove had been a favorite in European gardens since the Middle Ages. Where the name *foxglove* originated is a bit of a mystery. According to one etymology, *foxglove* derives from the Anglo-Saxon *foxes-gleow*, a type of musical instrument with bells, which foxglove flowers were said to resemble. Hmm ... At least the derivation of the Latin name of the genus is slightly clearer: *Digitalis* is Latin for "of or belonging to the finger," which is as good a way as any to describe the small thimblelike flowers. With its tall, graceful stalks and cascading bell-shaped flowers, the plant was always a popular ornamental, and it also doubled as a medicinal plant for healing bruises and as a heart stimulant. In the 19th and early 20th centuries, several cultivars were derived from the popular *D. purpurea* that added considerably to the available color palette: the white 'Alba' appeared as early as Breck's 1838 seed catalog; the spotted, large-flowered 'Giant Shirley' strain in white, crimson, and dark rose was introduced by the Rev. Henry Wilkes in the late 1800s; and the stunning 'Apricot' appeared in the early 1900s.

Once established, foxgloves will generally self-sow, at least that's what the catalogs always say. My experience has been entirely different—I've laboriously planted generation after generation in my garden, which bloom once and then disappear forever.

Foxglove

As foxgloves are shade plants, I had somehow always presumed that they would like damp soil. Nothing could be farther from the truth. Foxgloves, it seems, despise moisture around their base and will quickly rot in overly damp conditions. To avoid this problem, lighten the soil with sand to ensure proper growth, or simply plant them on a partly sunny slope. Foxgloves can be started from seed in either spring or late summer, but I prefer to sow them in September and hold the little plants over in a cold frame. Then, early in the following season, I plant out the seedlings, which will often bloom profusely that very year. (Technically, foxgloves are biennials, blooming, then dying, in their second year, although occasionally they last a few years longer. That's why either replanting or reseeding for two successive years is required for continual future bloom.) Zones 4–10.

DIANTHUS

The members of the large genus *Dianthus*, which includes pinks and carnations, are among the oldest of our garden flowers. Deriving their name from the Greek *dios* (meaning "divine") and *anthos* ("flower"), the delicately fragrant blooms of dianthus made their appearance in English gardens as early as the 11th century and on the Continent centuries before that. Two members of the genus arrived very early in American gardens, probably before 1700: *D. caryophyllus* (clove pink, gillyflower, or border carnation) and *D. barbatus* (the famous sweet William). I have grown the two at various times in the garden, enjoying them for their colorful flowers and, in the case of clove pinks, their heady fragrance. (Clove pinks, by the way, gave us the common name *pink*, which describes the color of their flowers, and are one of the parents of the modern carnation, which gives you some idea of their deliciously musky scent.)

Dianthus

Sweet Williams, which technically are perennials, are rather short lived and are best treated as annuals. The small individual flowers are carried on flat heads up to 5 inches across, in colors ranging from white through pink, red, and violet, including several bicolors. To ensure continual flowering from year to year, it's best to plant seeds in well-drained soil in full sun just after the current crop blooms in late spring, discarding the old plants when they begin to look ratty. You can also generally buy young plants from the nursery.

Clove pinks are tender perennials, supposedly hardy to Zone 6, although here in Zone 5b we can usually overwinter them (given some luck with the weather and a well-protected spot). Grow them from seed sown in spring, or by division. I have been told pinks layer well during late summer, but I have never tried that means of propagation.

LYCHNIS

Rose Campion

One of my all-time favorite plants in the garden is rose campion (*Lychnis coronaria*), not so much for its pretty magenta flowers held aloft on 2-foot stems but for its 6-inch-high woolly gray leaves, which, like lamb's ears (*Stachys byzantina*), make a wonderful foil for green foliage in the garden. Beloved in Europe for centuries, rose campion was blooming at Shadwell, Thomas Jefferson's birthplace, by 1767. The Victorians were especially fond of this flower, and clumps were often to be found gracing their gardens. I grow both the species and several cultivars in the garden (the white type dates to 1597 in England); one I particularly like bears white flowers with a pink eye and goes by various names in the trade (Thompson & Morgan calls it 'Dancing Lady'). If the truth be told, I actually prefer the cultivars to the common variety (lychnis derives its name from the Greek *lychnos*, or "lamp," which tells you something about the intensity of the flower color).

Rose campion is hardy in Zones 3–9. Sow seeds in flats in the spring for flowers the following year, or, if you have access to a greenhouse or a cold frame, seed in late summer for flowers the following spring. Whichever method you choose, transplant the seedlings into the garden when they are several inches high, spacing them about 12 to 15 inches apart. Rose campion should be planted in a light, well-drained soil, but it is indifferent to soil fertility. The species readily self-seeds if the stalks are left to bear seed—something I rarely allow, because I like to place lychnis at the front of the border, where the beautiful gray leaves can be appreciated.

HOLLYHOCKS

Perhaps no flower evokes the old-fashioned cottage garden more than the hollyhock (*Alcea* spp.). Native to China, hollyhocks appeared in Europe in the 14th century and eventually made their way to early Colonial America, where the plant was grown primarily as a medicinal, its flowers brewed to prevent miscarriages and to thin the blood. By the mid-1800s, hollyhocks were popular as border plants or for growing against trellises and stone walls, highly valued for their long season of bloom from early summer to fall. Since the 1930s, hollyhocks have been subject to extensive selection and crossbreeding, gaining considerably in color variety but losing in form: the tall, single-flowered varieties were sacrificed for the sake of heftier blooms. Some of the old singles still exist, though. Among these old varieties, look for the classic *A. rosea*, which comes in rose, pink, and white; and the stunning black (really a very dark purple) hollyhock, *A. nigra*, which was a favorite of Thomas Jefferson's.

Hollyhock

Hollyhocks love two things: a warm spot and rich, well-drained soil. Although technically they are biennials, given the right conditions they so readily self-seed that the average gardener often presumes they are perennials. For flowers the next growing season, sow plants in pots during late summer and winter, then overwinter them in a cold frame. Plant them out early the next spring.

LIATRIS

One of the key elements of good design is to include plants whose flowers rise above the general line of the border. In the same way that a skyline seems dull if all the buildings are of the same height, it's important to vary the shape and rhythm of flowers in the border. Of all the tall spiky types of flowers available, one of my favorites is *Liatris spicata*. Also called blazing star or gayfeather, this American native is equally at home in the border, meadow, or wild garden. Listed in catalogs as early as 1847, liatris probably appeared in gardens much earlier. The 2½-foot spikes of lovely purple blooms open from the top down and last right through the heat of summer. The flowers are exceptionally good for cutting, too.

Liatris is very easy to grow—hardy to Zone 3, indifferent to soil, and tolerant of drought. Its only demand is a nice sunny spot. Plants can be started from seed, or you can purchase young plants, which are common enough in most nurseries. There are several other species of liatris—*L. aspera*, *L. elegans*, and *L. pycnostachya*, among others—that are quite similar in form and habit to *L. spicata* and came into cultivation at about the same time.

Elecampane

Elecampane (*Inula helenium*, also known as wild sunflower and elfwort) arrived on our shores with the first settlers. This large perennial has been in cultivation since before Roman times, mostly for its roots—they contain a sweet starch called inulin, which was cooked and made into a popular candy. In fact, Helen of Troy was said to have been collecting elecampane when she was abducted (hence the species name). Pliny notes that the empress Julia Augusta "let no day pass without eating some of the roots candied, to help the digestion and to cause mirth." Throughout the Middle Ages, apothecaries sold the root made into sugary cakes, which were said to relieve asthma and indigestion. Culpepper, in his herbal of 1649, notes that it was "one of the most beneficial roots nature affords for the help of the consumptive." For those of you troubled by flower-stealing neighbors, Stephen Blake suggested another use in his 1664 work, *The Com-*

Liatris

Elecampane

plete Gardener's Practice: simply sprinkle dry powdered elecampane over a bunch of flowers with a lovely scent and give the bouquet to the offending party. Upon their first sniff of the fragrance, they will inhale the powder and will sneeze until "tears run down their thighs."

Not having the need to punish any horticulturally larcenous neighbors, I was unaware of this plant until several years ago, when I first saw it at Plimoth Plantation. I was immediately impressed by its large mass, towering over my head in a raised bed, its bright yellow flowers waving in the breeze. Elecampane makes a striking addition to any border with full sun and a moist and fertile soil. It can be sown from seed in the spring or divided from an existing plant in the fall. Yellow flowers appear in early summer. Zones 3–9.

TEASEL

Teasel (*Dipsacus sylvestris*) is another tall plant I first saw at a historic garden, this time Old Sturbridge Village. As I was looking around one of its historic gardens, there stood a 5-foot giant with some of the most interesting dried seedpods I'd ever seen—large and thistlelike, with what turned out to be viciously sharp thorns. (If you sense that I like big plants in the border, you're correct. I am always on the lookout for new and interesting material that will add vertical interest to the garden.) The plant's full common name, fuller's teasel, explains its former demand in the garden. These sharp heads were grown and harvested specifically to use as combs—the spines were perfect for "teasing," or raising the nap on woolen cloth. These days, the dried heads make spectacular additions to dried-flower arrangements.

Teasel

Native to Europe, fuller's teasel is a biennial, and it is easily started from seed. It also reseeds itself, but like foxgloves and all other biennials, you need to plant the seed two years in a row if you want to have flowers year after year. The first season, nothing much happens: the plant produces a low, flat rosette of serrated leaves that look very much like a thorny dandelion. But the second year, watch out! Up from this rosette rises a spiked stem to almost 5 feet, which produces a small oval head of purple flowers in the summer. Afterward, the heads turn brown and can be harvested.

DELPHINIUM

Delphiniums are another one of the best plants for vertical effects in the old-fashioned border, but I must be honest: until recently I have had miserable luck growing the bloody things. I think now I have discovered why (to be revealed below) and I am currently embarked on a new program to reestablish them at the rear of the long border along the drive to our office. To many people, nothing says "old-fashioned" like delphiniums. This association is rather remarkable, because the plants haven't been in our gardens for all that long, at least compared with some in this list. The first delphiniums (*Delphinium elatum*) were imported to England from their native Siberia about 1800. The original English delphiniums were available only in shades of white and blue, but they were soon subjected to long and poorly documented rounds of hybridization, which produced the two main

Delphinium

types found today: *D.* × *belladonna*, a shorter version of the original in white and all colors of blue (the famous Connecticut Yankee Series so often seen in catalogs is part of this group); and the multitude of *D. elatum* hybrids, which come in colors from white through pink, mauve, blues, and purples. Supposedly reds are under development, but I haven't seen any. The original *D. elatum* arrived in this country about 1850, and it is almost impossible to find these days. Chances are, any variety so named will in reality be one of the hybrids, and anyone wishing to plant an authentic Victorian garden must be satisfied with using one of the *D. elatum* hybrids in the original colors of blue or white.

Which leads us to the discussion of culture, and why I have historically failed so miserably with delphiniums. They are *voracious* feeders and require an extremely rich, well-drained soil heavily amended with manure and in *full* sun. This, of course, was my mistake: I presumed that these garden aristocrats could be fawned off with any old soil, and generation after generation simply scoffed at my meager offering and departed to the great delphinium beyond. (As with the foxgloves described earlier, I found to my chagrin that it pays to inform yourself about a plant's soil requirements. See "Soil Is Everything" on page 218 for tips on improving your soil.) I have now heavily enriched the soil and planted my delphiniums where they will get sunlight from dawn to dusk. We'll see. . . .

I am reliably informed by those who have actually grown them successfully that once they really begin to thrive, delphiniums will throw up multiple bloom spikes, often more than the plant can realistically support. Bloom spikes should be thinned to two or three when they are about 6 inches tall. Most delphiniums are propagated from seed, by either a spring or a fall sowing. The plants are hardy to Zone 3. The seed tends to be variable in quality, so if there are several plants in your garden that have shown promise, you can propagate these from cuttings of the new shoots to ensure getting the same plant in the next generation. Personally, I am just hoping to get that far!

ALCHEMILLA

The first time I read the etymology and history of alchemilla, I knew I had to have one in my garden: the name comes from the Arabic meaning "little magical one." This rather remarkable cognomen is due both to the herb's reputation as a healing agent for "women's problems" and to its habit of catching the morning dew in its leaves in precise little drops, while every other plant leaf around is completely dry. So remarkably mysterious was this trait that the water collected from alchemilla leaves was believed in the Middle Ages to have magical properties: alchemilla water was a crucial ingredient in the constant struggle to turn base metals into gold, important enough to

Alchemilla

give its name to the entire process: alchemy. Given alchemilla's widespread magical reputation, its healing qualities, and a healthy dose of the "if you can't beat them, join them" philosophy, the plant's name was eventually Christianized, hence its common name in English: lady's mantle.

When alchemilla arrived in this country is not known, but it was almost undoubtedly before 1800, and considering its widespread reputation, my guess is that it was probably much earlier than that. There are numerous species of alchemilla, although three are most commonly found in cultivation: *Alchemilla vulgaris*, *A. mollis*, and *A. alpina*. The oldest is probably *A. vulgaris*, although *A. mollis* may be equally old. *A. alpina* seems to date in cultivation to about 1850.

The reason for all these "probably's," "may be's," and "seems to's" is that alchemilla is one of those plants that can reproduce by apomixis—the ability to produce fertile seed without pollination (yet another bit of alchemilla's magic). This means that in any given location, the mother plant and any resulting generations are all genetically identical. Any regional differences may over time result in a slightly altered plant population, thus making the whole problem of classification rather difficult and unreliable—the same yet not the same, if you get the drift. The nomenclature in nurseries is certainly confused—I have seen countless plants labeled one way in one place and identical plants marked entirely differently in another. In general, *A. mollis* and *A. vulgaris* are similar: gray-green plants about 18 inches in height that send up delightful sprays of chartreuse flowers in early summer. *A. alpina* is slightly shorter, rising to only 12 inches, with slightly smaller leaves as well. Although not fussy about soil, alchemillas do like a bit of moisture and will tolerate partial shade, especially in hot climates. They are hardy in Zones 3–9.

LUPINE

It will surprise many people to learn that lupines, being so associated with English gardens, are actually North American natives. Discovered in British Columbia in 1825, they appeared as early as 1833 in American seed catalogs as tremendous novelties and were instantly popular. Tough and tolerant of the worst soils and even drought, the original variety, *Lupinus pollyphyllus*, grew to almost 5 feet, with stalks of pealike flowers in colors from white through red to purple. Owing to selective hybridization throughout the 1800s, an extended color range was developed, which included bicolors. Transported to Britain, where this American import was quickly included in English gardens, the program of hybridization was continued and intensified. The culmination of this process was the introduction of the Russell hybrids in the 1930s.

Unlike their ancestors, the Russell hybrids are shorter and prefer a moister, richer soil. They are available in an almost incredible mix of colors. To quote from Jo Ann Gardner's wonderful book *The Heirloom Garden* (see the Bibliography), in the words of a flower-show judge first seeing these new lupines in 1937: "Never before have I seen such marvelous colouring, or been thrilled by such exotic blendings … colours in rich pink, orange-yellow, strawberry-red; bi-colors of royal blue and gold, apricot and sky blue, rose-pink and amethysts, and dozens of intermediate shades and combinations on hundreds of massive spikes." High praise indeed, and no wonder that the Russell hybrids have almost completely eclipsed the original species in the garden.

Lupines are not difficult to grow, once you figure out the trick of getting the seed to sprout. Unlike most other plants whose seed you can just toss on the ground, lupine seed must be treated in order to sprout. The easiest way to do this is to freeze the seed for 2 to 3 days and then soak it overnight. Plant in pots or directly outside. You should see results in about 2 to 3 weeks, given a temperature in the 50s. (Lupine seeds are also different in that they don't like bottom heat, as do most other plants.) Seedlings will bloom in their second year. One note: Lupines generally don't do well in hot climates, preferring areas where the summers are cool and moist, although I have had fine success here in Southborough, where the summers are often neither cool nor moist. Clumps may be divided in the fall. Hardy in most of the country in Zones 4–6 and in the Pacific Northwest in Zones 8–9.

Lupine

Tulipmania

I had a long love-hate relationship with tulips, at least until I discovered some of the antique varieties that are once again available. My main objections to modern hybrids, with their waxy, scentless perfection, were that they are expensive and just too much work, considering that within the last several decades, tulips have become annuals. It seems that in breeding exciting new types and colors, hybridizers lost the perennial habit of the bulbs (their ability to come back every year). The majority of modern varieties are good for only one showing, at most two; after that, the main bulb disintegrates into tiny little bulblets that never seem to bloom again. Fed up with this laborious and expensive process, I had stopped planting tulips altogether. If you feel the same

Parrot Tulip

way I did, read on, because the tulips of our youth—those hardy, reliable souls that arose red and redolent each year in our mothers' gardens—are now available again.

Tulips have had one of the most spectacular up-and-down histories of any plant in cultivation. Imported to Europe in the middle of the 16th century from the Ottoman empire, tulips became an instant hit in northern Europe, especially Holland. Tulips became *de rigueur* in every fashionable garden, and the Dutch, smitten with the plant, started a speculative futures market in tulips, the collapse of which led to a major financial panic in 1638—the first modern "market crash." The popularity of tulips "crashed" as well after this collapse, so much so that for decades only a few English florists even bothered with the bulb. It's to cherished preservation and propagation of these growers during this period of disfavor that we owe the presence of tulips in our gardens today.

As Katherine Whiteside notes in her 1991 book, *Classic Bulbs*, the American colonists were too poor and preoccupied to participate in "Tulipmania," although tulips were present in gardens from the Colonial period onward. Many of the varieties were smaller and shorter than our modern-day tulips (the so-called species tulips) and bloomed much earlier. Others were prized equally for their color and their scent—the latter being a feature that is almost entirely (and regrettably) missing in tulips today.

As for planting schemes, tulips were often combined with other plants in the border during the Colonial era, though as the 19th century wore on, they were increasingly used in massed beds that were planted with annuals afterward. Traditionally, tulips were set out, allowed to flower, and then dug up and stored for the summer, the same bulbs being replanted in the fall. The main reason for digging up the tulips was not to replace them but rather to remove the unsightly foliage from view while the leaves died back. Personally, I think in most cases this is a lot of unnecessary work, and I prefer to plant my tulips either in places where I won't mind the foliage when it recedes or where it will be hidden by other plants.

According to Scott Kunst, founder of Old House Gardens in Ann Arbor, Mich., the chief trick to getting tulips to reappear year after year is keeping them dry in summer, which makes sense, given the bulbs' origins in the hot, rainless summers of the eastern Mediterranean region. To this I would add that the bulbs need to be planted deeply (at least 9 inches or so) in areas where they are not to be disturbed. For once in the garden, benign neglect is best!

Tulips

Historic Garden

The Garden Beautiful: The Glebe House

Gardens like these were the dream of everyone who ever read Gertrude Jekyll's books; unfortunately only a lucky few ever succeeded in maintaining gardens of this complexity.

How the 18th-century Glebe House in Woodbury, Connecticut, wound up with a late Victorian garden by one of the world's most famous English landscape designers is a fascinating tale. Constructed around 1750 as part of a clergyman's "glebe," or rural holding, the house has the distinction of being the birthplace of the Episcopal Church in America. It was used as a private residence for the better part of 150 years, but it fell into considerable disrepair. Threatened with demolition, the house almost succumbed to the wrecker's ball, but fortunately the home's religious significance saved the day. In 1923 a citizen's group, the Seabury Society for the Preservation of the Glebe House, was formed to purchase the structure and restore it as a museum.

One of the society's founding members, Anne Burr Jennings, decided that the property lacked a proper "old-fashioned garden." Ms. Jennings must have been something of a powerhouse within the society, because she was able to convince the committee to toss fairly extensive plans that had already

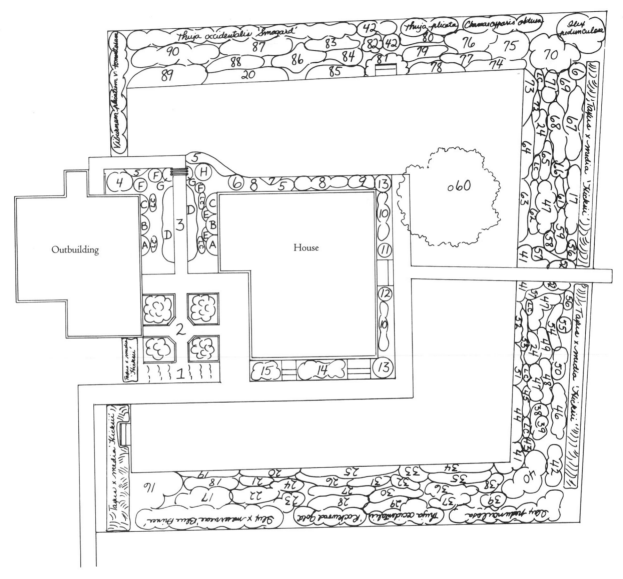

The Glebe House garden planted according to Gertrude Jekyll's plan. (Courtesy of the Glebe House. Used by permission.)

been drawn up, paid for, and partially executed and start afresh. She even traveled to England and managed to convince Gertrude Jekyll, who was then in her eighty-third year and near the end of her long career, to undertake the design of a garden that she had never seen (and never would see, except in photographs), on the other side of the Atlantic. A long correspondence ensued, and Miss Jekyll eventually produced a plan for a typical Edwardian-style garden—a series of elaborate garden rooms separated from the street by a hedge, with stone flagged paths and large, deep herbaceous borders featuring some of her signature color combinations of blue, white, and light gray.

For reasons still mysterious, after all that effort and expense, Jekyll's garden plan was never installed. In fact, it was not until garden historian Susan Schnare discovered the plans in the early 1980s that Jekyll's design came back to light. The discovery stirred up considerable controversy in the historical community and touched on a question common to museum houses and old-home owners alike: What constitutes an "appropriate" landscape for a historic structure? Is it best to replicate one "correct" period with exactness, or merely to invoke the romance of a bygone age by using elements of period design?

In the case of the Glebe House, the problem was even thornier, for although Jekyll had designed several other gardens in this country, only one was extant (and in private hands), so the chance to restore one of Jekyll's designs for public view was quite a temptation. On the other hand, this late Victorian/Edwardian garden was considered by some to be completely inappropriate for a house of this date, especially one whose interior had been carefully restored to reflect its late-18th-century appearance. Cost was also an issue—gardens of this type are quite expensive to install, and constant maintenance is required to keep them from falling rapidly into ruin. Furthermore, the garden had been designed by Jekyll to blend in with a slate blue-gray house, but the house had recently been repainted a vibrant ochre color. After much soul-searching, the Glebe House Board decided to proceed with Jekyll's plan. Now roses drape gracefully over arbors, the borders are flushed with bloom, and the small lawn is luxuriant, much as Jekyll had envisioned these elements almost a century earlier.

But what of the question of appropriateness of the landscape in relation to the house? For house museums and other structures where historical purity is deemed paramount, a conscious decision is generally made to limit the interpretation to a specific period, be it 1750, 1830, or 1900. This decision, however, is often purely arbitrary and is based on the time period that can best be documented and represented. For the average owner of an old house, the decision is even more complex. Obviously, Colonial houses existed through the late Victorian period and in fact could very well have had gardens of this type, had the owners been so inclined. Moreover, in the case of the Glebe House, Jekyll's garden plan is one that derives its success in part from her respect for the traditional precepts of architecture and the visual arts, especially those of painting. The classic lines of her scheme are very much in keeping with those of Colonial architecture: the house seems happily nestled in the landscape, comfortably embracing the plants around it. The planting style, although complex, manages not to overwhelm the small frame house.

Although you may be salivating at the lushness of Jekyll's plan and be tempted to replicate it in your own yard, you should be aware that this laid-back, cottage style of gardening is *extremely* difficult to pull off successfully. It is a given in gardening that whatever seems most "natural" is always much more difficult to create and to maintain. You are, after all, trying to imitate the work of nature rather than the work of man, and it's hard to play the garden god successfully.

Even the great Jekyll had her hands full—her own gardens at Munstead Woods fully occupied her talents and her finances, forcing her to employ a large gardening staff to tend and maintain them. The minute her back was turned, things started to decline, and after her death her famous gardens all but vanished, although a portion is now in private hands and is currently being restored. Add to these difficulties the cost of the plants themselves. The amount of material required to pull off these borders is staggering: their lush effects rely on large "drifts" of perennials (in multiples of 5, 7, 9, and 11), not to mention a huge supply of annuals to ensure bloom throughout the season.

Having said all this, it is also true that this style of garden is one of the most beautiful ever created, and the temptation to try at least one of these borders is almost impossible to resist. (I know—I speak from experience!)

The following list represents the Gertrude Jekyll Garden as planted in 1995–1996, and shown on page 174. Substitutions have been made where Jekyll recommended material not suitable to the Connecticut climate.

1. Kitchen herbs
   Tansy, thyme, golden oregano, lady's mantle, sweet basil and purple basil, golden sage, lavender, curly parsley, chives, garlic chives, rue, nasturtiums, heliotrope, feverfew, and muscari
2. Rose quadrants
   Rosa 'Nathalie Nypels', *Salvia horminum* 'Claryssa' and *Campanula rapunculoides*, *Iris* cultivar and *Tulipa* 'Lilac Wonder', *Ornithogalum*
3. Rose allée
   A. 'New Dawn'; B. 'Dortmund'; C. 'William Baffin'; D. 'White Pet'; E. 'Dainty Bess'; F. 'Thérèse Bugnet'; G. Arbor: 'Cuisse de Nymphe', Cape Cod rose, *Clematis* × *jackmanii*; H. 'Harison's Yellow'
   Perennials: *Dianthus arenarius* 'Snow Flurries'; *Clematis* 'Henryi', 'Bees Jubilee', and 'Comtesse de Bouchard'; *Lilium regale* 'Album'; *Iris* cultivar
   Bulbs: *Narcissus* 'Actrice', 'Actaea', 'Thalia', and Single Jonquil; *Muscari*; *Allium neapolitanum*

Perennial border:

4. *Buddleia alternifolia, B.* 'Lochinch'
5. *Convallaria majalis*
6. *Philadelphus coronarius*
7. *Helleborus orientalis, Allium bulgaricum, A. neapolitanum*
8. *Spiraea* × *bumalda* 'Anthony Waterer', *Lilium speciosum* var. *rubrum*
9. *Lavandula angustifolia* 'Munstead', *Rosa* 'Fru Dagmar Haustrup'
10. *Kalmia latifolia, Vinca minor, Anemone blanda, Corydalis, Narcissus* 'Ice Follies'
11. *Syringa microphylla*
12. *Syringa meyeri*
13. *Viburnum* × *burkwoodii*
14. *Rosa* 'Fru Dagmar Haustrup', *Phlox subulata, Thymus serpyllum* 'Coccineum', *T. pseudolanuginosus, Perovskia atriplicifolia, Saxifraga*
15. *Perovskia atriplicifolia, Rosa* 'Fru Dagmar Haustrup', *Phlox subulata, Thymus pseudolanuginosus, axifraga*
16. *Spiraea nipponica* 'Snowmound', *Aegopodium podagraria* 'Variegatum'
17. *Ilex crenata* 'Howardi'
18. *Erigeron speciosus* 'Prosperity'
19. *Iberis sempervirens* 'Snowflake'
20. *Euonymus fortunei* 'Variegatus'
21. *Iris germanica* var. *florentina*
22. *Anemone vitifolia* 'Robustissima'
23. *Dahlia* 'White Perfection', *D.* 'My Love'
24. *Chrysanthemum* × *superbum*
25. *Rudbeckia fulgida* 'Goldsturm'
26. *Helenium autumnale* 'Sunball'
27. *Hemerocallis flava*
28. *Phlox maculata* 'Miss Lingard'
29. *Alcea rosea* 'Nigra'
30. *Antirrhinum* 'Rocket Red'
31. *Iris* 'Gold Galore'
32. *Oenothera tetragona* 'Fireworks'
33. *Helenium* 'Moerheim Beauty'
34. *Polygonum affine* 'Border Jewel'
35. *Iris* 'Spartan'
36. *Monarda didyma* 'Gardenview Scarlet'
37. *Dahlia* 'Rosabella'
38. *Centranthus ruber*
39. *Weigela florida* 'Foliis Purpureus'
40. *Weigela florida* 'Red Prince'
41. *Bergenia cordifolia*
42. *Viburnum opulus* 'Sterile'
43. *Paeonia* 'Mrs. Roosevelt'
44. *Dianthus* cultivar
45. *Iris* cultivar
46. *Neillia siberica*
47. *Paeonia* 'Festiva Maxima'
48. *Alcea rosea* cultivar
49. *Antirrhinum* 'Rocket Rose'
50. *Sorbaria sorbifolia*
51. *Antirrhinum* 'Royal Carpet Pink'
52. *Stachys lanata*, flowering and nonflowering
53. *Geranium clarkei*
54. *Anemone hybrida* 'Honorine Jobert'
55. *Ligustrum vulgare* 'Cheyenne'
56. *Hedera helix* 'Arborescens'
57. *Lavandula angustifolia* 'Munstead'
58. *Campanula persicifolia* 'Alba'
59. *Alcea rosea* cultivar
60. *Platanus occidentalis* (This American sycamore, the ninth largest in Connecticut, is estimated to be more than two hundred years old.)
61. *Iris sibirica* 'Perry's Blue'
62. *Iris* cultivar

63. *Dicentra eximia*
64. *Geranium himalayense*
65. *Chelone lyonii, Antirrhinum* 'Rocket Pink'
66. *Dahlia* 'Le Castle'
67. *Weigela* 'Pink Princess'
68. *Anchusa azurea* 'Dropmore', *Lobelia siphilitica*
69. *Delphinium* Hybrids, 'Summer Skies', 'Galahad', and 'Connecticut Yankee Mix'
70. *Rosa virginiana*
71. *Paeonia* cultivar
72. *Iris germanica* var. *florentina*
73. *Hosta plantaginea*
74. *Dianthus* 'Her Majesty'
75. *Echinops ritro*
76. *Alcea rugosa*

77. *Salvia* × *superba* 'May Night'
78. *Nepeta* × *faassenii* 'Blue Wonder'
79. *Iris pallida*
80. *Campanula latifolia* var. *macrantha*
81. *Rosmarinus officinalis*
82. *Oxydendrum arboreum*
83. *Aquilegia* cultivars, with *Thalictrum rochebrunianum* 'Lavender Mist'
84. *Phlox paniculata* 'Fairest One'
85. *Hosta sieboldiana* 'Elegans'
86. *Paeonia* 'Seashell'
87. *Campanula persicifolia* 'Alba', *C. persicifolia* cultivars, *C. medium*, *C. rapunculoides*
88. *Iris* 'Glistening Icicles'
89. *Veronica* 'Snow White'
90. *Spiraea thunbergii*

LC = *Lilium candidum*

Additional perennials found throughout the garden: *Campanula rapunculoides, Iberis sempervirens, Polemonium caeruleum, Pulmonaria angustifolia*

Peonies

While many flowers vie for the title "Queen of the Garden," the peony may rank first—its breathtaking blooms, fascinating pedigree, interesting foliage and habit, disease resistance, hardiness, and dependability all combine to make it one of the outstanding flowers of garden and landscape.

Botanically, peonies are divided into two principal groups: herbaceous or "garden" peonies (sometimes confusingly called Japanese or Chinese peonies), and tree peonies. The former type is the one most people think of when they visualize peonies. It owes its existence to crosses made primarily from *Paeonia lactifolia*, which is native to regions of Siberia and Manchuria, and *P. officinalis*, which originated in southern Europe (*officinalis* means "of the pharmacist" and indicates a long history of medicinal use).

Peony

Tree (or Moutan) peonies are shrubby or woody plants from 3 to 10 feet high that originally came from China and Tibet, and in many ways they are quite different from their European cousins. For one thing, the stems of tree peonies do not die down to the ground like those of the garden variety, although the plants do lose their leaves in the winter. Both types are very cold-hardy; the garden type doesn't care much for the Deep South, however, where the winters are not cold enough to cause dormancy. (Tree peonies seem to do just fine in the Deep South.) Garden peonies prefer full sun. The tree varieties actually prefer dappled shade, and they make terrific understory plantings, but they often require several years to come into flower.

All peony varieties are described by the number of petals per flower. The types are, in ascending order, single, Japanese (a fuller type of single), semidouble, double, anemone (a double type with a full center surrounded by a ring of single petals), and bomb (extremely double, almost triple). Whichever type you choose, the uses for peonies in the landscape are myriad. They make an excellent addition to perennial beds, look well when massed, and can even be used as small shrubs in the general landscape.

Peonies have a fascinating history. According to legend, the flower was named for Paeon, a famous physician in Greek mythology who used its miraculous powers to cure wounds of the gods Pluto and Mars. The great encyclopedist Pliny the Elder, in his monumental work *Natural History* (A.D. 77), lists over twenty illnesses that peonies cured, with special emphasis on epilepsy. The medicinal use of peonies continued throughout the Middle Ages, and no good physic garden was considered complete without these plants. Peonies arrived in this country with the first settlers and were popular throughout the colonies—Thomas Jefferson listed them in his garden, for example. Because a large number of varieties are introduced each year, many older varieties are no longer grown and propagated. Here are some old-fashioned varieties still in common cultivation.

'Baroness Schroeder' (1889), white with yellow center
'Duchesse de Nemours' (1856), white with yellow center
'Edulis Superba' (1824), old rose-pink
'Félix Crousse' (1881), red
'Festiva Maxima' (1851), white
'Humei' (1810), cherry pink
'Monsieur Jules Elie' (1888), medium pink with creamy center
'Sarah Bernhardt' (1906), apple-blossom pink

Peony bush

The Knot Garden

The knot garden, or more accurately the parterre, is one of the oldest forms of garden in America—a direct descendant of the walled gardens of the Middle Ages. These gardens rose to prominence during the late Renaissance and became common in slightly different variations all over the continent by the 17th century. In America, a simplified form of the parterre arrived with the early colonists, and ever more elaborate versions, rivaling their European cousins, were common features in prosperous American gardens by the time of the Revolution.

At its most basic, a parterre is a symmetrically designed garden of richly patterned shapes that relies on strict geometry to achieve its charming effect. Long a staple of the formal or architectural garden, parterres are the perfect complement to most house styles (including, somewhat surprisingly, many modern houses). They are remarkably simple to lay out if you keep some basic concepts in mind.

Although historically classified into many subtypes, only two types of parterres are of interest in today's American garden: the true knot and what is often called the cutwork parterre. (The term *knot garden* is used for any geometrically arranged flower garden, but *parterre* is the correct general term.) True knot gardens are elaborate patterns of low-growing shrubbery in which the several different types of plant material in the borders have contrasting foliage and appear to cross over and under one another like threads in a weave. The interior spaces of these gardens are occasionally filled with flowers, but the main decorative feature is really the design of the edging pattern itself.

It is in the fall and winter that the knot garden truly comes into its own: the fluid geometry of its living line remains crisp and clear long after much of the garden has faded into brown nothingness. The illustrations on this and the following pages, from 17th-century manuals, provide interesting models for creating your own period knot garden.

The cutwork garden is the form of parterre more often seen in the United States. Although equally geometric and symmetrical, the pattern is formed by edged beds, typically bordered with a single type of low-growing shrub such as dwarf box or santolina. The edging material is generally wood, cobble, or some type of stone. The space in between the beds forms pathways, usually constructed of hard paving—stone, brick, or gravel. Turf may also be used as a path surface, but grass paths have to be mowed and sharply edged quite frequently, or the design will lose its crispness.

Parterres are often considered "formal," but the way in which the beds are planted, not the geometric design, actually determines the degree of formality. Spilling over with a wild riot of flowers and herbs, even the most rigidly shaped garden, lushly planted, is hardly what I would call formal! So go ahead and experiment with these historic gems. Knots and parterres, some of our most traditional garden features, remain fresh and integral parts of the modern American landscape.

Following is a step-by-step guide to laying out your own knot garden.

Step I: Forming the Square

Determine the general size and location of your parterre and roughly mark out the four corners with stakes. Choose one corner to be a starting point (point A on the diagram). Stretch a line from stake A to stake B and measure. (It's best if you use a measurement rounded to the foot.) This forms the first side of the parterre. Measure 3 feet from stake A along side 1 and mark with a new stake, E. Extend a 4-foot rope up from point A and swing the rope to form an arc; mark the resulting arc on the ground (powdered lime is very useful to mark the lines). Then with a 5-foot rope, swing another arc from point E to the spot where the 5-foot arc intersects with the 4-foot arc (point F). You have now formed a perfect 90-degree corner. Next, extend side 2 to the same length as side 1. Now repeat the 3-4-5 plottings at point B to form side 3. Form the final side, 4, by joining sides 2 and 3. You now have a perfect square!

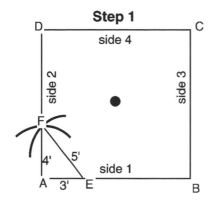

Step 1

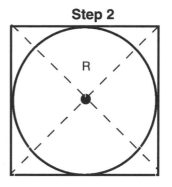

Step 2

Step 3

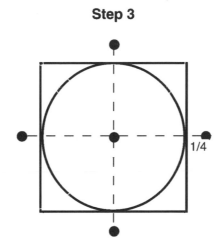

Step 4

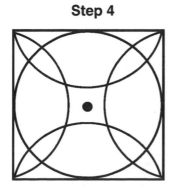

Step 5

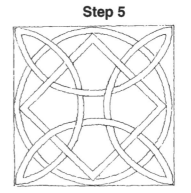

Step 2:
Making the Central Circle

Stretch a line diagonally from corner A to corner C and another line from corner B to corner D. Where the lines cross is the center of the square. Mark this spot with a stake. The distance from the center of the square to the center of each side is called the radius of the circle inside the square. Attach a line to the center stake, and mark a circle inside the square with lime.

Step 3: Making the Exterior Circles

Mark the center point of each of the four sides by dividing the sides in half. Then extend a line from the center stake of the central circle through the center point of each side to a distance beyond each side equal to one-quarter of the radius of the central circle from step 2. Mark the four resulting points and form a circle around each, using a circle identical to the central circle in step 2. This forms the four exterior circles.

Step 4: Forming the Central Diamond

To form the central diamond, simply connect the four center points of each side of the original square. Mark all the lines with lime.

Step 5: The Final Product

You've done it! Now plant with edging materials of different colors and textures for maximum effect.

So what do you plant in a knot garden? The simple answer is, anything you want. While the choice of edging materials is somewhat limited to dwarf and easily clipped plants—miniature box, rosemary, germander, lavender, and santolina are traditional choices—what goes inside is entirely up to you. For a more formal look, try mass plantings of a single species, such as roses; spring bulbs, followed by annuals, are another good choice. For a cottage feel, you might use masses of flowers and herbs. The only caveat is that whatever plant material you use should not grow to such a size as to entirely overwhelm the design of the borders. Generally, plants under two feet are best. You'll find too that if the inside plantings get too big and flop over onto the edging plants for extended periods, their growth will be thin and the clarity of the exterior line will be lost, so keep the tallest plants in the center of the beds and away from the edges.

How-to: Cottage Gardens

Cottage gardens are often held up as a perfect model for today's amateur gardener, but they really require a tremendous amount of skill and work to bring off successfully, especially if they consist entirely of flowers. It seems almost counterintuitive that something so wild- and carefree-looking should be so demanding, but it's true: cottage gardens are completely managed artifice. The continuous sequence of flowering, and the full, lush effect, depend on a planting scheme that is exceedingly tight.

Part of the charm of the cottage garden is that everything grows and blends together. The problem is that you have to be extremely knowledgeable about the growing habits and inclinations of each plant you use, or the whole thing rapidly declines into a weedy, ragged mess, where larger, more aggressive plants completely overwhelm their smaller neighbors. Correct sequencing of bloom is very difficult as well and necessitates a vast knowledge of plantsmanship to accomplish. For years I struggled with this type of garden in my own yard in Southborough. I have finally succeeded to a relative degree through careful planning and layout, and with the help of a few fortuitous discoveries.

If you are interested in laying out a cottage garden, the very first thing to do is to draw up the plan of the garden bed you intend to plant. As you think about the size and extent of the bed, don't underestimate the amount of work required. Flower gardens aren't any more difficult than other types of gardens, but they do require dedication and upkeep, either yours or someone else's. It's far better to start small and then decide later to enlarge your plot.

The country ideal: a lush Victorian cottage garden, complete with cottager.

Choosing what to plant is the next step, and this is often difficult for inexperienced gardeners. Defining selection criteria, such as a color scheme, is a good way to start. For this type of relaxed garden, I rather like to use a large range of colors, muted with gray-leaved or variegated plants—always keeping a wary eye out for any potentially glaring clashes. However, I have seen equally successful schemes that limit flower color to a single range. Whichever way you proceed, choosing the colors first will help limit your plant choices. Other possible selection criteria are introduction date, for those of you interested in historical accuracy; local growing conditions (that is, grow what grows well where you live); fragrance; suitability as cut flowers; or simply personal favorites. It doesn't really matter as long as you pay attention to how the plants are placed in the garden.

Plant placement is the most crucial element to good flower-garden design, and the most basic tenet I can offer is "Read the label!" Height indications and sun preferences are not wisely ignored. But you need to interpret the label information conservatively, and be wary of some plant descriptions that are deceptively ambiguous. What "shade tolerant" really means, for instance, is that the plant will sulk in the shade, that the growth will never be as lush or full as that of its neighbor in full sun, and that the plant may never bloom. "Prefers" is another wonderfully creative term. My personal belief is that these loose phrases were deliberately invented by the growers to lull the public into purchasing plants and installing them in poor locations where they will ultimately fail and need to be replaced, thus generating future sales! If you mentally change "tolerates" to "doesn't like" and "prefers" to "requires," you'll be far ahead of the game.

As for actually siting the plants in the garden, height is probably the most important consideration. In general, locate tall material near the rear of a one-sided border, or in the center if the bed will be viewed from both sides. This would seem fairly straightforward advice, but plants don't always grow to the size predicted. Depending on whether or not the plants are happy where they are located, they may be much shorter, taller, or less broad than expected. Furthermore, it typically takes several years for a plant to reach full height and width, so be patient. Judging eventual width and the best plant spacing is also something of a learned art, although less important than correctly estimating a plant's final height. You can always supplement or subtract from a planting by adding more material or dividing a plant. You can't, however, do much about a 5-foot hollyhock in front of a 2-foot rose. If, after all your planning and waiting (that is, after several seasons), a plant doesn't thrive or isn't the right size, simply move it. (Make sure you transplant it at the right stage in its growing cycle. Check a good guide for plant-specific timing advice.)

One other secret to the successful cottage garden is to use a liberal selection of annuals and biennials that are *grown in place from seed*. While potted annuals tucked in and about perennial material early in the season will help extend the flowering period, plants sown from seed directly into the spot where they are meant to grow will also help knit the various sections of the garden together in a way not achievable by any other means. This is truly one of the keys to the cottage garden, and something that it took me a long time to learn.

These days, the usual method of planting annuals and biennials is to raise or buy already potted material, lay it out, and then plant it in the garden. This is the method I always used, with very mediocre results. There are advantages to starting with plants instead of sowing seeds—you get a relatively good idea of how the plants will look in terms of foliage and flower color, and sometimes you get faster results. But you will almost certainly set the tiny plants in groups or clumps that defy a "natural" arrangement and that will never really blend together in the carefree way you want. However, if you scatter the seeds of some of your favorite annuals into the garden or, better yet, use plants that readily self-seed, this charming randomness occurs all by itself.

Why it took me so long to figure this out, I'm not quite sure. I had always known that historically, potted container plants were extremely rare and were used only for those varieties that didn't propagate easily any other way. Most plants in the traditional cottage garden were grown directly from sown seed. Yet nowadays, we are all so used to instant gratification in the garden that we simply don't consider other, more time-consuming alternatives, even when they yield better results. Many common annuals, such as cosmos, zinnias, sunflowers, marigolds, and flowering sweet peas, grow much better and flower more profusely when started directly from seed in the garden. They also often catch up to, and even surpass in size, their potted-out brothers and sisters! I first noticed this one summer when some marigolds seeded themselves. They were twice the size, bore twice the number of flowers, and had much deeper, richer foliage than the same variety I had started indoors that spring and so laboriously set out. Moreover, they were charmingly tucked in between two large stones that accented the flowers perfectly, and where I could never have inserted the small plants myself. If you want to duplicate the lovely nonchalance of the early American garden, the old-fashioned way—direct-sowing the seeds—is the *only* way to do it.

My general advice to would-be cottage gardeners is to start small, be prepared for the expense (these borders seem to eat plants for lunch), and be sure that you are ready to spend a lot of time in the garden! I would also highly recommend reading some of Gertrude Jekyll's works before you begin, especially *Colour in the Flower Garden* and *Colour Schemes for the Flower Garden*, as Jekyll's advice on color combinations and plant choice doesn't condense well. One other note, and this is an important one not often mentioned: To accommodate planting in "drifts" as advocated by Jekyll, the borders must be at least 8 feet wide, to allow for the successful blending of shape and color. Narrow perennial borders *simply cannot accomplish this*, and this is one of the main reasons most people fail in re-creating this style of garden. When initially laid out, these borders may seem huge, but you will be amazed at how quickly they will fill in, even during their first season.

$\mathcal{P}$roductivity

$\mathcal{I}$t is only within the last several decades that American gardens became largely ornamental in nature. Before this, they were expected to produce as well as to please. There are many reasons for this loss of productivity, principal among them being the prodigious supply of exotic and out-of-season foods that are now available to us throughout the year. Nowadays we can go to the market and buy not only common produce but also raspberries, blueberries, kumquats, and melons from all over the world, in all seasons. With the rise of global transport, people simply have become accustomed to buying everything and growing nothing.

There are two very good reasons to reconsider this stance: cost and quality. Cost is an interesting issue because, until recently, home gardening *never* really paid off, at least in the monetary sense. Stories of the $10/pound tomatoes and the $3 heads of lettuce are almost apocryphal among vegetable gardeners. The key to making a financial success of home gardening is three-fold: grow only what you like, what is expensive to buy, and what is not readily available at the market. People seem to feel somehow that because they are planting a vegetable garden, it needs to be nutritionally complete, with representatives of each of the vegetable groups, even if they normally don't like them. Instead, plant only what you enjoy, and plant only as much as you will realistically consume or store. As for availability and price, it most certainly makes sense to plant those raspberries everyone adores, which are easy to grow and are *very* expensive at the store; or your own gooseberries, which take up little space in the garden and are both costly and hard to find; or your own 'Fameuse' apples, which can't be had in the marketplace for love or money.

The pleasures of picking your own fruit can't be understated.

In regard to the second, and maybe the best, reason to grow your own—quality—you can grow foods yourself that taste better than almost anything you can possibly buy, and I am not talking just about freshness. Many varieties of fruits and vegetables that you can grow are simply not available in stores, because produce intended for the market is bred first and foremost for shipping durability and shelf life. That's why heirloom varieties are making such a comeback—these classic varieties that our ancestors enjoyed may not ship well, but they do yield unique produce whose flavor is beyond comparison with what you can buy in the store. (While this may sound like an exaggeration, it's not: until you have bitten into your own homegrown peach, whose juicy flavor almost explodes in your mouth, or eaten a 'Brandywine' tomato, still redolent from the vine, you can't imagine what a taste experience it is. Words do indeed fail.) And if you're concerned about chemicals in your food, there are only two real options: go to a certified grower and pay a huge premium for your produce, or grow your own. While it's unlikely that you will want to grow the household's entire fruit and produce supply, you will be amazed at what you can grow with relative ease.

Of course, nothing comes from nothing. Productive gardens require more thought and effort than those that merely sit around like a green plastic yard ornament. To get something, you generally have to give something in return. Having a productive garden does not necessarily mean churning up part of the lawn for a huge vegetable garden, although that certainly is an option, albeit one that would require a large amount of time and effort. There are many ways that you can make your garden productive, some with practically no work at all, others with a modest initial investment that amply justifies the expenditure of time and labor.

For instance, berry bushes, such as highbush blueberries, are often quite ornamental and make lovely additions to the garden. Why not plant a few where you were intending to put that plain old forsythia? For the same effort, you get flowers, berries, and fall color! Fruit trees are another good example: many people plant ornamentals such as crab apples, when instead they could have a beautiful *apple* tree that would flower in the same delightful way *and* produce an edible crop with no additional work. Incorporating other plants such as asparagus is not quite as effortless, but your labors will pay off well in the end: a weekend's worth of spadework spent on preparing an asparagus bed will guarantee pounds of delicious shoots for twenty years or more. The point is that, short of plastic plants, all gardens require some "sweat equity," and if you are going to expend it, why not get something in return?

> ## FINE FRUIT
>
> *Fine fruit is the flower of commodities. It is the most perfect union of the useful and the beautiful that the earth knows. Trees full of soft foliage; blossoms fresh with spring beauty; and finally, fruit: rich bloom-dusted, melting and luscious; such are the treasures of the orchard and garden, temptingly offered to every landholder in this bright, sunny, though temperate climate.*
>
> —A. J. Downing
> *Fruits and Fruit Trees of America (1845)*

All productive plants are worthwhile in the garden, but growing ancient heirloom plants brings a pleasure all its own. Of all the plants known to humankind over the millennia, food crops have been the most closely associated with our history. These plants have nourished, cured, and clothed us for centuries, and some, such as corn, have lore and history that dates far back in human memory. While few of us have the budget and the ability to possess antiques or artwork with great historical significance, the garden is far more democratic: we can *all* own a piece of history out-of-doors. Do you fancy owning the same pear that Louis XVI dangled over the lips of Marie-Antoinette? How about the apples that graced George Washington's table, or the asparagus that Queen Victoria daintily munched on the lawn at Osborne? No problem in the garden. The actual descendants of these plants or even a grafted *piece of the very same plant* that graced a garden hundreds or thousands of years ago is yours for the planting. Talk about preserving a piece of history! All this *and* the pleasure of growing a product far superior in taste and quality to almost anything on the market. What more can you ask?

So then, with hopefully a whetted appetite, here is a short selection of some crops drawn from our gardening past to make your garden more productive—for you, your family, and the environment as a whole. You can pick and choose projects to suit your needs, pleasures, energy, time, and budget. As you plan out or work in your garden, give some thought to making *each* space produce something—whether it be fruit, vegetable, or flower. Given the amount of time and money the average American gardener gives to the landscape, it seems a real shame that often the landscape doesn't give something back. It used to, and it can again: the garden is certainly bountiful, if you but ask.

Favorite Heirloom Fruits

One of the first things I did when I bought my house in Southborough was to plant an orchard of antique fruit trees. Some people at the time thought that strange, especially since this 1852 house had neither working plumbing nor electrical systems, and the house and outbuildings from rooftop to foundation were under renovation. While the workmen felled rain-soaked walls, ripped out damaged sills, and otherwise made a complete disaster of the interior, I, oblivious to all except the mounting expenses of the renovation, blithely cleared and prepared a piece of overgrown land and set out the trees I had purchased even before I'd closed on the house. Friends and neighbors would stop by and note the progress of the house renovation, and then cast a bemused glance in my direction as I worked away at my orchard.

There was, you see, method to my madness. The previous winter I had been bitten by the antique apple bug, seduced by catalog descriptions of luscious long-forgotten apples that were old when the Colonies were young. These were deliciously redolent apples not only for eating out of hand but also for baking, cider, cooking, and general storage, fruit of sonorous name and historic associations such as 'Roxbury Russet', 'Tompkins' County King', 'Cox's Orange Pippin', and 'Duchess de Oldenburg'. The books and catalogs promised culinary delights unknown to the modern purchaser of our hard, nearly flavorless supermarket varieties, notable only for their cosmetic appeal.

Now the first real apple harvests are in, and friends and neighbors doubt my sanity no longer, as they are too busy marveling over these magnificent, long-lost varieties and wondering why they themselves don't have a tree or two in their backyards. This is a very good question, because as recently as fifty years ago, no homeowner or gardener of note would have been without a small home orchard, with apples, cherries, peaches, and pears. (Take a look at almost any of the period landscape plans in this book and you will see indications for at least a few fruit trees on even the smallest property.) At the time, of course, this planting was a matter of culinary necessity. Fruit was often expensive and impossible to find out of season, and every industrious homemaker harvested and preserved her own if she wanted fruit in winter.

These days the necessity is based not on availability but on quality. If you wish to experience fruit flavor, aroma, and texture unlike that of any store-bought apple, peach, or plum, you must grow your own historic fruit trees.

When I ask my clients if they have considered growing fruit trees in the landscape, their answer is almost invariably "Yes, but they are so much trouble and so messy that we never tried." While it is true that fruit trees require a bit of care, their needs aren't really that demanding, and the rewards of having a few trees of your own justify the efforts. As to the mess, once you taste some of these antique varieties, rest assured that there will be few if any left on the ground. (Owners of horses and other animals take note: Windfalls make great feed.)

The best reason for growing fruit trees is the taste. Modern fruits such as the 'Delicious' apple (which really isn't) are selected only for cosmetic appearance and shelf life, but heirloom varieties were developed not only for taste

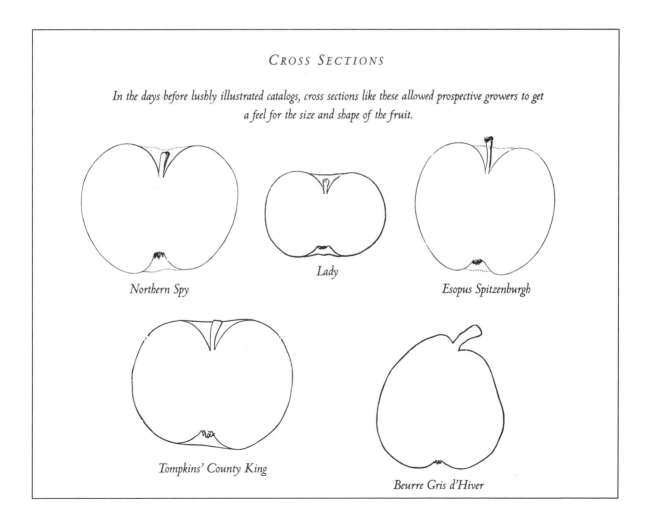

Cross Sections

In the days before lushly illustrated catalogs, cross sections like these allowed prospective growers to get a feel for the size and shape of the fruit.

Northern Spy

Lady

Esopus Spitzenburgh

Tompkins' County King

Beurre Gris d'Hiver

but for purpose. Specialty apples were selected for cooking, general eating, pressing for cider, winter storage, and, the king of all uses, as dessert apples. The list of formerly common varieties is almost endless, and remarkably, thanks to the work of some hardy souls who refused to see their favorite varieties pass into oblivion, a goodly number are still available today for purchase. Just be sure that when you choose your trees, you purchase dwarf (8- to 10-foot) or semidwarf (12- to 15-foot) species, even if you plan to devote a considerable space to the enterprise. Both sizes have their own set of advantages. Dwarf trees produce much more fruit per square foot than their full-size counterparts and much sooner, too, so you can have many more varieties and harvest earlier than with standard-size trees. Personally, though, I prefer semidwarfs; they don't need to be staked as dwarfs do, they produce a nicer-looking tree, and they are still small enough to be picked without too much trouble.

Although the specifics of growing apple and fruit trees are outside the scope of this book, there are many excellent sources that demystify the whole process, including Lewis Hill's *Fruits and Berries*, Stella Otto's *The Backyard Orchardist* and *The Backyard Berry Book*, and Lee Reich's *Uncommon Fruits Worthy of Attention*. (See the Bibliography for details.)

Below I've listed some of my favorite antique fruit trees, with dates of introduction and short descriptions. The ripening dates are estimated for Boston and will vary considerably depending on your location and the weather. As you find yourself becoming a fruit connoisseur, you'll realize the extremely subjective nature of the debate over the "best" varieties, so by all means investigate the hundreds of other cultivars now available as well. Just be sure when you make your selection that you pay attention to a few points: climate preferences (some trees do much better in the South than others); pollination requirements (some trees need other varieties nearby in order to bear fruit); bearing season (apples, for instance, bear over a long season, generally from late August to late November, so be sure to choose a range of bearing dates to better stagger the harvest); and, finally, use requirements (there's no point planting a good baking apple if you never bake).

APPLES

Arkansas Black (1870) A medium to large, waxy, dark-skinned apple with yellow flesh that keeps well. Extremely hard when picked but softens and improves in storage. Not a highly prolific tree, but noted for disease resistance. A good, late, no-spray apple.

Ben Davis (1860) For many years after the Civil War, this striped red apple was the most popular eating apple in the South. An exceptional keeper, and one of the best apples south of the Mason-Dixon line. Not for northern gardens, however. **Black Ben Davis** is a seedling from 1880 that is darker and makes terrific apple butter. Both ripen in mid-October.

Black Gilliflower (1700) Also called 'Sheepnose', this large, dark red, conical apple originated in Connecticut, but it does well in the South, too. The flesh is firm and sweet and is good for drying. Ripens very late.

Black Limbertwig (before 1900) A spicy, fragrant apple that was once very popular in the South. Good for fresh eating, cider, and apple butter. Ripens in early fall.

Buckingham (1817) Another great southern apple, which may have originated with the Cherokee. The fruit is large, crisp, and juicy; yellow/green with occasional red stripes. An average keeper, this apple ripens in early fall.

Calville Blanc d'Hiver (1627) As *d'Hiver* implies, one of the best apples for winter storage; considered the classic dessert apple in France. 'Calville' actually predates 1627, when Le Lectier grew it for Louis XIII. A large apple that is pale green at picking and turns pale yellow in storage. Tender, spicy flesh with an extremely high vitamin C content—greater than an orange's! Good for cider and cider vinegar. A late apple, maturing in October or November.

Carolina Red June (before 1900) This old southern baking apple has small fruit with yellow/red stripes and pink/white flesh. Very early, and best used right away.

Chenango Strawberry (1854) This medium conical fruit is *very* fragrant. The skin is pink over white, the flesh juicy and tender, although the fruit must be picked precisely when the skin turns milky white, or else it disappoints. Great for desserts. Named after Chenango County, New York.

Cort Pendu Plat (ancient) This apple may date to the Roman Empire. Its French name aptly describes its appearance: hanging, short, and flat. The fruit is yellow, blushed with red, and very flavorful. According to one source, this variety was often known in England as the "wise apple" because its late budding and flowering allowed it to escape late-spring frosts. Also late bearing.

Cox's Orange Pippin (before 1830) A premier English variety, which, according to Robert Nitschke of Southmeadow Fruit Gardens, is "of red and yellow skin, unsurpassed in tender juiciness of its yellow textured flesh that lingers on the tongue like ice cream." More difficult to grow but worth trying. Bears toward the end of September.

Fameuse (1730) This so-called snow apple was brought to Canada from France. Dark red skin and white flesh occasionally streaked with red. This variety is best eaten just picked. Ripens in October.

Golden Russet (1850s) Once the most famous of the russets (a name that conjures delight in any American apple lover), 'Golden Russet' bears crisp yellow fruit with the merest hint of green; the flesh is delicious and very juicy. Excellent for eating out of hand, dessert, and keeping. A must-have for the small garden.

Grimes Golden (1804) One of the best yellow apples for general use, universally praised, with clear yellow skin, tender flesh, and a delicious aroma. Originated in West Virginia. Ripens in early fall. (N.B.: Make sure your tree is grafted onto collar-rot-resistant rootstock.)

King David (1894) Reputed to be a cross between a 'Jonathan' and an 'Arkansas Black', this southern favorite has long been gracing gardens there with its medium-size, dark red, spicy fruit. 'King David' keeps very well and bears early.

Lady (ancient) One of the oldest apples in existence, 'Lady' dates to imperial Rome. Grown throughout the Middle Ages, the variety was especially prized by ladies of the French court because of its small size—it fit easily into the pockets of their dresses. Small and flatish, with a reddish green skin. The flesh is white, crisp, and very juicy. Known in Colonial America as a "fancy apple," it was used for dessert at the holidays and added to decorative wreaths. A very late apple, ripening in November.

Mother (1844) This Massachusetts native was one of the most popular apples of the late 1800s, which does nothing to explain its almost complete disappearance from the American orchard until very recently. 'Mother' ripens midseason and is great for fresh eating, but it does not keep overly well.

Newtown Pippin (before 1750) Regarded by many authorities as the all-around best-tasting American apple, this extremely long keeper was popular on sailing ships before the days of refrigeration. The fruit is green with a reddish tint and requires a long, warm growing season to ripen successfully.

Northern Spy (before 1850) One of the best apples for colder climates, this crisp, juicy apple has red skin and fine white flesh. Patience is required, though, as trees take 4 to 5 years to come to bearing age. Ripens late.

Roxbury Russet (1700) Originating in Roxbury, Massachusetts, this apple was once one of the premier commercial varieties. Today, unless you grow it yourself, you won't be able to partake of what one noted apple connoisseur called its "austere perfection and refinement of character." A great keeper, this October ripener will still grace the dessert table in April.

Smokehouse (1837) The first known specimen grew next to the smokehouse on the farm of William Gibbons in Lancaster, Pennsylvania, thus its name. One of the few apples that bear well even on poor soil. The fruit is yellow with red stripes and is very juicy, with an oddly "chewy" texture and a flavor similar to apple cider. Considered one of the best apples for the South. Ripens early to mid fall.

Sops of Wine (1200) The name of this apple aptly describes the result of taking a bite; great for cooking, cider, and apple wine as well as dessert use. Ripens very early.

Spitzenburg (1700) A great, spicy dessert apple with yellow and red stripes that keeps well. A favorite of Thomas Jefferson's. Ripens late in the season.

Summer Rambo (1600s) This large, bright red, striped apple was one of the first grown in this country. The trees are very prolific and bear early.

Tompkins' County King (before 1800) To describe this apple, I will yield to Robert Nitschke of Southmeadow Fruit Gardens: "To my taste, 'Tompkins' King' has no superior for size, beauty, or flavor. It always seems to bring back boyhood memories of the way a real apple ought to taste. In addition to being of delicious flavor for eating out of hand, it is one of the finest of apples for sauce, pies, and 'apple kuchen.' It is large, often very large, red striped, crisp, and juicy." Andrew Jackson Downing, the 19th-century authority, noted the "rich vinous flavor unexcelled by any other apple for home use." What more can I add, except get one! Ripens in late October.

Wealthy (1860) I've always admired this apple, if for no other reason than its name. Originating in Excelsior, Minnesota, it is extremely hardy. Its fruit is bright red with very white flesh. Good flavor with a hint of strawberry, great for general eating. Delish! Ripens in October.

Westfield Seek No Further (1750) Originating in Westfield, Massachusetts, this creamy yellow apple streaked with red is crisp and juicy. Not a cooking apple, but great for eating in hand. Average keeper. Ripens in October.

Winter Banana (1876) One of my very favorites, this large yellow apple with a rose blush actually smells and tastes something like a banana! Good for fresh eating and great for cider. Keeps rather well. Ripens in September or October.

Yellow Newton Pippin (before 1750) This apple was bred by the American colonists for export to Britain, and it had to meet fussy British standards and tolerate the long ocean voyage. Grown by Franklin and Jefferson, this variety is considered by many to be the "best American apple." It certainly is the best storer—the solid green fruit with a blush of red will keep until May. Excellent for cider, cooking, and general use.

York Imperial (1830) This highly prolific tree bears medium to large, rather lopsided, pink/red apples with yellow flesh, ideal for applesauce. One of the latest apples to ripen, with a renowned storageability.

Although most of the work of researching and rescuing old varieties has been conducted on apples, many old varieties of peaches, pears, plums, cherries, and interesting natives such as the pawpaw have been investigated as well, and they are now being restored to their rightful place in the home landscape.

OTHER ANTIQUE FRUITS TO GROW

Apricots		Fondante d'Automne	1835
Large Early Montgamet	1765	Josephine de Malines	1830
Nectarines			
Early Violet	1659	*Plums*	
		Angelina Burdett	1850
Peaches		Count Althann's Gage	1867
Champion	1880	General Hand	1790
George IV	1820	Imperial Epineuse	1883
Grosse Mignonne	1667	Imperial Gage	1790
Late Crawford	1821	Jefferson	1825
Lola Queen	1876		
Oldmixon Free	before 1800		
		Sweet Cherries	
Pears		Downer's Late Red	1808
Bartlett	before 1800	Early Purple Gean	1830
Belle Angevine	1700	Early Rivers	1872
Beurre Gris	before 1680	English Morello	1600s
Flemish Beauty	before 1850	Governer Wood	1842
		Kirtland's Mary	1843

Berries, Berries, Everywhere

Berries were once a common sight in almost every American garden. Look closely at many of the old plans in this book and you will see berry plants tucked here, there, and everywhere. Some of these berries are still familiar to today's gardener, such as raspberries, strawberries, blackberries, and blueberries. But there were others you would be hard pressed to find in the store today: lingonberries, elderberries, currants (white, red, and black), mulberries, and gooseberries, to name just a few. These delicious delights are available today only if you grow them yourself, and they're worth the time and trouble to track down (see Suppliers in the appendices).

Hansell Raspberries

Berries are one crop for which the reward far outstrips the effort. Stale, store-bought berries that have been harvested unripe and shipped hundreds or thousands of miles can in no way compare to the luscious berries from your own garden. As for the financial benefits, given the cost of berries at the market these days, growing your own is like picking money off the

Black Champion Currants

Industry Gooseberries

trees (or bushes, or plants). And many of these delectable delicacies are available *only* if you grow your own.

While the culture of each differs, in general berries are united by two common characteristics: they are incredibly tasty, and they are extremely easy to grow. Raspberries, which are members of the weedy bramble family, are pretty close to "plant and pick." Strawberries, once established, form a thick carpet, which many a wise gardener has used as a berry-bearing ground cover.

Elderberries are so simple that some experts don't even bother to list growing instructions (just many mouthwatering recipes): simply plant in a moist spot where little else will grow! Blueberries are somewhat fussy about their soil conditions, but compared with most plants, berries are easy as pie. Just select the best varieties for your climate and give them the growing conditions they need. You would be wise to consult a good guide such as Stella Otto's *The Backyard Berry Book* (see the Bibliography). Fruit from the gods, practically for free. What could be better?

Growing Grapes

For years I never even considered growing grapes in my own garden—after all, Boston was hardly the sunny Mediterranean, where as a youth I had happily tramped through many a redolent vineyard at harvesttime. Grapes somehow just didn't seem like something that would

Niagara grapes

grow in the harsh winters of New England. Fortunately my father, a lover of Concord grapes, pointed out the error of my ways (pretty stupid, actually, given the fact that Concord, Massachusetts, which gave the grapes their name over a century and half ago, is but 20 miles away!) and now I mouth silent thanks to my dad each time I pass under my grape arbor. (He was also kind enough to build the arbor, so he gets a double vote of thanks.) Grapes are in fact a wonderful, historically appropriate addition to almost every American garden, from Colonial to modern. They are remarkably hardy too: although the European family of wine grapes (those in the *vinifera* clan) tolerate lows only to −5° F., members of the American bunch grape family (which is what most of us buy at the store), both the seeded varieties like Concord and Edelweiss, and the seedless types like Interlaken and Romulus, are much hardier—several can tolerate temperatures to −25° F.

Grapes are not particularly difficult to grow either, especially if, like me, you simply enjoy the vines for the lovely, glossy foliage on an arbor or trellis, and consider the grapes an incidental bonus. Those truly interested in maximizing the harvest would do well to consult a guide like *The Backyard Berry Book*, which describes in easy-to-understand terms the essentials of vine selection, planting, and pruning. The hardest part about growing grapes may be choosing between some of the wonderful varieties now available. A word in the ear of all you historical gardeners—unless you have an absolute necessity for a historical variety, consider using some of the more modern cultivars in addition to the old favorites. Grapes are one of the areas where plant breeding has tremendously enhanced the disease resistance and bearing capabilities of the plant, without sacrificing taste, flavor, or overall appearance. Just be sure to choose a variety appropriate to the length of your growing season, and one that bears fruit for your intended purpose—whether eating out of hand, juice, jellies, jams, or even wine. And don't forget about the decorative qualities of grapes—the distinctive exfoliating vines and shiny leaves can be trained on a trellis to form a unique living fence, and are great for screening more utilitarian areas of the garden from view. Grapes are also perfect for forming a shady terrace roof for porch or pergola.

THE POMONAL RICHES
OF THE DAY

He who owns a rood of proper land in this country, and, in the face of all the pomonal riches of the day, only raises crabs and choke-pears, deserves to lose the respect of all sensible men.

—A. J. Downing
Fruits and Fruit Trees of America (1845)

Bee-utiful

Beekeeping is an ancient art. Both the Greeks and the Romans practiced a primitive sort of bee culture and wrote extensively about bees, although most of their accounts centered around poetic descriptions of the bees' diligence and industry. All that was really known with any certainty was that bees produced honey, which was a much-valued commodity in the days before the use of sugar. This state of ignorance continued until well into the 19th century:

Bees have been part of gardens since Roman times. Note the bee skeps in this 17th-century engraving. Traditional bee skeps like these were common before modern hives were invented. But in order to harvest the honey, you had to destroy the hive.

beekeeping consisted of trapping feral colonies in the forest and transferring them to hollowed-out logs, straw bee skeps, or wooden boxes, where the honey could be more easily harvested. Nor was the fascinating social hierarchy of the hive, with its single queen, female worker bees, and male drones, at all understood.

This situation changed radically when L. L. Langstroth discovered the concept of "bee space" during the 1850s, which led to the invention of the modern beehive. Before then the man-made hives were essentially empty shells that the bees filled willy-nilly with honeycomb, pollen, and brood. There was often no way to remove the honey without fatally damaging the hive. Through keen observation, Langstroth had noticed that bees required just ⅜ inch for walking or crawling; other space in the hive was filled with honeycomb. By devising a simple box with easily removable internal frames that respected the bees' space, he invented a harvestable hive that essentially remains unchanged to this day.

An early beehive model

Given the fact that honey is no longer our primary sweetening staple, why should you want to keep bees today? For your garden! Through pollination, bees play an *essential* role in producing most of the fruits and vegetables we consume every day, and the number of bees in this country is in dramatic decline. Overuse of pesticides, recently introduced parasitic mites, and diseases have decimated the population of honeybees. With no bees, fruit and vegetable harvests can often decline markedly, especially in the home garden. Most gardeners don't realize it, but many plants require multiple visits from pollinators in order to set full, flavorful fruit. If your tomatoes have been tasteless lately, your cucumbers tiny, and your apple trees bare, chances are you don't have enough bees and other pollinators.

Beekeeping makes a terrific hobby and is one that has fascinated me ever since boyhood when I first saw a glass-sided demonstration hive at the zoo. The summer I bought my house, I set up my first hive, and I have kept bees ever since. Beekeeping is not particularly difficult, and equipment and expert guidance are readily available (see Suppliers in the appendices).

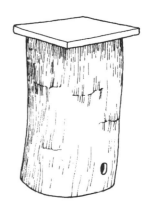

Covered hollow wooden logs were another common hiving method in the Colonial era.

The first question everyone asks is whether or not I get stung. It's important to understand that unlike other stinging species (such as those pesky yellow jackets), honeybees are generally indifferent to human activity and sting only when directly threatened. Yes, occasionally you do get stung when working the hives (after all, you are trying to steal the bees' honey), but after one or two times, the beekeeper develops a tolerance for the stings that makes them no worse than fly bites. Nor is bee care particularly time consuming, although the hives must be tended now and then. By and large, the bees take care of themselves, providing me with plenty of honey, an extremely fruitful garden and orchard, and a terrific feeling of contentment as I watch them busily at work.

For those inclined to a more passive approach, there are other ways to attract native pollinators, such as bumblebees, to the garden. Many species, including honeybees, were actually imported to this country early in the Colonial period. Our native pollinators don't build large hives or produce much honey, but they do play a very important role in the pollination of food crops. To encourage native species such as the orchard mason bee in your garden, simply take a piece of soft wood such as pine, drill several dozen ⁵⁄₁₆-inch holes about 5 inches deep into the wood, and attach the block to a tree trunk at roughly head height. The holes simulate the natural nesting place of these solitary bees, and with any luck you'll soon have your own industrious group of garden pollinators.

For more information, Richard Bonney's *Beekeeping: A Practical Guide* is a good place to start. (See the Bibliography for details.)

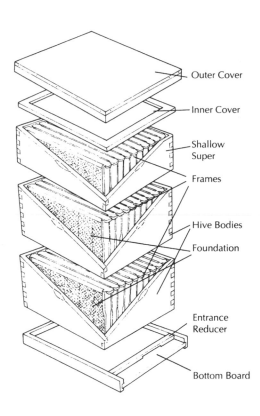

Outer Cover

Inner Cover

Shallow Super

Frames

Hive Bodies

Foundation

Entrance Reducer

Bottom Board

The modern hive allows the beekeeper to harvest the honey without harming the bees or the hive. It has changed very little since it was invented in the mid-19th century. (Line drawings on pages 203 and 204 by Brigita Fuhrman, from *Bee Keeping: A Practical Guide,* © 1993 by Richard E. Bonney. Reprinted with permission of Storey Communications.)

Remembering Rhubarb

It is said that lilacs are the mother of memory, and I have to agree—at least where the sense of smell is concerned. With just one whiff of their sweet fragrance, I am instantly transported back to Milwaukee on a warm spring day, playing tag with my grade school friends through streets rich with the heady scent. But when it comes to matters of taste, nothing can match rhubarb's power to charm me back to the carefree springtimes of my youth. Its sour stalks, lightly cooked and sweetened, were transformed by my mother into a wonderfully piquant sauce—a special treat to be poured over fruit in the morning before school. Whenever that crimson-colored delight appeared on the table, I knew summer vacation couldn't be far behind.

Our family garden was never without rhubarb. Each of the three times we moved, a portion of the original plant would accompany us to our next garden. Once, having forgotten to take the rhubarb with us, we even made a special trip to our former house to beg a division from the new owners—such was the displacement each of us felt without its familiar presence.

Commonly mistaken for a fruit, rhubarb is actually a vegetable—a member of the buckwheat family (*Polygonaceae*)—and is closely related to garden sorrel. Although many species are grown throughout the world, it is the common garden-variety rhubarb, *Rheum rhabarbarum*, also known as *R. rhaponticum*, with which we are most familiar here in the United States.

Rhubarb hasn't changed much since it first arrived in gardens. In fact, one of today's most common varieties, Queen Victoria, was introduced in 1863.

As with many plants, rhubarb's origins date back to ancient China, where its roots (rhizomes) and stalks (petioles) were prized for their purgative and other medicinal qualities. While several species are native to parts of Siberia, northern India, and Nepal (some found as high as 14,000 feet), it is the Chinese variety—*R. palmatum*—that first made it to Europe. Marco Polo, who traveled throughout China in the 13th century, was a big fan of rhubarb and wrote extensively about it in his journals. By the mid-1500s, rhubarb's use as an intestinal aid was already widely known throughout Europe. It was to these laxative properties that Shakespeare's Macbeth clearly refers when he cries out, "What rhubarb, senna, or what purgative drug would scour these English hence?"

The plant's history is so old that even its etymology is somewhat obscured. In the English language, the word *rhubarb* made its first appearance around the mid-1400s. According to one theory, the genus *Rheum* derives from *Rha*—the ancient name for the Volga river in Russia, on whose banks the plant was said to grow. Others claim the name comes from the phrase *rha barbarum*, or "of the bearded peoples," referring to all those rhubarb-eating, "bearded" (Latin: *barbarus*) tribes in northern Europe.

For all its medicinal and ornamental attributes, in America rhubarb has always been grown primarily for its taste. Introduced into New England between 1790 and 1800, the hardy plant endeared itself to the early settlers and by 1822 was widely available in Massachusetts produce markets. Its thick, fibrous stalks were stewed and sweetened to make everything from preserves and compotes, to wine, to that great American culinary icon: the rhubarb pie.

With its large, attractive leaves, bright red or crimson-colored stalks, and the tall, spiky flowers of ornamental varieties such as *R. officinale* and *R. emodi*, it is no wonder that in England rhubarb has long been a favorite of the perennial border. And although still somewhat hard to find, ornamental varieties have been cropping up in American gardens, too, in recent years. (The only source I know of in the United States for ornamental varieties is Heronswood Nursery in Washington State (see Suppliers). For you heirloom fans, one of the most common varieties found in nurseries today is 'Victoria', dating to 1863.)

GROWING RHUBARB

Very few plants could be easier to grow, or give so much for so little in return. A cool-season perennial crop, rhubarb grows from April through September and requires temperatures below 40 degrees in the winter to stimulate bud break and below 90 degrees in the summer to sustain active growth. Once established, rhubarb is generally untroubled by pests and is extremely long lived. Plants are productive for 8 to 15 years.

Rhubarb is produced from crowns consisting of rhizomes and buds—never mind trying to grow it from seed. Set root divisions about 3 feet apart in well-drained soil that is heavily composted with manure or peat. The crown bud should be about 2 inches below the surface. Good drainage is essential to help ensure against crown rot, and planting in raised beds is ideal.

Harvesting occurs throughout the spring, although you should cease by early summer to let the plant regenerate for the next year. Ideally, you should forgo harvesting the plant until the second year to allow it to establish itself. When harvesting, cut the stalks at the soil line and pull them out one at a time. All of the stalks may be harvested at one time, or as needed over a 4- to 6-week period. Be sure to trim the leaves off immediately upon harvesting; they contain oxalic acid, which is highly poisonous.

When Hop Was King

Those were the days when the "hop was king," and the whole countryside was one great hop yard, and beautiful. . . .

—James Fenimore Cooper
Reminiscences of Mid-Victorian Cooperstown

It's puzzling that a vine so lovingly tended for centuries in Europe, and once a mainstay in the American landscape, should today be almost unknown to American gardeners. This is truly a shame, because along with providing one of the key ingredients in beer (the reason behind hops' agelong cultivation), the vine's hardiness, rapid growth, and attractive foliage make it a valuable addition to almost any garden.

Native to Europe, *Humulus lupulus* is closely related to another plant with an equally long history, the infamous cannabis. In fact, the handsome vine, with its five-lobed, green, serrated leaves, bears some resemblance to its notorious cousin. Hops are hardy perennials, but unlike most other perennial climbers, the vines die back to the ground each year. Twining clockwise, hops require a strong support such as a pole, trellis, or heavy cord; once the plants are established, their growth rate is prodigious, with the vines reaching heights of 30 feet and often growing more than 2 feet in a single week! On a warm early-summer day, you can literally watch the vines grow.

The reason for the historic hops hoopla is found in the flower: during August or early September, hops produce a greenish bloom, properly called a strobile, that looks like a flattened, papery pinecone about an inch or two long. Although generally barren of seeds, the cones contain oils that are used to add aroma to beer and counteract the sweet taste of the malt. While most varieties of hops look pretty much the same to the untrained eye, each produces a slightly different-shaped cone whose distinctly different flavor plays a unique role in the brewing process.

Who first thought of making beer with hops is lost in history, but in Bavaria the plant has been in commercial production since the 11th century. Cultivation of hops eventually spread throughout the Continent to England, although the plant did not cross the channel without a fight. Unlike Dutch and German beers, English ale had traditionally been made with a combination of malt and bitter herbs such as wormwood. English brewers long thought hops were a "wicked weed" that would spoil the taste of ale and "endanger the people." In fact, growing or importing hops was illegal in England until the 16th century, when its people, who had acquired a taste for hops-flavored beers during the many long wars on the Continent, forced Parliament to lift the ban. So great was the public's thirst that demand for English hops soon outstripped production, and expensive foreign hops had to be imported. Ever watchful for ways to make a profit at their competitors' expense, the English sent the first European hops to their newly formed colony at Massachusetts Bay in 1629.

Hops production boomed in America throughout the 17th and early 18th centuries. Grown in fields spotted with T-shaped poles, hops became a major American industry: more than 1.5 million pounds were being produced by the mid-1800s, with over 1 million pounds coming from New York State alone. If this doesn't sound like a large operation, remember that the flower cones of hops are as light as paper and had to be meticulously picked by hand and quickly dried to just the right degree, as incorrectly harvested cones rapidly spoil. Special types of drying barns were constructed for the process, whose distinctive rooflines can still be found today in places such as Cooperstown, New York, once known as "Hops City." Large-scale commercial production came to an end on the East Coast around 1920, when diseases such as downy mildew pushed production to the drier valley areas of the Pacific Northwest. Today hops production is still concentrated in this region, although small-scale operations are scattered throughout the country.

Besides their use in beer, hops have had medicinal, culinary, and craft uses

A 19th century hops yard

as well. The fresh flowers were used by Native Americans in tranquilizers, while the dried blooms were used as a toothache remedy. The plant has long been known for its sleep-inducing powers, and hops are one of the traditional ingredients in "sleepy time" potpourris and cachets. The fresh sprouts are considered quite a springtime delicacy in many parts of northern Europe, where they are blanched and added to salads. And since the vines die back to the ground each year, hops always produce a good supply of vines for wreath making, far easier to work with than the much less supple grapevines so commonly used in craft applications.

The plant is hardy from Zones 4 to 9. As propagation is by root division, you should purchase hops stock from a reliable source and plant it outside in spring around your frost-free date. Provide a sunny spot with well-drained soil of general fertility and a pH level between 6.0 and 7.0, and adequate water. Plant with the buds pointed up and cover with 1 inch of loose soil. In the first year of growth, hops will require frequent light watering. When the new shoots reach a foot or so, provide support. Hops are generally untroubled by insects, although aphids and mites can become a problem and Japanese beetles do seem to like to munch the leaves of mine occasionally. The major concern is downy mildew, which looks like black fuzz under the leaves. If any appears—thankfully I have never seen it—cut out and carry away any infected spikes. Organic copper sprays or standard fungicides will prevent recurrence, but be very careful what you spray on the plant if you expect to harvest the cones for beer. If you wish to propagate additional plants, bury several stems in a shallow trench late in the season and mark their location. In the spring, simply dig them up and cut into 4- to 5-inch sections, each with at least one bud. Although varietal differences are not a concern to the average gardener (except for the ornamental golden vari-

The hops vine from a 19th century illustration

eties, all hops look pretty much alike), for those interested in home brewing, hops varieties are generally classed into three types: aromatic, bittering, or a combination of the two. As their names suggest, each adds either scent or taste to the final product. Often several types of hops are used in a single brew. Here's a small selection:

BITTERING TYPES

- 'Galena'—the most popular bittering hops; high alpha acid content; high yield; midseason
- 'Nuggett'—the second most popular; stores well, late to mature; high yield; midseason

AROMA TYPES

- 'Cascade'—one of the most popular, although stores poorly; high yield; midseason
- 'Eastwell Golding'—developed before 1889 in Kent, England
- 'Fuggle'—another English hop, from 1875, the oldest in the United States; grows well in cool weather; resistant to mildew; low yield; early
- 'Willamette'—the most widely grown aroma type in the United States; moderate yield; midseason

DUAL-PURPOSE TYPES

- 'Brewer's Gold'—good general variety
- 'Cluster'—one of the oldest hops varieties in the United States; susceptible to downy mildew
- 'Perle'—recent German introduction; moderate yield; midseason

Although the complexities of great beer brewing are akin to those for wine making, here's a simple recipe to whet your taste buds on: Hop cones are ready for harvest when they start to dry and turn a light golden color. Add about 30 grams (1 ounce) of the hop cones to 1 liter of boiling springwater. Wait 15 minutes. Dissolve 500 grams (1 pound) of sugar in the hop water, then add 2 liters of cold springwater plus 1 tablespoon of brewer's yeast. Keep in a warm spot for 12 hours, then bottle. Be sure to use sterilized bottles, and keep your beer refrigerated until consumed.

In addition, there are several golden-leaved ornamental varieties: 'Aureus', an older cultivar, and two newly introduced selections—'Sunbeam' and 'Bianca', which have yellow foliage and reddish stems throughout the season. Unlike their sun-loving cousins, though, the ornamental varieties should be grown in dappled sunlight for best foliage color and color retention.

The Japanese hop, *H. japonicus,* is a related species and another fine vine for quick cover. Generally grown as an annual, it will reach almost 20 feet in a season. There is also a variegated variety, *H. japonicus* 'Variegatus', whose seven-lobed leaves are splashed with white.

Whatever your aspirations, the best reason by far for the average gardener to grow hops is that they make a terrific decorative plant wherever a good, fast vine is needed. I grow mine up an unsightly telephone pole outside the greenhouse. During early summer, the pole soon becomes covered with beautiful greenery to the height of almost 25 feet; during late summer, the attractive flower cones appear (which I have yet to harvest for my own beer, but I intend to try soon). In the fall and winter you can clear away the dead vines, or you can leave them on the trellis, as I do. They provide a wonderfully sculptural support for the next year's growth, and have a marvelously poetic way of catching the first light snows.

Historic Garden

A Productive Garden: Monticello

The greatest service which can be rendered [any country] is to add a useful plant to its culture.
—Thomas Jefferson

So how do you go about finding ways to make your landscape more productive? To a large extent, simple trial and error forms a key part of this process, and no one better illustrates the success that this type of horticultural experimentation can bring than Thomas Jefferson. Not content with a purely ornamental landscape, Jefferson used the vegetable gardens at Monticello as a veritable laboratory of productivity: he was constantly experimenting with new varieties of plants that would increase the productivity of his garden and, as a fringe benefit, provide new culinary delights for the table. Figs from France, squashes and broccoli from Italy, beans and salsify collected by the Lewis and Clark Expedition, and peppers from Mexico all arrived to improve the gardens, and the tables, of Monticello. At one point, Jefferson was growing twenty varieties of beans and fifteen types of English pea to see which would best flourish in his garden. All told, Jefferson grew more than two hundred and fifty varieties of some seventy different species of vegetables. Slouches were not tolerated—any varieties that produced mediocre results were eliminated and replaced with better types.

Jefferson's vegetable garden was no small affair: a 1,000-foot-long terrace, hewn from the side of the mountain and supported at places by a stone wall over 12 feet high, it was described as a "hanging garden" with a dramatic "sea view." From the beautiful detailed pavilion at the garden's center, one could gaze across the 8-acre orchard, vineyard, and berry plots to the rolling Piedmont hills beyond. The main part of the 2-acre vegetable garden was divided into twenty-four squares, or growing plots, arranged in neat Jeffersonian fashion by what type of plants grew there: "fruits" (including such crops as tomatoes, melons, and beans), "roots" (beets, carrots, and radishes), and "leaves," such as lettuce and cabbage. The siting of the garden on a south-facing slope allowed Jefferson to greatly extend the growing season at both ends. There were early peas for annual pea contests (those who were first able to bring a crop to table would host a dinner party featuring the prize peas) and such tender, long-season varieties as the French artichoke.

Nor was this garden purely practical. The presence of the garden pavilion, where Jefferson often retired to read, assures us that the space was used for pleasure and enjoyment. A large arbor with multicolored scarlet runner beans was proposed; a "long, grass walk" shaded by cherry trees was installed. Even the vegetables were arranged for the pleasing effects of color and texture: broccoli in shades of green, white, and purple; white and purple eggplant; tomatoes bordered with sesame and okra.

The vegetable garden at Monticello that visitors see today has been re-created through extensive and time-consuming research that began in 1979. Two years of archaeological work attempted to confirm details known through Jefferson's voluminous garden records and correspondence. The result is extremely accurate in showing the overall structure of the garden as it existed between 1807 and 1814. The plantings, too, closely follow those of Jefferson's time, although the loss of various antique plant types and changes in labor practice have made some modern substitutions inevitable. As a whole, however, the composite gives perhaps the most accurate representation in America of what a garden in the early part of the 19th century looked like, and it provides today's visitor with a chance to view one of this country's premier gardens—a productive space, artfully decorated, that simultaneously pleases sight, smell, *and* palate. And although the scale of Jefferson's garden may not be suitable to today's landscape, the adventuresome spirit of productivity that motivated its creation is something that should be part of every modern garden.

VARIETIES JEFFERSON ACTUALLY GREW THAT ARE STILL IN CULTIVATION

Artichoke	Red
Bean	Arikara, Asparagus, Refugee, Scarlet Runner, Sieva
Beet	Early Scarlet Turnip-rooted
Broccoli	Green-sprouting, Purple-sprouting, White-sprouting
Carrot	Long Orange
Cucumber	Long Green, West Indian Gherkin
Eggplant	White
Endive	Broad-leaved Balavian, Green Curled
Fig	Angelique, Marseilles
Lettuce	Tennis-ball, White Cos
Melon	Citron, Winter

Onion	Egyptian or Tree
Pea	Blue Prussian, Dwarf White Sugar, Prince Albert
Pepper	Bullnose, Long Red Cayenne
Spinach	Prickly-seeded
Squash	Yellow Crookneck
Strawberry	Alpine, Chile

SOME 19TH-CENTURY VARIETIES USED AS SUBSTITUTIONS IN THE GARDEN TODAY

Artichoke	Green Globe
Bean	Cascknife, Cutshort ("Long Speckled Snap"), Flageolet, Hyacinth, Lazy Wife, Red Cranberry, Wild Goose
Cabbage	Drumhead, Early Flat Dutch, Early Jersey Wakefield, Early Round Dutch, Glory of Enkhuizen, Red Drumhead, Winnigstaedt
Carrot	Early Scarlet Horn
Cauliflower	Dwarf Erfurt
Cucumber	Early Cluster, Evergreen White
Eggplant	New York Improved
Leek	London Flag
Melon	Jenny Lind, Green Nutmeg, Persian
Okra	Cow's Horn
Onion	Large Red Wethersfield, White Portugal
Pea	Alaska, Champion of England, Early May
Pumpkin	Cheesecake, Connecticut Field
Radish	Early Scarlet Turnip-rooted
Squash	Acorn, Hubbard, White Scallop, Yellow Crookneck
Strawberry	Carolina Pine, White Pine
Tomato	Large Red, Ponderosa

Aspire to Asparagus

I have a fascination with asparagus. Somehow I never seem to tire of those luscious spears. I wait for them each spring, repeatedly venturing out to the still largely sleeping garden and returning disappointed, until one fine day, the wait is over. Hurrah! Sound the trumpets! *The* season has arrived!

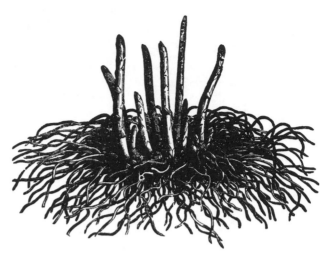

Asparagus, a favorite since Roman times, shown here with new shoots and roots.

Now, all this hysteria may sound strange to you, unless you are one of the select few privileged enough to have picked the fresh spears out of your own garden, cooked them in boiling water for a few minutes until just soft, and eaten them at once, lightly buttered and salted (or with fresh hollandaise, for the gourmands among us). Then you would understand my jealous passion, because you would share it as well, for there is no comparison between freshly picked asparagus from your own garden and the kind you commonly buy in the grocery store.

Nor am I alone in this mania; asparagus has been in gardens for over 2,000 years. Native to the Mediterranean area of southern Europe, asparagus was gathered wild by the ancient Greeks, who prized it both for its obvious culinary delights and for some rather interesting medicinal qualities—the plant reputedly had the power to repel stinging bees and to cure toothaches. The Romans seem to have been the first to domesticate the plant; the agricultural writer Cato the Elder wrote a treatise on asparagus culture before 150 B.C. that would hold up to scrutiny today. Because this vegetable was always considered something of a luxury owing to its short harvest period (the plants yield for less than a month once a year in the very early spring), ingenious ways were invented throughout the centuries to extend the usable season. King Louis XIV of France even went so far as to have his gardeners grow asparagus in special greenhouses so that he could enjoy asparagus year-round. By the 1700s asparagus had arrived on our shores with the Dutch and English colonists, and by the 1850s it had made it as far as northern California, which became a center for commercial production in the United States.

GROWING ASPARAGUS

Despite its aristocratic associations, asparagus is really a rather democratic plant, happily growing in most parts of the country except the Deep South. One interesting factor is its longevity. It is often said with complete truth that a *well-made* asparagus bed will outlast its planter. The key to success, however, lies in the term *well-made*. As with rhubarb, or any long-term planting, the soil has to be particularly well dug and amended; and that, to be frank, is not work for the fainthearted. Asparagus requires—and there is no getting around this—soil that is extremely rich in rotted manure and compost (at least one part manure to one part soil) and a bed that is *at minimum* 2 feet deep. That necessitates a lot of work and, as my Uncle Guy from Oklahoma would say, a whole heap and a peck of manure. I can hear the overworked backs groaning all the way from here. But take heart: you don't have to dig 2 feet down. In many sections of the country (such as here in rocky New England), you couldn't do this to save your soul. The answer is simply to build upward. Asparagus is a perfect candidate for the raised-bed method, which also makes for much better drainage, faster harvesting, and easier maintenance.

After ordering my one-year-old asparagus crowns through the mail, I dug my beds about as far as they could go (about 1 foot), removed stones and other debris, and then boxed the trench with simple painted pine boards staked every couple of feet or so. The boards will ultimately rot, but I prefer the labor of replacing them to the long-term dangers of using pressure-treated wood near food crops. I then filled the beds to the tops of the boards with rotted manure and tilled it in. After making a trench about 15 inches deep, I spaced the plants roughly 18 inches apart with the roots spread out, covered them with just enough soil to hold the plants in place, and watered them. As the spears appeared, I continued to fill in the trench until the soil bed was level.

Asparagus beds require patience. The plants need to rest unharvested for two years—try to control yourself when they pop up the first spring. Just keep them well watered and weeded. The fernlike fronds that appear are actually quite pretty and make a pleasant addition to the garden. In the third year, and in every year thereafter, you'll have your payoff. Interestingly enough, salt traditionally was applied to asparagus beds in the spring, at the rate of ½ pound per square yard. This supposedly was of some benefit to the asparagus, and it served to keep down all but the most salt-tolerant weeds. I haven't tried this myself, because I mulch heavily with half-rotted leaves and compost, which both controls weeds and provides nourishment. But those of you without access to large quantities of compost may want to experiment with this salt method.

Before I planted my beds, I had been told that modern asparagus varieties are almost care-free; the old ones were susceptible to rust and fusarium wilt. But here is one of those occasions where *almost* is a very vague word. The Achilles' heel of asparagus is the asparagus beetle, a nasty little red bug about ¼ inch long whose black larvae will defoliate an entire stand of asparagus, "faster than you can cook asparagus"—or *"citius quam asparagi coquentur,"* to quote the Roman emperor Augustus. There is only one recourse for this beetle: spraying. Try a natural pyrethrum spray, for starters. Fortunately, the problem doesn't usually get too bad until after harvest, but left unchecked it will destroy the bed. Removing all the dead foliage in the fall and lightly cultivating the soil after a frost helps to discourage the beetle.

How-to: Soil Is Everything (Well, Almost)

There is a natural temptation when creating any type of garden to want to hurry it to completion. That's to be expected, given the amount of dreaming, wishing, and eager anticipation that accompanies most garden planning. In the rush, though, it's easy to skip the more arduous, less glamorous steps, such as soil preparation. What would you rather do—dig those big rocks out of the ground or plant those sexy lilies? Besides, how bad could the current soil be, right? Many people look out and figure that if there are things growing in the ground now, things can't be too awful: let's just add the new plants and a little fertilizer, do a bit of shallow hoeing (or the modern-day equivalent, a quickie rototill) and see what happens. Unfortunately, the result is—not much.

While it's true that many plants can survive in mediocre or poor soil, to get things to really thrive, good soil preparation and enhancement is key. For shrubs, this means following the old adage about digging a hole twice as wide as the root ball, removing rocks and other debris, and enhancing the soil with compost or manure. (I also like to use a little superphosphate or bonemeal to promote root growth.) Remember, this tree or shrub is there forever (at least as far as it's concerned), and the first few years of crucial growth will depend on how well you prepared the hole.

For perennial plantings, the old *double-digging* method, as arduous as it sounds, is really the only way to achieve the results you see all the time in those glossies. Anyone who tells you to the contrary is perpetuating the age-old art of wishful thinking. Nor will tilling alone, with the average small-size tiller, be sufficient—a small tiller just won't penetrate deeply enough to allow for good root growth, and it is just this growth that yields all those beautiful flowers and fruits. While double digging is a lot of work, take my word that it is worth every bit of effort, and it will save you many a disappointment in the long run. I know this from personal experience.

When I first moved to Southborough, I was in a rush to prepare the courtyard garden, and in my haste I gave the soil a very minimal going-over. While the garden growth the first year was adequate, the lack of good preparation soon revealed itself—in subsequent years the flowers have been sparse and stunted, the plants susceptible to disease, and to top it all off these puny specimens require twice the amount of water as their counterparts in the better-prepared beds. This last problem is an important one to consider for those of you who live in areas prone to dry summers: the difference between a well-dug border and a poorly prepared one in a drought is dramatic. The deeply prepared bed is able to survive and thrive despite the lack of water, because the roots can penetrate much more deeply than otherwise would be the case. The moral of the story is that last fall I had to rip up the entire garden and amend the soil, which is twice the amount of work it would have taken to do it properly in the first place.

DOUBLE DIGGING

For those of you with the luxury of time, double digging the beds the previous fall and setting the plants out the following spring is ideal, although you can prepare the beds as soon as the soil is workable in the spring, as long as you give them several weeks to settle before planting. To begin, find a willing spouse, partner, or suitably bribed teenager and dig a 2- by 2-foot square as deeply as you can (2 feet deep is optimal). Put the first 4 inches or so of topsoil in a wheelbarrow for later use. Add to the remaining subsoil a large quantity of rotted compost or manure. By "large" I really do mean a lot—a ratio of two parts compost to one part existing soil is usually sufficient to bring the ground level up to just about where it was when you started. These days, finding well-rotted manure or compost in sufficient quantities for this procedure is frequently the hardest part of the whole operation. We keep several horses around just for this purpose (or so it seems, sometimes), but you can often get the manure you need from a local riding stable. Cow manure is even better (fewer weed seeds) if you can find it, but local dairy farmers are few and far between these days. Fortunately, many towns are now composting their leaves and selling the product, which has opened up a new source of supply. In any event, you will need much more compost/manure than you can usually lug home in those plastic bags, so it pays to make a few calls to see what you can have delivered.

Once you have added the compost or manure to the first square, move on to the next; dig out and place the first few inches of topsoil on top of the square you just completed, and repeat the procedure. At the final square, take the topsoil from the first square (still in the wheelbarrow) and add it to the last square. For final mixing, you can rototill the plot for good measure if you have a machine available. Don't worry that the soil level is higher than when you started: the action of wind, rain, and worms will soon settle it back down. Yes, soil preparation is a lot of work, but once done correctly, you can sit back and relax on your laurels (or lilies, liatris, or lilacs) for many years to come.

$\mathcal{S}$tewardship

$\mathcal{T}$here is one last defining principle of historic American gardens. It's somewhat more nebulous than the rest, more of an attitude than an action, and perhaps the best way to introduce it is with a story.

For the last several years, I have had the great fortune to spend a part of each summer at the home of a wonderful friend in northwestern Montana. It's an almost magical place: built at the turn of the century, the main lodge and so-called cabins are located on a deep, clear, 12-mile-long lake, which gently laps secluded, wooded shores. The closest town is Big Fork, which in the last decade has changed from a typical sleepy western village to a bustling resort center and artists' colony, complete with a terrific gourmet restaurant, a summer theater, and even a sidewalk *crêperie*. Some people lament the passing of the rugged-around-the-edges town, but personally I don't mind too much. Local businesses, usually the first casualty of gentrification, seem to be thriving, and most of the old buildings have been beautifully preserved, renovated, and reused. I admit that I like having my copy of the *Wall Street Journal* and a good crêpe or bagel after my morning bike ride. There is only one problem with all this quaint loveliness—it's becoming more and more of an island. Beyond the town center, which is protected by zoning laws and covenants, a large portion of the bucolic countryside is being lost to trashy development. Everywhere you go in this area, you see For Sale signs in front of farms and ranches. These properties are not just being transferred from one owner to another—they are being subdivided for houses, golf courses, and shopping complexes.

I tell you this tale of Montana not as a travelogue but because it struck me with horrifying certainty that if this destruction of our scenic lands has spread all the way to the remoteness of Montana, time is truly running out. I don't mind the development so much in itself. Given our apparent unwillingness or inability to control the size of our population, I am rather resigned to the fact that ever larger numbers of people are going to require ever larger numbers of houses, shops, and so forth. What I do mind, though, and what I am determined to fight against, is the awful sprawl of gas stations, shopping malls, stores, and cardboard housing subdivisions, all surrounded by mile after mile of asphalt, dotted with horrible little stick shrubs and sickly red mulch. This type of progress may have to exist, but it doesn't have to be such an eyesore and to take up so much valuable natural space.

It should be plain to see that we need beauty in our lives—whether the man-made beauty of a well-designed home and garden; the natural beauty of rolling farm fields, meadows, and woodlands; or the still-wild beauty of untouched nature. Anyone who has been in a national park recently, such as Glacier in Montana, which is one of the *lesser*-visited parks and still received over a million visitors last year, realizes that many people continue to feel this need for beautiful, natural surroundings. Yet our national parks may soon be the only places where such loveliness exists. Equally beautiful natural areas are found all over the country, but they are being eaten up by shortsighted developers who care nothing about the long-term effects of their building, as long as their own profits are secure—and we all pay the price. But there is something that each and every one of us can do, literally right in our own backyards. We can beautify our home grounds in an environmentally sensitive way, for the enrichment of both ourselves and our neighbors. This is one of the surest ways to fight the general aesthetic degradation we see all around us. We should do this not only for the present but for the future.

There was once a concept common to almost every culture found in this country, although most prevalent perhaps in the Native American peoples: the idea of *stewardship*, that we are merely *tenants* of the land, temporary holders of the earth, water, and air around us, with a responsibility to pass on our space to future occupants in the same condition as we found it or, better yet,

Wonderful trees like this don't occur in the home landscape by themselves. You have to plant them, if not for yourself, then for your children.

improved. This idea is no longer in vogue—most people are too focused on the present and on their "rights." I find it ironic that as parents, many people spend nearly every ounce of their efforts trying to secure the future for their own children, while neglecting the future of the world in which their children must ultimately live their lives. Will it really matter if Johnny gets into Harvard when the world into which he graduates will be an impoverished wasteland? Perhaps we are just too concerned with our own problems, or perhaps the issues that we face seem so daunting, that we forget about our surroundings. But certainly, if we are to survive on this planet, we must embrace the concept of stewardship again, for ourselves, for our children, and for everyone else's children as well.

Faced with these formidable prospects, it is hard to figure out where to begin. Although this may sound simplistic, one of the best ways to get started is to plant a tree. I don't mean one of those fast-growing varieties we see everywhere, such as poplars and birches. There is nothing wrong with these trees; it's just that they will give pleasure and sustenance only to us and not to future generations. When we are old, they will be, too, and we will both be dust together. The types of trees that I am talking about may take a hundred years or more to mature—oaks, maples, hemlocks, firs, and many others, depending on your climate. They are the majestic trees we see today in the park, along the boulevards, and, if you are very lucky, right in your own backyard, thoughtfully planted generations ago for our enjoyment. These trees lend an air of peace and contentment to a space that no amount of good design or money can supply.

Here in Southborough, I have several huge trees in my yard—one large ash, several great maples, a gigantic *Pinus rigida*, and a huge elm, one of the largest I have ever seen. These trees were planted 150 years ago, when the house was young, by the foresighted first owners, who saw value in planting for the future. These caretakers of the land never received any direct benefit from these plantings, other than watching their selfless gift grow, but their successors here certainly have. Several generations have lived and loved, laughed and even died beneath the cool welcoming embrace of the shade these giants provided.

Today these trees are my pride and joy—yet I am afraid that my pleasure is to be short lived. Several of the largest are nearing the end of their useful lives; the ash in particular has a newly imported disease for which there is no cure. All of these trees are about the same age, and all will go at about the same time, and then the place will seem bare and denuded. This could have been avoided if the owners just before me had not neglected their duty as stewards. No large trees were planted during their tenancy, and now there are no successors coming along to replace them. I have planted numerous trees that will one day shade the future inhabitants of this house, but that day is

In the Victorian neighborhood, gardens were designed to draw the eye from one property to the next, and to contribute to the sense of interesting, shared space.

far off, and in the meantime, there will be nothing to replace the old giants. The ash especially will leave a huge gap—the late arrival and early departure of its leaves are perfectly designed to maximize the much-desired early-spring and late-fall sun, while carefully shading the house during the torrid summer. When the ash dies in a few years, I shall indeed bake, and with every drop of sweat that falls from my brow, I'll mumble a silent curse at those who forgot about us.

In this day and age, we plant for ourselves and not for others, and that must stop. We need to plan and plant *for the future*, and not only trees, either. The individual landscape can be planted with an eye toward the public weal. We, as gardeners, so concerned with beauty, should be the first to see that. Look at the delight we take in reading about and visiting other people's gardens, in seeing the joy and beauty that others are able to create through nature. So why do we so often hide all our efforts behind high walls and fences, leaving the front yards and public spaces of our landscape neglected, barren, and boring? Why do we allow our streetscapes to be dull and dreary, devoid of flowers? Of course, portions of our gardens should be designed as private pleasures, to be shared judiciously. But if other areas can serve a dual role and vicariously please our neighbors, why not? The Victorians, especially, were aware of the advantages of mutual landscape improvements, and they deliberately opened up the more public portions of their front gardens in order to improve the general neighborhood. Everyone benefited—the owners, the neighbors, and passersby alike. This is why all those old Victorian streetscapes look so inviting to tired modern eyes. They welcome us into the common landscape and allow us to participate. By all means, create a private paradise for yourself—but don't forget to spend equal effort on a landscape to share with others.

And speaking of streetscapes and creations on a larger scale, it is important that those of you with time and resources become involved in your local planning, zoning, and historical boards or commissions. These local groups have tremendous influence over how much or how little environmental desecration we have to endure outside our property boundaries. They regulate such things as commercial store locations, density of office parks, landscaping required around commercial structures, minimum residential lot size, and wetland protection. Creating a beautiful garden is all well and good, but the beauty of your community, town, city, or county depends entirely on people like you

> ## FOR POSTERITY
>
> *I thank you for the seeds. . . . Too old to plant trees for my own gratification, I shall do it for my posterity.*
>
> —Thomas Jefferson
> From a letter to Samuel Constantine
> Rafinesque *(1822)*

participating in these governing bodies. Serving on these boards and committees requires dedication and effort, but if we don't become involved very soon, there won't be much left to save.

I am not saying that we have to shut down all development and economic growth. What I am saying is that these things can be achieved without completely destroying the beauty once found in both our cities and our countrysides. Shops and stores can survive and even prosper without destroying historic structures. Houses and subdivisions can be designed and built to preserve as much open space as possible, in styles with some historical resonance. Roads can be constructed around instead of through wetlands (or better yet, commuter rail lines can be built instead). Commercial zones can be concentrated together instead of strung out infinitely along our once-scenic highways. Our city centers can be rehabilitated and rejuvenated, thereby helping to remove the development pressure on our farmland and to preserve it to feed future generations, an important and growing concern.

Finally, our historic landscapes, many of which are facing an uphill battle against neglect and development, must be protected and restored. If we have the ingenuity and resourcefulness to chart the mysteries of the Martian landscape, we can certainly figure out how to preserve, protect, and enhance our own landscape here on Earth. The quiet gardeners must speak out. We have all benefited from the glories of our American gardening past—the lovely parks, the gardens overflowing with fruit and flower, the beautiful old homes nestled in their landscapes, the historic tree-lined squares and boulevards. These things were conserved for us, handed down in trust. It's now time to renew this heritage. Our gardening forebears have shown us the way—they were *our* stewards, and now it's our turn to assume the role. No one is going to make the effort for us, though. This is one row we have to hoe ourselves, and if ultimately we fail, our only excuse will be that we never really cared enough to try.

$\mathcal{H}$istoric Plant Compendium

$\mathcal{U}$sers of this compendium should note that in general plant introduction dates are *not* an exact science. Unlike interiors, where often one can determine within months when a particular fabric or wallpaper was introduced, the ever-changing nature of the garden presents quite a different story. For one thing, many of the plants commonly found in American gardens today are natives—when exactly they were "introduced" into American gardens is almost impossible to determine. The story is even more complicated due to the fact that early in our history, many of our native plants were discovered and sent back to Europe, where they were propagated and "re-introduced" into American gardens via the British Isles, the Netherlands, or Spain! This also leads to the question of when certain plants that were first propagated in Europe or discovered by European explorers in other parts of the globe actually made it to our shores. Often there was a lag of twenty years or more between the first "introduction" of a particular variety and the time when the plant in question actually became common in American gardens. Then of course there is the issue of regional differences in the United States (early on, the East received many new plants far earlier than the West, for example—later on, for many species, the reverse was true).

All these factors make studying plant introduction dates a *very* inexact science. By and large, the best means to determine what was actually growing when and where is by examining old letters, plans, and other original documents such as antique nursery catalogs. This of course is a time-consuming and laborious process, and the serious research required is just now being done in this country. In the meantime, we must content ourselves with some basic assumptions.

In general, the later the date, the more certain the year. Throughout this compendium, where I list a specific year, such as 1861, chances are good that there is precise documentation behind that number. Where I list a rounded number ending in 0, such as 1750 or 1900, then you may assume that I have ascribed a conservative limit based on various secondary sources. I have tried in all cases to choose the latest of the dates given where various authorities list different dates or date ranges, on the assumption that most people would prefer to know that something was *almost certainly* in American gardens at a specific time, rather than *almost probably*. Where zone information is not clearly known or is conflicting, a question mark occurs. Most of all, I would like to state that this is a work in progress, and that if any readers have more information about plants listed in this compendium, or information regarding plants I have not listed, they are encouraged to contact us at our Web site, www.traditionalgardening.com, as I will be constantly updating the database. I hope you enjoy using this compendium as much as I enjoyed piecing together this amazing jigsaw puzzle of horticultural history.

Annuals

Botanical Name	Common Name	Year of Introduction
Abelmoschus esculentus	Lady's finger	1800
Abelmoschus manihot	Sunset hibiscus	1800
Abronia umbellata	Sand verbena	1900
Abutilon × hybridum 'Souvenir de Bonn'		1900
Acalypha wilkesiana 'Macrophylla'	Copperleaf	1900
Acalypha wilkesiana 'Musaica'	Giant redleaf	1900
Adonis aestivalis	Summer adonis	1800
Adonis annua	Pheasant's eye	1800
Adonis autumnalis	Pheasant's eye	1900
Ageratum houstonianum	Flossflower, pussy-foot	1800
Agrostemma githago	Common corn cockle	1800
Allium cepa	Onion	1700
Allium porrum	Leek	1700
Alternanthera amoena	Telanthera	1900
Alternanthera bettzickiana		1900
Alternanthera bettzickiana 'Aurea'		1900
Alternanthera bettzickiana 'Aurea Nana'		1900
Alternanthera versicolor	Copper alternanthera	1900
Amaranthus caudatus	Tassel flower, love-lies-bleeding	1800
Amaranthus hybridus var. erythrostachys	Prince's feather	1800
Amaranthus hypochondriacus	Prince's feather	1900
Amaranthus tricolor	Joseph's coat	1800
Anagallis arvensis	Scarlet pimpernel	1750
Anagallis arvensis f. caerulea	Blue pimpernel	1750
Anethum graveolens	Dill	1750
Anthemis cotula	Mayweed	1750
Anthriscus cerefolium	Chervil	1750
Antirrhinum asarina	Clammy snapdragon	1900
Antirrhinum majus	Common snapdragon	1800
Apium graveolens var. dulce	Celery	1850
Apium graveolens var. rapaceum	Celeriac	1800
Argemone grandiflora	Showy prickly poppy	1800
Argemone mexicana	Prickly poppy	1900
Atriplex hortensis	Orach	1750
Avena sterilis	Animated oats	1900

Botanical Name	Common Name	Year of Introduction
Begonia semperflorens	Begonia vernon	1900
Begonia × *tuberhybrida*	Tuberous begonia	1900
Borago officinalis	Borage	1750
Brachycome iberidifolia	Swan River daisy	1900
Brassica alba (hirta)	White mustard	1750
Brassica nigra	Black mustard	1750
Brassica oleracea Acephala Group	Wild cabbage/colewort	1750
Brassica rapa	Turnip	1750
Briza maxima	Big quaking grass	1900
Browallia americana	Amethyst browallia	1900
Calandrinia ciliata	Desert rock purslane	1900
Calandrinia grandiflora	Common rock purslane	1900
Calendula officinalis	Pot marigold	1750
Callirhoe pedata	Poppy mallow	1800
Callistephus chinensis	China aster	1900
Callistephus hortensis	Cassini	1800
Cannabis sativa	Hemp, hashish, marijuana	1800
Capsella bursa-pastoris	Shepherd's purse	1750
Capsicum spp.	Peppers	1800
Carthamus tinctorius	Safflower	1750
Celosia cristata	Crimson cockscomb	1800
Celosia lutea	Yellow cockscomb	1900
Centaurea cineraria	Dusty miller	1800
Centaurea cyanus	Cornflower, bachelor's button	1800
Centaurea gymnocarpa	Dusty miller	1900
Centaurea moschata	Sweet sultan	1800
Centaurea moschata 'Alba'	White sweet sultan	1800
Chamaelirium luteum	Blazing star	1800
Cheiranthus cheiri	Wallflower	1750
Chenopodium botrys	Oak of Jerusalem	1750
Chrysanthemum carinatum	Tricolored chrysanthemum	1900
Chrysanthemum coronarium	Crown daisy	1900
Chrysanthemum indicum	Lady Skipwith's pride	1800
Cichorium endiva	Endive	1750
Citrullus lanatus	Watermelon	1800
Clarkia amoena ssp. *lindleyi*	Lindley's godetia	1900
Clarkia pulchella	Beautiful clarkia	1900
Clarkia rubicunda	Ruddy godetia	1900
Clarkia unguiculata	Rose clarkia, elegant clarkia	1900
Cleome gynandra	Spider wisp	1900
Cleome hasslerana	Spider flower	1900
Cnicus benedictus	Blessed thistle	1750

Botanical Name	Common Name	Year of Introduction
Coix lachryma-jobi	Job's tears	1900
Coleus blumei 'Golden Bedder'		1900
Coleus blumei 'Kirkpatrick'		1900
Coleus blumei var. *verschaffeltii*	Butterfly coleus, painted nettle	1900
Collinsia grandiflora	Blue lips	1900
Collinsia heterophylla	Pagoda collinsia	1900
Colocasia esculenta	Elephant's ear	1900
Consolida ambigua	Annual larkspur	1800
Consolida regalis		1762
Convolvulus tricolor	Dwarf morning glory	1800
Coreopsis basalis	Goldenwave coreopsis	1900
Coreopsis tinctoria	Plains coreopsis	1900
Coreopsis tinctoria 'Atropurpurea'	Purple plains coreopsis	1900
Coriandrum sativum	Coriander, cilantro	1750
Corydalis aurea	Yellow fumitory, golden corydalis	1850
Corydalis sempervirens	Glaucus fumitory, Roman wormwood	1900
Crucianella stylosa	Crosswort	1900
Cucurbita pepo var. *ovifera*	Gourd	1700
Cuphea platycentra	Cigar flower	1900
Datura ceratocaula	Horn-stalked datura	1900
Datura inoxia var. *quinquecuspidata*	Downy thorn apple	1900
Datura quercifolia	Jimsonweed	1900
Datura stramonium	Jimsonweed	1800
Dianthus chinensis	Chinese pink	1800
Dioscorea alata	Yam	1800
Dolichos lablab	Hyacinth bean	1800
Downingia elegans	Elegant clintonia	1900
Downingia pulchella	Pretty clintonia	1900
Dracocephalum austriacum	Austrian dragon's head	1850
Dracocephalum moldavica	Moldavian balm	1900
Echeveria gibbiflora cv. 'Metallica'	Hen-and-chickens	1900
Echeveria secunda var. *glauca*	Hen-and-chickens	1900
Emilia javanica	Tassel flower	1900
Emilia sagittata	Tassel flower	1850
Eruca vesicaria	Rocket	1750
Eschscholzia californica	California poppy	1900
Eschscholzia californica 'Crocea'	Orange California poppy	1900
Euphorbia marginata	Snow-on-the-mountain	1900
Foeniculum vulgare	Fennel	1750
Foeniculum vulgare var. *azoricum Foeniculum vulgare*	Florence fennel	1800
Fumaria officinalis	Fumitory	1750

Botanical Name	*Common Name*	*Year of Introduction*
Gaillardia pulchella	Painted gaillardia	1900
Gaillardia pulchella var. *picta*	Sweet gaillardia	1900
Geranium carolinianum	Carolina cranesbill	1800
Gilia capitata	Headed gilia	1900
Gilia tricolor	Bird's eyes	1900
Gladiolus × *hortulanus*	Gladiolus, sword lily	1900
Glycine max	Soybean	1800
Gomphrena globosa	Globe amaranth	1800
Gossypium barbadense	Sea Island cotton	1800
Gossypium herbaceum	Levant cotton	1800
Gossypium hirsutum	Upland cotton	1800
Hedeoma pulegioides	American pennyroyal	1800
Helianthus annuus	Common sunflower	1750
Helianthus annuus 'Nanus'	Dwarf common sunflower	1850
Helichrysum bracteatum	Strawflower	1700
Helichrysum bracteatum 'Monstrosum'	Large everlasting	1900
Heliotropium peruvianum	Common heliotrope	1800
Hibiscus trionum	Flower-of-an-hour, bladder ketmia	1800
Iberis amara	Rocket candytuft	1800
Iberis odorata	Scented candytuft	1800
Iberis umbellata	Globe candytuft	1800
Impatiens balsamina	Garden balsam	1800
Ipomoea purpurea	Common morning glory	1800
Ipomoea quamoclit	Cypress vine	1800
Iresine spp.	Bloodleafs	1900
Lactuca sativa	Garden lettuce	1800
Lantana camara cv. 'Hybrida'	Dwarf lantana	1900
Lathyrus luteus		1850
Lathyrus odoratus	Sweet pea	1800
Lavatera olbia	Tree lavatera	1800
Lavatera trimestris	Herb tree mallow	1800
Lepidium latifolium	Dittander, pepperwort	1750
Lepidium sativum	Garden cress/pepperwort	1750
Limnanthes douglasii	Meadow foam	1900
Linanthus liniflorus	Flax-flower linanthus	1900
Linum grandiflorum	Flowering flax	1900
Linum usitatissimum	Flax	1750
Lobelia erinus	Edging lobelia	1900
Lobularia maritima	Sweet alyssum	1800
Lobularia maritima 'Variegata'	Variegated sweet alyssum	1900

Botanical Name	Common Name	Year of Introduction
Lupinus albus	White lupinus	1900
Lupinus hartwegii	Hartweg's lupine	1900
Lupinus hirsutus	Great blue lupinus	1900
Lupinus mutabilis var. cruckshanksii	Cruckshank's lupine	1900
Lupinus texensis	Texas bluebonnet	1900
Lychnis coeli-rosa	Rose of heaven	1800
Lycopersicon esculentum	Tomato	1800
Malcolmia maritima	Virginia stock	1800
Malope trifida	Grand flowering malope	1900
Malope trifida 'Alba'	White malope	1900
Malva rotundifolia	Round-leaved mallow	1800
Malva verticillata var. crispa	French mallow	1750
Matthiola incana 'Annua'	Ten-weeks stock	1800
Mentzelia lindleyi	Lindley mentzelia	1900
Mesembryanthemum crystallinum	Common ice plant	1900
Mirabilis jalapa	Common four-o'clock	1767
Mirabilis longiflora	Sweet four-o'clock	1800
Musa ensete	Banana plant	1900
Myosotis arvensis	Forget-me-not	1900
Myosotis sylvatica	Woodland forget-me-not	1900
Nemophila maculata	Five-spotted nemophila	1900
Nemophila menziesii	Baby-blue-eyes	1900
Nemophila menziesii var. atomaria	Baby-blue-eyes	1900
Nicotiana longiflora	Long-flowering tobacco	1900
Nicotiana rustica	Tobacco	1800
Nicotiana tabacum	Tobacco	1800
Nierembergia spp.	Cupflowers	1900
Nigella damascena	Love-in-a-mist	1800
Nigella hispanica	Fennel flower	1900
Nigella sativa	Fennel flower	1800
Nolana paradoxa	Dark blue nolana, Chilean bellflower	1900
Ocimum basilicum	Sweet basil	1750
Ocimum basilicum 'Minimum'	Basil	1900
Oenothera longiflora	Evening primrose	1900
Oenothera tetraptera	Evening primrose	1900
Origanum majorana	Sweet marjoram	1750
Oxalis corniculata var. atropurpurea	Purple creeping oxalis	1900
Papaver dubium	Smooth poppy	1900
Papaver rhoeas	Flanders poppy	1900
Papaver somniferum	Opium poppy	1781
Pelargonium zonale	Horseshoe geranium	1900

Botanical Name	Common Name	Year of Introduction
Perilla frutescens var. *crispa*	Perilla	1900
Persicaria orientalis		1737
Petunia violacea	Violet-flowered petunia	1850
Petunia × *hybrida*	Garden petunia (many varieties)	1900
Phlox drummondii	Drummond phlox	1900
Platystemon californicus	Creamcups	1900
Polygala lutea	Yellow annual milkwort	1850
Polygonum hydropiperoides	Smartweed	1750
Polygonum orientale	Prince's feather	1800
Portulaca grandiflora	Rose moss, eleven-o'clock	1900
Portulaca oleracea	Purslane	1672
Proboscidea fragrans	Unicorn plant	1900
Proboscidea louisianica	Unicorn plant	1900
Raphanus sativus	Radish	1800
Reseda odorata	Common mignonette	1800
Ricinus communis	Castor bean	1900
Salpiglossis sinuata	Painted tongue	1900
Salvia coccinea	Texas sage, scarlet sage	1900
Salvia hispanica	Spanish sage	1850
Salvia lyrata	Lyre-leaved sage	1850
Salvia splendens	Scarlet sage	1900
Satureja hortensis	Summer savory	1750
Scabiosa atropurpurea	Sweet scabious, mourning bride	1800
Schizanthus pinnatus	Butterfly flower	1900
Schizopetalon walkeri		1900
Senecio elegans	Purple ragwort	1800
Senecio leucostachys	Centauria	1900
Silene armeria	Sweet William catchfly	1900
Silene pendula	Nodding catchfly	1900
Silybum marianum	Blessed thistle, milk thistle	1800
Solanum hispidum	Devil's fig	1900
Stellaria media	Stitchwort	1750
Tagetes erecta	African marigold	1800
Tagetes patula	French marigold	1900
Tagetes tenuifolia	Signet marigold	1860
Thlaspi arvense	Field pennycress	1750
Tolpis barbata	Purple-eyed brepis	1900
Trachymene coerulea	Blue laceflower	1900
Trigonella foenum-graecum	Fenugreek	1900
Tropaeolum majus	Common nasturtium	1800
Ursinia anthemoides		1900
Valerianella locusta	Corn salad	1750

Botanical Name	Common Name	Year of Introduction
Verbena canadensis	Rose verbena	1840
Verbena peruviana	Peruvian verbena	1900
Vinca rosea	Madagascar periwinkle	1900
Viola tricolor var. *hortensis*	Pansy	1900
Xeranthemum annuum	Immortelle	1800
Zea mays	Indian corn	1800
Zinnia elegans	Common zinnia	1900
Zinnia peruviana	Red zinnia, yellow zinnia	1800

Biennials

Botanical Name	Common Name	Year of Introduction
Alcea ficifolia	Antwerp hollyhock	1800
Anchusa officinalis	Bugloss	1750
Angelica atropurpurea	Purple-stem angelica	1800
Apium graveolens var. *dulce*	Celery	1750
Arctium lappa	Great burdock	1750
Arctium minus	Smaller burdock	1750
Barbarea vulgaris	Winter cress	1750
Campanula medium	Canterbury bells	1800
Campanula pyramidalis	Chimney bellflower	1850
Campanula rapunculus	Rampion	1700
Campanula trachelium	Coventry bells	1850
Carum carvi	Caraway	1750
Cochlearia officinalis	Scurvy grass	1900
Cynoglossum officinale	Hound's tongue	1900
Daucus carota var. *sativus*	Carrot	1750
Dianthus barbatus	Sweet William	1800
Dianthus superbus	Lilac pink	1800
Digitalis lutea	Straw foxglove	1850
Digitalis purpurea	Common foxglove	1797
Digitalis purpurea 'Alba'	White foxglove	1850
Dipsacus sativus	Fuller's teasel	1750
Dracocephalum parviflorum	Dragonhead	1800
Echium vulgare	Bugloss	1750
Gentianopsis crinita	Fringed gentian	1750
Heracleum maximum	Cow parsnip	1750
Lunaria annua	Honesty	1750
Lychnis coronaria	Rose campion	1760
Lychnis coronata	Crown campion	1850
Matthiola incana	Stock gillyflower	1750
Oenothera biennis	Common evening primrose	1800
Oenothera pallida		1830
Petroselinum crispum	Curly parsley	1750
Picris echioides	Ox tongue	1750
Reseda luteola	Dyer's rocket	1900
Salvia sclarea	Clary	1750
Senecio jacobaea	Ragwort	1800
Silene compacta	Small-flowered catchfly	1900
Tragopogon pratensis	Goatsbeard	1750
Verbascum lychnitis	Mullein	1750

Bulbs

Botanical Name	Common Name	Year of Introduction	Zone
Allium ampeloprasum	Wild leek	1750	4
Allium canadense	Wild garlic	1750	3
Allium moly	Yellow moly	1700	5
Allium sativum	Garlic	1700	4
Allium schoenoprasum	Chive	1750	2 or 3
Amaryllis belladonna	Belladonna lily	1800	9
Belamcanda chinensis	Blackberry lily	1800	5
Bulbocodium vernum	Spring meadow saffron	1900	6
Canna × *generalis* 'City of Portland'	Canna hybrid	1915	9
Canna × *generalis* 'Firebird'	Canna hybrid	1911	9
Canna × *generalis* 'Florence Vaughan'	Canna hybrid	1893	9
Canna × *generalis* 'Richard Wallace'	Canna hybrid	1902	9
Canna × *generalis* 'Roi Humbert'	Canna hybrid	1902	9
Canna × *generalis* 'Wyoming'	Canna hybrid	1906	9
Chasmanthe aethiopica		1800	7
Claytonia caroliniana	Carolina spring beauty	1800	6
Colchicum luteum	Yellow autumn crocus	1800	7
Colchicum variegatum		1800	6
Corydalis bulbosa		1850	6?
Crinum amabile 'J. C. Harvey'		1902	8
Crinum × *powellii* 'Album'		1888	7
Crocus chrysanthus 'Snowbunting'		1914	4
Crocus susianus	Cloth-of-gold crocus	1900	4
Crocus tommasinianus		1847	4
Crocus vernus	Common crocus	1800	4
Crocus vernus 'Mammoth Yellow'		1800	4
Crocus vernus 'Mont Blanc'		1853	4
Crocus vernus 'Paulus Potter'		1920	4
Crocus vernus 'Purpureus Grandiflorus'		1870	4
Crocus vernus 'Queen of the Blues'		1916	4
Crocus versicolor	Common crocus	1900	4
Endymion hispanicus	Spanish squill	1850	?
Endymion italicus	Italian squill	1850	?
Endymion non-scriptus		1850	?

Botanical Name	Common Name	Year of Introduction	Zone
Fritillaria imperialis	Crown imperial	1800	5
Fritillaria imperialis 'Aurora'		1865	5
Fritillaria meleagris	Snake's-head fritillary	1840	4
Fritillaria meleagris 'Alba'		1840	4
Galanthus nivalis	Common snowdrop	1800	3
Galanthus nivalis 'Flore Pleno'		1800	3
Galanthus nivalis 'Magnet'		1890	3
Hyacinthoides non-scripta	English bluebell	1800	6
Hyacinthus orientalis	Common hyacinth	1800	4
Hyacinthus orientalis 'Bismarck'		1875	4
Hyacinthus orientalis 'Chestnut Flower'		1880	4
Hyacinthus orientalis 'City of Haarlem'		1893	4
Hyacinthus orientalis 'Distinction'		1880	4
Hyacinthus orientalis 'General Kohler'		1878	4
Hyacinthus orientalis 'Grand Monarque'		1863	4
Hyacinthus orientalis 'King of the Blues'		1863	4
Hyacinthus orientalis 'L'Innocence'		1863	4
Hyacinthus orientalis 'Lady Derby'		1875	4
Hyacinthus orientalis 'Lord Balfour'		1883	4
Hyacinthus orientalis 'Marconi'		1900	4
Hyacinthus orientalis 'Marie'		1860	4
Hyacinthus orientalis 'Perle Brilliante'		1895	4
Hyacinthus orientalis var. *albulus*	Roman hyacinth	1850	7
Leucojum aestivum	Summer snowflake	1900	4
Leucojum aestivum 'Gravetye Giant'		1920	4
Leucojum autumnale	Autumn snowflake	1800	5
Leucojum vernum	Spring snowflake	1800	4
Leucothoe axillaris	Coast leucothoe	1765	6
Lilium auratum	Gold-band lily	1900	4
Lilium auratum 'Platyphyllum'		1900	4
Lilium bulbiferum	Bulbil lily	1800	3
Lilium canadense	Canada lily	1800	3
Lilium candidum	Madonna lily	1800	4
Lilium catesbaei	Catesby lily	1800	8
Lilium chalcedonicum	Chalcedonian lily	1800	7

Botanical Name	Common Name	Year of Introduction	Zone
Lilium henryi	Yellow speciosum	1889	4
Lilium martagon	Martagon lily	1900	3
Lilium michauxii	Carolina lily	1800	7
Lilium philadelphicum	Wood lily	1800	4
Lilium pomponium	Lesser Turk's-cap lily	1800	5
Lilium regale	Regal lily	1905	4
Lilium speciosum	Lily	1900	4
Lilium speciosum 'Rubrum'	'Rubrum' lily	1830	5
Lilium superbum	Turk's-cap lily	1800	5
Lilium tigrinum	Tiger lily	1800	3
Lilium tigrinum var. *splendens*	German catchfly	1800	3
Lycoris radiata	Red spider lily	1900	7
Lycoris squamigera	Hall's amaryllis	1900	5
Muscari armeniacum	Grape hyacinth	1878	4
Muscari botryoides	Grape hyacinth	1800	4
Muscari botryoides 'Album'		1800	4
Muscari comosum 'Plumosum'	Feather hyacinth	1767	4
Muscari racemosum	Southern grape hyacinth	1800	5
Narcissus 'Albus Plenus Odoratus'		1861	4
Narcissus 'Avalanche'		1900?	7–9
Narcissus 'Barrii Conspicuus'		1869	4
Narcissus 'Beersheba'		1923	4
Narcissus bicolor		1800	6?
Narcissus bulbocodium ssp. *bulbocodium*	Petticoat daffodil	1800	6
Narcissus 'Butter and Eggs'		1777	4
Narcissus 'Elvira'		1902	4
Narcissus 'Emperor'		1865	4
Narcissus 'Franciscus Drake'		1921	4
Narcissus 'Golden Spur'		1885	4
Narcissus 'Grand Soleil d'Or'		1900	4
Narcissus × *incomparabilis*		1800	4
Narcissus × *intermedius* 'Texas Star'		1816	7–9
Narcissus jonquilla	Jonquil	1700	
Narcissus jonquilla 'Minor Plenus'	Jonquil	1700	4
Narcissus 'King Alfred'		1899	4
Narcissus 'Laurens Koster'		1906	6–8
Narcissus 'Mary Copeland'		1914	4
Narcissus × *medioluteus* 'Twin Sisters'		1700	6–8
Narcissus moschatus		1800	6
Narcissus × *odorus*		1700	6

Botanical Name	Common Name	Year of Introduction	Zone
Narcissus × *odorus* 'Plenus'		1700	6
Narcissus 'Orange Queen'		1908	6–8
Narcissus poeticus	Poet's narcissus	1800	5
Narcissus poeticus ssp. *radiiflorus*		1800	6
Narcissus 'Princeps'		1878	4
Narcissus pseudonarcissus	Daffodil	1800	4
Narcissus 'Queen of the North'		1908	4
Narcissus 'Silver Chimes'		1914	4
Narcissus 'Sir Watkins'		1884	4
Narcissus tazetta	Polyanthus narcissus	1800	8
Narcissus tazetta 'Double Roman'		1800	8
Narcissus tazetta 'Paper-white'	Paper-white narcissus	1900	8
Narcissus tazetta var. *orientalis*	Chinese sacred lily	1800	8
Narcissus tazetta var. *polyanthos*	Polyanthus narcissus	1900	8
Narcissus 'Telamonius Plenus'		1700	4
Narcissus triandrus	Angel's tears	1800	4
Narcissus triandrus 'Thalia'		1916	4
Narcissus 'W. P. Milner'		1869	4
Ornithogalum umbellatum	Star-of-Bethlehem	1750	4
Polianthes tuberosa	Tuberose	1736	9
Polianthes tuberosa 'Mexican Single'		1750	9
Polianthes tuberosa 'Pearl'		1870	9
Scilla autumnalis	Squill	1850	?
Scilla bifolia	Two-leaved squill	1850	4
Scilla peruviana	Squill	1850	?
Scilla siberica	Siberian squill	1900	3
Tulipa 'Bleu Aimable'		1916	4
Tulipa 'Clara Butt'		1889	4
Tulipa 'Couleur Cardinal'		1845	4
Tulipa 'Diana'		1909	4
Tulipa 'Dillenburg'		1916	4
Tulipa 'Duc Van Thol Max Cramoisie'		1700	4
Tulipa 'Duc Van Thol Orange'		1700	4
Tulipa 'Duc Van Thol Red'		1700	4
Tulipa 'Duc Van Thol Rose'		1700	4
Tulipa 'Duc Van Thol Violet'		1700	4
Tulipa 'Duke of Wellington'		1925	4
Tulipa 'Electra'		1905	4
Tulipa 'Fantasy'		1910	4
Tulipa 'Generaal de Wet'		1904	4

Botanical Name	Common Name	Year of Introduction	Zone
Tulipa 'Greuze'		1891	4
Tulipa 'Keizerskroon'		1750	4
Tulipa 'Lac van Rijn'		1700	4
Tulipa 'Mr. Van der Hoef'		1911	4
Tulipa 'Peach Blossom'		1890	4
Tulipa 'Prince of Austria'		1860	4
Tulipa 'Schoonoord'		1909	4
Tulipa schrenkii		1700	4
Tulipa sylvestris	Florentine tulip	1700	4
Tulipa 'Van der Neer'		1860	4
Tulipa 'Zomerschoon'		1700	4

Perennials

Botanical Name	Common Name	Year of Introduction	Zone
Achillea ageratum	Sweet yarrow	1900	7
Achillea filipendulina	Fern-leaf yarrow	1900	4
Achillea millefolium	Yarrow, milfoil	1750	2
Achillea ptarmica	Sneezeweed	1750	3–10
Achillea tomentosa	Woolly yarrow	1900	3
Aconitum japonicum	Monkshood, wolfsbane	1900	4
Aconitum lycoctonum	Wolfsbane, monkshood	1800	3
Aconitum napellus	Common or English monkshood, helmet flower	1750	2–9
Aconitum rostratum	Monkshood	1900	?
Aconitum uncinatum	Wild or clambering monkshood	1800	6
Aconitum variegatum	Monkshood	1900	?
Acorus calamus	Sweet flag	1750	3
Actaea pachypoda	White baneberry	1900	2–9
Actaea rubra	Red baneberry	1800	3
Actaea spicata	Black baneberry	1800	5
Adenophora confusa	Ladybells	1900?	3–9
Adiantum pedatum	Maidenhair fern	1750	5
Adonis vernalis	Pheasant's eye, spring adonis	1900	2 or 3
Aegopodium podagraria	Goutweed, bishop's weed	1900?	3
Aegopodium podagraria 'Variegatum'	Silveredge goutweed	1900?	4
Agave americana	American aloe	1800	6
Agrimonia eupatoria	Agrimony	1750	7
Ajuga reptans	Carpet bugleweed	1750	2 or 3
Alcea rosea	Hollyhock	1750	5
Alchemilla alpina	Mountain lady's mantle	1850?	3
Alchemilla mollis	Common lady's mantle	1800?	3–9
Alchemilla vulgaris	Lady's mantle, dewcup	1800?	4
Althaea officinalis	Marshmallow	1750	5
Amsonia tabernaemontana	Blue star	1800	3–9
Anaphalis margaritacea	Common pearly everlasting	1800	3–9
Anchusa azurea	Italian bugloss	1900	3–10
Anemone blanda	Greek windflower	1900	6–10
Anemone coronaria	Poppy anemone	1800	8
Anemone hortensis	Garden anemone	1800	5
Anemone hupehensis var. *japonica*	Japanese anemone	1900	5
Anemone nemorosa	European wood anemone	1900	3
Anemone patens	Spreading pasqueflower	1900	5
Anemone pulsatilla	European pasqueflower	1800	5

Botanical Name	Common Name	Year of Introduction	Zone
Anemone quinquefolia	American wood anemone	1800	4
Anemone sylvestris	Snowdrop	1800	5
Anemonella thalictroides	Rue anemone	1900	4
Angelica archangelica	Garden angelica	1800	4
Angelica sylvestris		1800	3–9
Antennaria canadensis	Live-forever	1750	3
Anthemis tinctoria	Golden marguerite	1900	3 or 10
Anthericum liliago	St. Bernard's lily	1900	6 or 7
Anthoxanthum odoratum	Sweet vernal grass	1800	3
Apocynum androsaemifolium	Spreading dogbane	1800	3
Apocynum cannabinum	Hemp dogbane	1800	4
Aptenia cordifolia	Baby sun rose	1900	9
Aquilegia alpina	Alpine columbine	1800	3
Aquilegia caerulea	Rocky Mountain columbine	1900	3–10
Aquilegia canadensis	American columbine	1750	4
Aquilegia chrysantha	Golden columbine	1900	3–10
Aquilegia flabellata	Fan columbine	1900?	3–10
Aquilegia glandulosa	Altai columbine	1900	2 or 3
Aquilegia vulgaris	European columbine	1900	2 or 3
Arabis caucasica	Wall rockcress	1900?	4–9
Arabis procurrens		1900?	3–9
Aralia hispida	Bristly sarsaparilla	1800	3
Aralia nudicaulis	Wild sarsaparilla	1750	3
Aralia racemosa	Spikenard, American sarsaparilla	1800	4
Arctostaphylos uva-ursi	Bearberry	1800	2–6
Arenaria montana	Mountain sandwort	1900?	4
Arenaria verna	Moss sandwort	1900	3
Arisaema draconitum	Dragonroot	1750	4
Arisaema triphyllum	Jack-in-the-pulpit	1750	4
Armeria maritima	Common thrift, sea pink	1900	3
Armoracia rusticana	Horseradish	1800	5
Artemisia abrotanum	Southernwood	1750	6–10
Artemisia absinthium	Wormwood	1750	4–10
Artemisia dracunculus	Tarragon	1750	5
Artemisia ludoviciana	Western sage	1900	3
Artemisia stelleriana	Dusty miller	1900	3–10
Artemisia vulgaris	Mugwort	1750	3
Aruncus dioicus	Sylvan goatsbeard	1900	3–9
Asarum canadense	Wild ginger	1900	2–9
Asarum europaeum	European wild ginger	1900	5
Asarum virginicum	Virginia wild ginger	1800	5
Asclepias curassavica	Bloodflower	1900	7

Botanical Name	Common Name	Year of Introduction	Zone
Asclepias incarnata	Swamp milkweed	1900	4
Asclepias syriaca	Common milkweed	1860	3
Asclepias tuberosa	Pleurisy root	1860	3
Asparagus officinalis	Garden asparagus	1750	5
Asphodeline lutea	King's spear	1850	6
Aster cordifolius	Blue wood aster	1900	4
Aster divaricatus	White wood aster	1850	4
Aster ericoides	Heath aster	1850	3
Aster linarii folius	Savory leaf aster	1850	4
Aster macrophyllus	Bigleaf aster	1850	4
Aster novae-angliae	New England aster	1800	3
Aster novi-belgii	New York aster	1800	3
Aster puniceus	Swamp aster	1850	3
Astilbe japonica	Spirea	1900	5
Astrantia major	Masterwort	1750	6
Atropa belladonna	Deadly nightshade	1800	6
Aubrieta deltoidea	Purple rockcress	1900	4–9
Aureolaria flava	False foxglove	1800	4
Aurinia saxatilis	Goldentuft, basket-of-gold	1800	4–10
Baptisia australis	Blue false indigo	1850	3–10
Bellis perennis var. *hortensis*	English daisy	1850	5
Bellium bellidioides	Stolon bellium	1900?	6
Bergenia cordifolia	Heartleaf saxifrage	1900	3–10
Bergenia crassifolia	Siberian tea	1900?	4
Boltonia asteroides	White boltonia	1900	3–10
Bouteloua gracilis	Mosquito grass	1900?	4
Cajanus cajan	Pigeon pea	1800	10
Calamintha nepeta	Calamint	1750	6
Calla palustris	Water arum	1750	2
Calluna vulgaris	Heather	1900	6
Calopogon tuberosus	Grass pink orchid	1800	3
Caltha palustris	Marsh marigold	1850	4
Campanula carpatica	Carpathian harebell	1850	3
Campanula glomerata	Clustered bellflower	1850	3
Campanula lactiflora	Milky bellflower	1850	5
Campanula persicifolia	Peach-leaved bellflower	1850	3
Campanula persicifolia 'Alba Plena'		1900	3
Campanula rapunculoides	Creeping bellflower	1850	3
Campanula rotundifolia	Bluebells of Scotland	1900	3
Campanula versicolor		1850	5
Canna indica	Indian shot	1800	?
Cardamine pratensis	Cuckoo bittercress	1900	4

Botanical Name	Common Name	Year of Introduction	Zone
Cassia fasciculata	Partridge pea	1800	6
Cassia marilandica	Wild senna	1800	3
Catananche caerulea	Cupid's dart	1850	4
Cedronella canariensis	Balm of Gilead	1900	9
Centaurea americana	Basket flower	1800	4
Centaurea americana 'Alba'	White-flowered centaurea	1800	4
Centaurea dealbata	Persian cornflower	1900?	3
Centaurea jacea	Brown knapweed	1766	4
Centaurea macrocephala	Globe centaurea	1800	2–3
Centaurea montana	Mountain bluet	1850	4
Centaurea nigra	Black knapweed	1800	5–10
Centranthus ruber	Red valerian	before 1800	5
Cerastium bierbersteinii	Mouse ear	1900	3
Cerastium tomentosum	Snow-in-summer	1900	3
Ceratostigma plumbaginoides	Leadwort	1900	6
Chamaemelum nobile	Chamomile	1750	4
Chasmanthium latifolium	Sea oats	1900	5
Chelidonium majus	Celandine, swallow wort	1750	4
Chelone glabra	Red-and-white turtlehead	1800	3
Chimaphila maculata	Spotted wintergreen	1800	4
Chrysanthemum balsamita	Maudlin	1750	4
Chrysanthemum coccineum	Pyrethrum, painted daisy	1900?	?
Chrysanthemum leucanthemum	Oxeye daisy	1750	3
Chrysanthemum maximum	Shasta daisy	1900	5
Chrysanthemum × morifolium	Garden mum	1900?	5
Chrysanthemum parthenium	Feverfew	1750	4
Chrysogonum virginianum	Golden star	1900	5
Cichorium intybus	Chicory, succory	1750	3
Cimicifuga racemosa	Black snakeroot	1850	4
Circaea lutetiana	Enchanter's nightshade	1800	?
Cistus ladanifer	Gum rock rose	1800	7
Colchicum autumnale	Autumn crocus	1800	4
Colutea arborescens	Bladder senna	1570	5–7
Commelina coelestis	Blue spiderwort	1900	8
Commelina virginica	Dayflower	1800	7
Comptonia peregrina	Sweet fern	1800	2
Convallaria majalis	Lily-of-the-valley	1750	2 or 3
Coreopsis grandiflora	Big-flowered coreopsis	1850	4
Coreopsis lanceolata	Lance coreopsis	1850	?
Coreopsis verticillata	Threadleaf coreopsis	1850	6
Coronilla emerus	Scorpion senna	1800	5
Coronilla varia	Crown vetch	1850	3

Botanical Name	Common Name	Year of Introduction	Zone
Cortusa matthioli	Purple cortusa	1800	6
Cunila origanoides	Common dittany	1800	5
Cyclamen purpurascens	European cyclamen	1800	5
Cymbalaria muralis	Kenilworth ivy	1800	3
Cynara scolymus	Artichoke	1750	6–10
Cynoglossum virginianum	Wild comfrey	1800	4
Cypripedium acaule	Pink lady's slipper	1800	3–8
Cypripedium calceolus var. *pubescens*	Yellow lady's slipper	1738	3
Cypripedium reginae	Showy lady's slipper	1760	2–3
Daboecia cantabrica	Irish heath	1800	5
Daucus carota	Queen Anne's lace	1750	3
Delphinium carolinianum	Carolina delphinium	1800	6
Delphinium elatum	Candle larkspur	1850	3
Delphinium nudicaule	Orange larkspur	1850	8
Delphinium speciosum		1850	8
Dennstaedtia punctilobula	Hay-scented fern	1900	4
Dianthus alpinus	Alpine pink	1850	3
Dianthus caryophyllus	Clove gillyflower, clove pink	1750	8
Dianthus deltoides	Maiden pink	1800	3–10
Dianthus fragrans		1839	3
Dianthus plumarius	Cottage pink	1800	4–10
Dicentra canadensis	Squirrel corn	1850	4
Dicentra cucullaria	Dutchman's breeches	1850	3
Dicentra eximia	Fringed bleeding heart	1800	4
Dicentra formosa	Bleeding heart	1900?	4
Dicentra spectabilis	Bleeding heart	1880	4
Dictamnus albus	Gas plant	1750	4
Dictamnus albus 'Ruber'	Red-flowering gas plant	1850	4
Digitalis ferruginea	Rusty foxglove	1850	4
Digitalis grandiflora	Yellow foxglove	1900?	4
Dionaea muscipula	Venus's flytrap	1763	8
Dodecatheon meadia	Shooting star	1800	4–9
Doronicum cordatum	Leopard's bane	1900?	4
Dracocephalum grandiflorum	Bigflower dragonhead	1850	2
Dryopteris filix-mas	Male fern	1750	3
Echinacea augustifolia		1850	4
Echinacea purpurea	Purple coneflower	1850	4
Echinops ritro	Globe thistle	1800	4
Echinops sphaerocephalus	Great globe thistle	1850	4
Empetrum nigrum	Black crowberry	1762	3
Epimedium grandiflorum	Barrenwort	1900	3
Equisetum hyemale	Horsetail	1750	3

Botanical Name	Common Name	Year of Introduction	Zone
Eranthis hyemalis	Winter aconite	1700	4
Erica carnea	Winter heath	1763	5
Erica ciliaris	Fringed heath	1773	7
Erica cinerea	Twisted heath	1750	5
Erica × darleyensis	Darley heath	1894	6
Erica mediterranea	Mediterranean heath	1765	7
Erica tetralix	Cross-leaf heath	1789	3
Erica vagans	Cornish heath	1811	5
Erigeron species	Fleabane	1900?	5
Eryngium alpinum	Alpine eryngium	1900	5
Eryngium maritimum	True sea holly	1700	5
Erythronium americanum	Yellow adder's tongue	1750	3
Erythronium dens-canis	Dogtooth violet	1700	3
Euonymus fortunei 'Vegetus'	Bigleaf wintercreeper	1876	5
Eupatorium aromaticum	Wild horehound	1850	5
Eupatorium coelestinum	Mistflower	1850	6
Eupatorium maculatum	Joe-Pye weed	1900	4
Eupatorium perfoliatum	Boneset	1800	3
Eupatorium purpureum	Joe-Pye weed	1800	4
Eupatorium rugosum	White snakeroot	1900	4
Euphorbia corollata	Flowering spurge	1900	3
Ferns, many varieties		1900	varies
Filipendula palmata	Siberian meadowsweet	1850	2
Filipendula rubra	Queen-of-the-prairie	1900?	3
Filipendula ulmaria	Queen-of-the-meadow, meadowsweet	1850	4
Filipendula vulgaris	Dropwort	1800	4
Frasera caroliniensis	Green gentian	1800	5
Fuchsia magellanica	Magellan fuchsia	1800	6
Gaillardia aristata	Blanket flower	1788	2 or 3
Galega officinalis	Goat's rue	1800	3
Galium odoratum	Sweet woodruff	1900	5
Galium verum	Bedstraw	1750	2 or 3
Gaura lindheimeri	White gaura	1900	5
Gentiana acaulis	Stemless gentian	1900	3
Gentiana andrewsii	Bottle gentian	1900	3
Gentiana catesbaei	Sampson's snakeroot	1850	7
Gentiana lutea	Great yellow gentian	1800	6–9
Gentiana saponaria	Soapwort	1765	4
Gentiana septemfida		1850	3
Geranium maculatum	Spotted geranium	1800	4
Geranium robertianum	Herb Robert	1750	3
Geranium sanguineum	Blood red geranium	1850	3

Botanical Name	Common Name	Year of Introduction	Zone
Geranium sanguineum var. *striatum*		1850	4
Gillenia stipulata	American ipecac	1800	4
Gillenia trifoliata	Bowman's root	1800	4
Gladiolus communis	Corn flag	1800	9
Glechoma hederacea	Ground ivy	1750	3
Glycyrrhiza glabra	Licorice	1750	9
Gnaphalium obtusifolium	Fragrant cudweed	1750	5
Goodyera pubescens	Downy rattlesnake plantain	1758	3
Gratiola aurea	Golden hedge hyssop	1800	3
Gynandriris sisyrinchium	Crocus-footed iris	1850	7?
Gypsophila paniculata	Baby's breath	1900	3
Hedyotis michauxii	Creeping bluets	1800	6–8
Hedysarum coronarium	French honeysuckle	1789	3
Helenium autumnale	Common sneezeweed	1800	3
Helenium hoopesii	Orange sneezeweed	1900	3
Helianthemum nummularium	Common sun rose	1800	5 or 6
Helianthus atrorubens	Dark-eye sunflower	1850	6
Helianthus decapetalus	Thinleaf sunflower	1850	4
Helianthus giganteus	Giant sunflower	1850	3
Helianthus maximiliani	Maximilian sunflower	1900	3
Helianthus salicifolius	Graceful sunflower	1900	3
Helianthus tuberosus	Jerusalem artichoke	1750	4
Helleborus foetidus	Bear's-foot hellebore	1800	6
Helleborus niger	Christmas rose	1800	3–9
Helleborus orientalis	Lenten rose	1850	6
Helleborus viridis	Green hellebore	1800	6
Helonias bullata	Swamp pink	1800	6
Hemerocallis fulva	Tawny daylily	1800	3
Hemerocallis lilioasphodelus	Lemon daylily	1800	3
Hemerocallis minor	Grass-leaf daylily	1840	3
Hemerocallis thunbergii	Late yellow daylily	1900	3
Hepatica acutiloba	Sharp-lobed hepatica	1800	4
Hepatica americana	Round-lobed hepatica, liverwort	1750	4
Hesperis matronalis	Dame's rocket, sweet rocket	1738	2 or 3
Heuchera sanguinea	Coralbells	1900?	3
Hibiscus militaris	Halberd-leaved rose mallow	1800	4–9
Hibiscus moscheutos	Common rose mallow	1800	5
Hibiscus palustris	Marsh mallow	1800	4–9
Hibiscus rosa-sinensis	Chinese hibiscus	1850	9
Hibiscus speciosus	Scarlet rose mallow	1800	7
Hibiscus syriacus	Rose-of-Sharon	1790	5–8
Hibiscus syriacus 'Ardens'	'Ardens' shrub althea	1873	5

Botanical Name	Common Name	Year of Introduction	Zone
Hibiscus syriacus 'Boule de Feu'	'Boule de Feu' shrub althea	1846	5
Hibiscus syriacus 'Coelestis'	'Coelestis' shrub althea	1887	5
Hibiscus syriacus 'Duc de Brabant'	'Duc de Brabant' shrub althea	1872	5
Hibiscus syriacus 'Souvenir de Charles Breton'	'Souvenir de Charles Breton' shrub althea	1886	5
Hibiscus syriacus 'Totus Albus'	'Totus Albus' shrub althea	1855	5
Hieracium pilosella	Mouse ear	1750	3
Hosta caerulea	Blue plantain	1900	3
Hosta plantaginea	Fragrant plantain	1900	4
Hosta sieboldiana	Plantain lily	1900	4
Hydrastis canadensis	Goldenseal	1800	5
Hymenocallis caroliniana	Inland spider lily	1800	5
Hypericum hypericoides	Saint Andrew's cross	1800	6
Hypoxis hirsuta	Little yellow starflower	1800	4
Hyssopus officinalis	Hyssop	1750	3–10
Iberis germanica var. *florentina*	Florentine candytuft	1850	5
Iberis gibraltarica	Gibraltar candytuft	1732	7
Iberis pruitii	Tenore candytuft	1850	5
Iberis sempervirens	Edging, evergreen, or perennial candytuft	1731	3–10
Impatiens capensis	Jewelweed	1800	2
Inula helenium	Elecampane	1750	3
Iris cristata	Dwarf crested iris	1800	4
Iris fulva	Copper iris	1800	7
Iris germanica	German iris	1800	4
Iris germanica var. *florentina*	Orris	1800	4
Iris kaempferi	Japanese iris	1900	5
Iris pallida	Orris	1830	7?
Iris prismatica	Blue flag	1750	3
Iris pseudacorus	Yellow flag	1750	5
Iris pumila	Dwarf bearded iris	1800	4
Iris sibirica	Siberian iris	1800	3
Iris susiana	Mourning iris	1800	5
Iris verna	Violet iris	1800	5
Iris versicolor	Blue flag	1800	3
Iris virginica	Virginia iris	1800	7
Iris xiphium	Spanish flag	1850	7?
Jeffersonia diphylla	Twinleaf	1800	5
Kniphofia × *corallina*	Torch lily, red-hot poker	1900	6
Kniphofia uvaria	Torch lily, red-hot poker	1900	6
Kniphofia uvaria var. *grandiflora*	Torch lily, red-hot poker	1900	6
Lamium maculatum	Spotted dead nettle	1700	5

Botanical Name	Common Name	Year of Introduction	Zone
Lathyrus grandiflorus	Everlasting pea	1850	5
Lathyrus latifolius	Perennial pea vine	1800	3
Lathyrus maritimus	Beach pea	1770	5
Leontopodium alpinum	Edelweiss	1900	4
Leonurus cardiaca	Motherwort	1800	4
Levisticum officinale	Lovage	1750	6
Liatris elegans	Pink-scale gayfeather	1850	7
Liatris pycnostachya	Kansas gayfeather	1900	4
Liatris scariosa	Tall gayfeather	1850	3
Liatris spicata	Spike gayfeather	1800	4
Liatris squarrosa		1850	4
Ligularia japonica	Grounsel	1900	?
Lilium parryi	Lemon lily	1900	7
Limonium latifolium	Sea lavender	1900	4
Limonium vulgare	Purple-cupped statice	1800	7
Linaria vulgaris	Toadflax, wild snapdragon	1750	3
Linum perenne	Perennial flax	1800	5
Lithospermum canescens	Indian paint	1800	3–9
Lithospermum officinale	Hoary gromwell	1900	3
Lobelia cardinalis	Cardinal flower	1800	2
Lobelia siphilitica	Blue cardinal flower	1800	5
Lobelia spicata	Pale-spike lobelia	1850	4
Lobelia splendens	Mexican lobelia	1850	8
Lupinus luteus	European yellow lupine	1800	6
Lupinus perennis	Wild lupine	1800	4
Lupinus polyphyllus	Lupine	1830	4
Lychnis alpina		1847	5
Lychnis chalcedonica	Jerusalem cross	1800	3
Lychnis flos-cuculi	Ragged robin	1800	3
Lychnis flos-jovis	Flower of Jove	1800	5
Lychnis fulgens		1850	5
Lychnis × *haageana*	Haages campion	1850	3
Lychnis viscaria	German catchfly	1800	3
Lychnis viscaria 'Flore Pleno'	German catchfly	1800	3
Lysimachia nummularia	Creeping Charlie	1750	3
Lythrum salicaria	Purple loosestrife	1900	3
Macleaya cordata	Plume poppy	1900	3
Maianthemum canadense	Wild lily-of-the-valley	1800	3
Malva moschata	Musk mallow	1750	3
Malva moschata 'Alba'	Musk mallow	1900	3
Manfreda virginica		1800	6
Marrubium vulgare	Horehound	1750	3

Botanical Name	Common Name	Year of Introduction	Zone
Medeola virginica	Indian cucumber root	1800	3
Medicago sativa	Alfalfa	1800	5
Melissa officinalis	Lemon balm	1750	4
Mentha × *piperita*	Peppermint	1900	3
Mentha pulegium	Organie, pennyroyal	1750	7
Mentha spicata	Spearmint	1750	3
Mertensia maritima		1850	5?
Mertensia virginica	Virginia bluebells	1800	3–10
Mimosa pudica	Touch-me-not, sensitive plant	1800	10
Mimulus cardinalis	Scarlet monkey flower	1900	?
Mimulus moschatus	Musk plant	1900	?
Miscanthus sinensis	Maiden grass	1900	4
Miscanthus sinensis 'Gracillimus'		1900	4
Miscanthus sinensis 'Variegatus'		1900	4
Miscanthus sinensis 'Zebrinus'	Zebra grass	1900	4
Mitchella repens	Partridgeberry	1761	3
Mitella diphylla	Common miterwort	1800	3
Monarda didyma	Bee balm, bergamot	1800	4–10
Monarda fistulosa	Wild bergamot	1850	4–10
Monarda punctata	Horsemint	1850	6
Monarda ruselliana		1830	5?
Myosotis azorica	True forget-me-not	1900	5?
Myosotis scorpioides	Perennial forget-me-not	1850	2
Myrrhis odorata	Sweet cicely, myrrh	1750	4
Napaea dioica	Glade mallow	1800	3–6
Nasturtium officinale	Peppergrass, watercress	1750	4
Nelumbo lutea	American lotus	1800	3–10
Nepeta cataria	Catnip	1750	3
Nerine sarniensis	Guernsey lily	1800	9
Nymphaea spp.	Hardy water lilies	1800	varies
Nymphoides indica	Water snowflake	1900	9
Oenothera fruticosa	Common sundrops	1900	4–10
Oenothera missouriensis	Ozark sundrops	1900	4–10
Oenothera speciosa	Showy evening primrose	1900	5–10
Omphalodes verna	Creeping navelseed	1850	7
Ononis rotundifolia	Coinleaf ononis	1800	4
Ophioglossum vulgatum	Adder's tongue fern	1750	7
Opuntia humifusa var. *austrina*	Hardy prickly pear cactus	1900	4
Orchis rotundifolia		1750	3
Orchis spectabilis		1750	3
Origanum dictamnus	Dittany	1750	8
Origanum heracleoticum	Winter sweet marjoram	1900	6

Botanical Name	Common Name	Year of Introduction	Zone
Origanum onites	Pot marjoram	1750	8
Origanum vulgare	Wild marjoram	1750	3
Osmunda regalis	Royal fern	1900	2
Oxalis acetosella	European wood sorrel	1750	5?
Pachysandra terminalis	Spurge	1882	3–8
Paeonia lactiflora	Chinese peony	1800	2–10
Paeonia officinalis	Common peony	1750	2–10
Paeonia tenuifolia	Fern-leaved peony	1775	4–10
Panax quinquefolius	American ginseng	1740	3
Papaver alpinum	Alpine poppy	1850	5
Papaver nudicaule	Iceland poppy	1850	3
Papaver orientale	Oriental poppy	1741	3
Papaver orientale var. *bracteatum*		1850	3
Paradisea liliastrum	St. Bruno's lily	1900	3
Pelargonium peltatum	Ivy-leaved geranium	1900	10
Pelargonium spp.	Scented geraniums	1850	10
Pennisetum setaceum	Fountain grass	1900	7
Penstemon barbatus	Bearlip penstemon	1900	3
Penstemon barbatus ssp. *torreyi*		1900	3
Penstemon cobaea	Cobaea penstemon	1850	5
Penstemon digitalis	White penstemon	1850	3
Penstemon hirsutus	Hairy penstemon	1850	3
Penstemon murrayanus	Cutleaf penstemon	1850	6
Penstemon speciosus	Showy penstemon	1850	5?
Perovskia atriplicifolia	Russian sage	1904	4
Phalaris arundinacea var. *picta*	Ribbon grass	1900	4
Phlomis fruticosa	Jerusalem sage	1800	8
Phlox carolina	Thick-leaved phlox	1800	4–9
Phlox divaricata	Wild blue phlox	1800	4–9
Phlox glaberrima	Smooth phlox	1800	4
Phlox maculata	Wild sweet William	1800	3–9
Phlox paniculata	Summer phlox	1800	3–9
Phlox × *procumbens*	Creeping phlox	1900	5
Phlox subulata	Moss pink	1800	2 or 3
Phragmites australis ssp. *australis*	Common reed	1800	5
Phragmites communis	Common reed	1800	5
Physalis alkekengi	Japanese lantern	1900	2 or 3
Physalis franchetii	Chinese lantern	1900?	5
Physostegia denticulata		1850	7?
Physotegia virginiana	False dragonhead, obediant plant	1850	?
Phytolacca americana	Pokeweed	1760	?
Pimpinella anisum	Anise	1750	5–9

Botanical Name	Common Name	Year of Introduction	Zone
Piqueria trinervia var. *variegata*	Stevia	1900	10
Plantago major	Plantain, white man's foot	1750	3
Platycodon grandiflorus	Balloon flower	1900	3
Podophyllum peltatum	Common mayapple	1800	3
Polemonium caeruleum	Jacob's ladder	1750	2 or 3
Polemonium reptans	Greek valerian	1750	2
Polygala senega	Seneca snakeroot	1751	4
Polygonatum biflorum	American Solomon's seal	1800	3
Polygonatum multiflorum	Eurasian Solomon's seal	1800	3
Potentilla atrosanguinea	Himalayan cinquefoil	1840	?
Potentilla nepalensis		1850	?
Potentilla reptans	Cinquefoil	1750	4
Potentilla russelliana		1850	?
Poterium sanguisorba	Salad burnet	1900	3
Primula auricula	Auricula primrose	1800	3
Primula elatior	Oxlip	1800	5
Primula farinosa	Birds-eye cowslip	1850	4
Primula halleri	Long-leaved primrose	1850	4
Primula japonica	Japanese primrose	1900	5
Primula × polyantha	Polyantha primrose	1850	3
Primula scotia	Scottish primrose	1850	5
Primula sieboldii	Siebold primrose	1850	4
Primula sinensis	Chinese primrose	1850	8
Primula veris	Cowslip	1800	5
Prunella vulgaris	Self-heal	1750	3
Pteridium aquilinum	Brake fern	1750	3
Pulmonaria officinalis	Common lungwort	1800	3
Pulmonaria saccharata	Bethlehem sage	1800	3
Ranunculus aconitifolius	Fair maids of France	1800	5
Ranunculus acris 'Flore Pleno'	Yellow bachelor's button	1800	3
Ranunculus asiaticus	Persian buttercup	1800	8
Ranunculus repens 'Flore Pleno'	Creeping buttercup	1850	3
Rheum palmatum	True Turkey rhubarb	1900	4?
Rheum rhabarbarum	Garden rhubarb	1900	3
Rheum rhaponticum	Rhubarb	1750	3
Rhexia virginica	Meadow beauty	1800	3
Rosmarinus officinalis	Rosemary	1750	6
Rubia tinctorum	Madder	1750	6
Rudbeckia fulgida	Showy coneflower	1830	4
Rudbeckia hirta	Coneflower, black-eyed Susan	1800	3
Rudbeckia laciniata	Cutleaf coneflower	1800	3
Rudbeckia laciniata 'Hortensia'	Golden glow	1900	3

Botanical Name	Common Name	Year of Introduction	Zone
Rumex acetosa	Broadleaf sorrel	1750	3
Rumex patientia	Patience, monk's rhubarb	1750	5
Rumex scutatus	French sorrel	1900	4
Ruta graveolens	Rue	1750	4
Sabatia stellaris	Sea pink	1830	6
Sagittaria latifolia	Arrowhead	1800	4
Salvia azurea	Blue sage	1800	4
Salvia officinalis	Sage	1750	4–8
Salvia pratensis	Meadow sage	1900	3
Sanguinaria canadensis	Bloodroot	1830	3 or 4
Sanicula marilandica	Black snakeroot	1800	5?
Santolina chamaecyparissus	Santolina, lavender cotton	1750	6
Santolina virens	Santolina	1900	6
Saponaria ocymoides	Rock soapwort	1850	3
Saponaria officinalis	Soapwort, bouncing Bet	1750	3
Saponaria officinalis 'Plena'		before 1850	3
Sarracenia purpurea	Common pitcher plant	1800	3
Satureja montana	Winter savory	1750	5
Saxifraga cotyledon	Pyramidal saxifrage	1850	6
Saxifraga granulata	Meadow saxifrage	1850	5
Saxifraga granulata 'Flore Pleno'	Fair maids of France	1850	5
Saxifraga hypnoides	Mossy saxifrage	1850	5
Saxifraga stolonifera	Strawberry saxifrage	1850	5
Saxifraga umbrosa	Londonpride saxifrage	1830	7
Saxifraga virginiensis	Virginia saxifrage	1750	3
Schrankia uncinata	Sensitive brier	1800	5?
Sedum acre	Stonecrop	1800	3
Sedum sieboldii	Siebold stonecrop	1850	3
Sedum spectabile	Showy stonecrop	1800	4
Sedum telephium	Live-forever	1750	4
Sempervivum tectorum	House leek	1750	4
Sida hermaphrodita	Virginia mallow	1800	6
Silene alba	Evening campion	1800	3
Silene dioica	Red campion	1800	5
Silene virginica	Fire-pink catchfly	1800	3
Silphium laciniatum	Compass plant	1800	5
Sisyrinchium angustifolium	Rush lily	1800	5
Sisyrinchium graminoides		1800	5
Sium sisarum	Skirret	1750	5
Smilax laurifolia	Bay-leaved smilax	1800	7
Solidago bicolor	Silver goldenrod	1850	3
Solidago odora	Sweet goldenrod	1750	3

Botanical Name	Common Name	Year of Introduction	Zone
Sphaeralcea coccinea	Prairie mallow	1800	5
Spigelia marilandica	Pinkroot spigelia	1800	8
Stachys byzantina	Lamb's ears	1850	5
Stachys grandiflora	Big betony	1850	3
Stachys officinalis	Betony	1750	4
Stokesia laevis	Stokes' aster, cornflower aster	1900	5
Succisa australis	Devil's bit scabious	1750	5
Symphytum officinale	Comfrey	1750	3
Symplocarpus foetidus	Skunkweed	1800	4?
Tanacetum vulgare	Tansy	1700	3
Taraxacum officinale	Dandelion	1700	3
Tephrosia virginiana	American goat's rue	1800	7
Teucrium chamaedrys	Germander	1900?	5
Teucrium flavum	Tree germander	1850	6?
Thalictrum dioicum	Early meadow rue	1800	4
Thalictrum flavum		1800	5?
Thalictrum polygamum	Meadow rue	1850	3
Thalictrum speciosissimum	Dusty meadow rue	1900	5
Thermopsis caroliniana	Carolina lupine	1800	4
Thymus serpyllum	Mother-of-thyme	1750	4
Thymus serpyllum var. *argenteus*	Silver mother-of-thyme	1900	5
Thymus serpyllum var. *aureus*	Golden mother-of-thyme	1900	5
Thymus serpyllum var. *variegatus*	Variegated mother-of-thyme	1900	5
Thymus vulgaris	Common thyme	1800	5
Tiarella cordifolia	Allegheny foamflower	1840	4
Trachelium caeruleum	Throatwort	1750	8
Tradescantia virginiana	Virginia spiderwort	1800	4
Trifolium pratense	Clover grass	1750	3
Trillium erectum	Purple trillium	1800	4
Trillium sessile	Toad trillium	1800	6
Trollius asiaticus	Siberian globeflower	1850	3
Trollius europaeus	Common globeflower	1800	5
Tussilago farfara	Coltsfoot	1750	3
Typha angustifolia	Cattail	1900	4
Urtica dioica	Nettle	1750	3
Valeriana officinalis	Valerian, garden heliotrope	1750	5
Veratrum viride	Hellebore	1750	3
Verbascum phoeniceum	Purple mullein	1850	6
Verbascum thapsus	Flannel mullein	1750	5
Verbena hastata	Blue verbena	1750	3
Verbena officinalis	Vervain	1750	5
Veronica gentianoides	Gentian speedwell	1850	4

Botanical Name	Common Name	Year of Introduction	Zone
Veronica longifolia var. *subsessilis*	Longleaf veronica	1850	4
Veronica spicata	Spike speedwell	1850	3
Veronica spuria	Bastard speedwell	1900	5
Veronicastrum virginicum	Culver's root	1850	4
Viburnum veitchii	Veitch viburnum	1901	5
Vinca major	Large periwinkle	1789	7–9
Vinca minor	Common periwinkle or myrtle	1800	3–8
Viola cornuta	Tufted pansy, horned violet	1800	6
Viola lanceolata	Lance-leaved violet	1850	3
Viola odorata	Sweet violet	1750	6
Viola pedata	Bird's-foot violet	1800	5
Viola primulifolia	Primrose-leaved violet	1850	3
Viola pubescens	Downy violet	1850	3
Viola tricolor	Johnny-jump-up	1767	4
Vitex agnus-castus	Chaste tree	1700	6
Vitex negundo	Chaste tree	1700	6
Vitis rotundifolia	Muscadine grape	1800	6
Waldsteinia fragarioides	Barren strawberry	1900?	5
Watsonia meriana	Meriana bugle lily	1800	8
Yucca filamentosa	Adam's needle	1800	5
Yucca recurvifolia	Yucca	1900	8?
Zephyranthes atamasco	Atamasco lily	1739	8
Zephyranthes candida	White rain lily	1850	7
Zephyranthes grandiflora	Pink rain lily	1850	8

Shrubs

Botanical Name	Common Name	Year of Introduction	Zone
Abutilon	Indian mallow	1800	10
Acacia farnesiana	Opopanax	1800	8
Acanthopanax sieboldianus	Five-leaved aralia	1859	5
Acer ginnala	Amur maple	1860	2–8
Aesculus pavia	Red buckeye	1711	4–8
Alnus rugosa	Speckled alder	1769	4
Amelanchier alnifolia	Saskatoon serviceberry	1918	5
Amelanchier arborea	Juneberry, downy serviceberry	1746	4–9
Amelanchier canadensis	Shadblow serviceberry	1776	3–7
Amelanchier laevis	Allegheny serviceberry	1870	4
Andromeda glaucophylla	Downy andromeda	1800	2
Andromeda polifolia	Bog rosemary	1786	2
Aronia arbutifolia	Red chokeberry	1700	4–9
Aronia melanocarpa	Black chokeberry	1700	3–8
Baccharis halimifolia	Groundsel tree	1800	5–10
Berberis koreana	Korean barberry	1905	4
Berberis × *mentorensis*	Mentor barberry	1924	5–8
Berberis thunbergii	Japanese green barberry	1656	4–8
Berberis thunbergii 'Atropurpurea'	Red barberry	1926	4–8
Betula humilis		1800	9
Bruckenthalia spiculifolia	Spike heath	1900?	5
Buddleia alternifolia	Fountain buddleia	1914	5
Buddleia davidii	Butterfly bush	c. 1900	5–9
Buddleia globosa	Globe butterfly bush	1774	7
Buddleia × *weyeriana*		c. 1920	7
Buxus microphylla	Littleleaf boxwood	1860	5
Buxus sempervirens	Common boxwood	1750	5
Buxus sempervirens 'Aurea'	Golden boxwood	1800	6
Buxus sempervirens 'Suffruticosa'	True dwarf boxwood	1750	6
Callicarpa americana	American beautyberry	1800	7
Calycanthus floridus	Common sweet shrub	1800	5
Capparis spinosa	Caper bush	1800	8
Caragana arborescens	Siberian pea shrub	1752	2
Caryopteris × *clandonensis*	Hybrid bluebeard	1933	6
Caryopteris incana	Common bluebeard	1844	7
Ceanothus americanus	New Jersey tea	1713	4
Cephalanthus occidentalis	Buttonbush	1800	5
Chaenomeles speciosa	Common flowering quince	1800	4–8
Chamaecyparis obtusa 'Nana'	Dwarf fernspray cypress	1900	4–8

Botanical Name	Common Name	Year of Introduction	Zone
Chamaedaphne calyculata	Leatherleaf	1761	2
Citrus aurantiifolia	Lime	1800	10
Clethra alnifolia	Summersweet	1731	3–9
Clethra alnifolia 'Paniculata'	'Paniculata' summersweet	1770	3–9
Clethra alnifolia 'Rosea'	Pink summersweet	1800	4
Clethra barbinervis	Japanese clethra	1870	5
Clethra tomentosa	Woolly summersweet	1731	5
Cneorum tricoccon	Widow wail	1800	9
Collinsonia canadensis	Citronella horse balm	1800	5
Cornus alba	Tartarian dogwood	1741	3
Cornus canadensis	Bunchberry	1750	3
Cornus sanguinea	Blood-twig dogwood	1800	4
Cornus sericea	Red osier dogwood	1656	3
Cornus sericea 'Flaviramea'	Golden-twig dogwood	1899	3
Corylopsis glabrescens	Fragrant winter hazel	1905	5–8
Corylopsis griffithii	Griffith winter hazel	1879	7
Corylus avellana 'Contorta'	Harry Lauder's walking stick	1870	4
Cotinus coggygria	Common smokebush	1656	6
Cotinus coggygria 'Pendulus'	Weeping smoke tree	1885	5–8
Cotinus obovatus	American smoke tree	1782	4–8
Cotoneaster adpressus	Creeping cotoneaster	1896	5
Cotoneaster apiculatus	Cranberry cotoneaster	1910	5
Cotoneaster dammeri	Bearberry cotoneaster	1900	5
Cotoneaster divaricatus	Spreading cotoneaster	1907	5
Cotoneaster horizontalis	Rockspray cotoneaster	1880	5
Cotoneaster lucidus	Hedge cotoneaster	1840	3–7
Cotoneaster multiflorus	Many-flowered cotoneaster	1900	6
Cotoneaster salicifolius	Willowleaf cotoneaster	1908	6
Cyrilla racemiflora	Leatherwood	1767	5–10
Cytisus decumbens	Prostrate broom	1775	5
Cytisus × kewensis	Kew broom	1891	6
Cytisus multiflorus	White Spanish broom	1752	6
Cytisus nigricans	Spike broom	1730	6
Cytisus × praecox	Warminster broom	1867	6
Cytisus procumbens	Ground broom	1900	6
Cytisus purgans	Provence broom	1750	5
Cytisus purpureus	Purple broom	1792	5
Cytisus scoparius	Scotch broom	1750	6
Danae racemosa	Alexandrian laurel	1713	8–9
Daphne cneorum	Rose daphne	1752	4
Daphne genkwa	Lilac daphne	1843	5
Deutzia × lemoinei	Lemoine deutzia	1891	3–8

Botanical Name	Common Name	Year of Introduction	Zone
Deutzia × magnifica	Showy deutzia	1909	5
Daphne mezereum	February daphne	1800	5
Daphne odora	Winter daphne	1771	7
Deutzia gracilis	Slender deutzia	1840	4–8
Deutzia parviflora	Mongolian deutzia	1883	4–8
Deutzia × rosea 'Eximia'	Pink-choice deutzia	1898	5
Deutzia scabra	Fuzzy deutzia	1822	5
Deutzia scabra 'Candidissima'	Snowflake deutzia	1822	5
Diervilla sessilifolia	Southern bush honeysuckle	1844	4–8
Dirca palustris	Leatherwood	1750	4–9
Elaeagnus multiflora	Cherry elaeagnus	1862	4
Elsholtzia stauntonii	Staunton elsholtzia	1905	4–8
Enkianthus campanulatus	Red-vein enkianthus	1870	6
Enkianthus deflexus	Bent enkianthus	1878	6
Enkianthus perulatus	White enkianthus	1870	5
Epilobium angustifolium	Fireweed	1850	3
Escallonia virgata	Twiggy escallonia	1866	7
Eucryphia glutinosa		1859	8
Euonymus alatus	Winged burning bush	1860	4
Euonymus americanus	Strawberry bush	1697	6
Euonymus atropurpurea	Wahoo	1756	4
Euonymus bungeanus	Winterberry euonymus	1883	4
Euonymus fortunei 'Coloratus'	Coloratus wintercreeper	1914	5
Euonymus fortunei 'Minimus'	Minimus wintercreeper	1912	5
Euonymus japonicus	Japanese euonymus	1804	8
Euonymus kiautschovicus	Running strawberry bush	1860	5–8
Euonymus latifolius	Broadleaf euonymus	1730	5
Euonymus nanus var. turkestanicus	Dwarf euonymus	1830	2
Euonymus obovatus	Running strawberry bush	1800	3
Euonymus yedoensis	Yeddo euonymus	1865	4
Exochorda racemosa	Common pearlbush	1849	4–8
Fatsia japonica	Japanese fatsia	1838	8
Forsythia × intermedia	Border forsythia	1875	5
Forsythia × intermedia 'Densiflora'	'Densiflora' border forsythia	1888	5
Forsythia × intermedia 'Spectabilis'	Showy border forsythia	1906	5
Forsythia × intermedia 'Vitellina'	'Vitellina' forsythia	1899	5
Forsythia ovata	Early forsythia	1917	4
Forsythia suspensa var. sieboldii	Weeping forsythia	1905	5
Forsythia viridissima	Greenstem forsythia	1845	5
Fothergilla gardenii	Dwarf fothergilla	1765	5–8
Fothergilla major	Large fothergilla	1900	5
Gardenia jasminoides	Common gardenia	1800	8–9

Botanical Name	Common Name	Year of Introduction	Zone
Gaultheria procumbens	Wintergreen, checkerberry	1762	4
Gaylussacia brachycera	Box huckleberry	1796	5
Genista pilosa	Silkyleaf woodwaxen	1789	4
Genista tinctoria	Woodwaxen	1750	4
Hamamelis japonica	Japanese witch hazel	1862	5–8
Hamamelis mollis	Chinese witch hazel	1879	5–8
Hamamelis vernalis	Vernal witch hazel	1908	4–8
Hamamelis virginiana	Common witch hazel	1736	3–8
Hebe buxifolia	Boxleaf hebe	1885	7
Hebe traversii	Travers hebe	1868	7
Hippophae rhamnoides	Sea buckthorn	1800	3
Hydrangea arborescens	Smooth hydrangea	1736	3–9
Hydrangea arborescens 'Grandiflora'	Hills-of-snow	1900	3–9
Hydrangea macrophylla	Blue hydrangea	1790	6
Hydrangea macrophylla 'Coerulea'	'Coerulea' lacecap hydrangea	1846	6
Hydrangea paniculata	Peegee hydrangea	1861	4
Hydrangea paniculata 'Grandiflora'	'Grandiflora' peegee hydrangea	1862	3–8
Hydrangea paniculata 'Praecox'	'Praecox' peegee hydrangea	1893	3–8
Hydrangea quercifolia	Oakleaf hydrangea	1803	5–9
Hydrangea serrata		1870	6
Hypericum calycinum	Aaron's beard	1676	6
Hypericum frondosum	Golden St.-John's-wort	1776	5
Hypericum hookerianum	Hooker's St.-John's-wort	1853	6
Hypericum hypericoides	St. Andrew's cross	1800	7
Hypericum patulum var. *henryi*	Henry St.-John's-wort	1898	6
Hypericum perforatum	St.-John's-wort	1750	3
Hypericum prolificum	Shrubby St.-John's-wort	1800	4
Hypericum stans	St.-Peter's-wort	1750	6–9
Hypericum × *moserianum*	Gold-flower	1887	7
Ilex ciliospinosa		1908	5
Ilex coriacea	Large gallberry	1800	7
Ilex cornuta	Chinese holly	1846	7
Ilex crenata	Japanese holly	1864	6
Ilex crenata 'Convexa'	Convex-leaved Japanese holly	1919	5
Ilex decidua	Possum haw	1760	5
Ilex glabra	Inkberry	1759	4–9
Ilex montana	Mountain winterberry	1800	5
Ilex opaca	American holly	1744	5
Ilex pedunculosa	Longstalk holly	1892	6
Ilex rugosa	Prostrate holly	1895	3
Ilex serrata	Finetooth holly	1866	5
Ilex verticillata	Common winterberry	1736	3–9

Botanical Name	Common Name	Year of Introduction	Zone
Ilex vomitoria	Yaupon	1700	7
Ilex yunnanensis	Yunnan holly	1901	6
Illicium anisatum	Japanese anise tree	1790	7–9
Illicium floridanum	Florida anise tree	1771	8–9
Indigofera amblyantha	Pink indigo	1908	5
Indigofera incarnata 'Alba'	White Chinese indigo	1878	5
Indigofera kirilowii	Kirilow indigo	1899	4
Itea japonica	Dwarf sweetspire	1850?	6
Itea virginica	Virginia sweetspire	1744	5
Juniperus chinensis	Chinese juniper	1767	4
Juniperus chinensis 'Pfitzeriana'	Pfitzer juniper	1767	4
Juniperus chinensis 'Pfitzeriana Aurea'	Golden Pfitzer juniper	1923	4
Juniperus chinensis 'Sargentii'	Sargent juniper	1892	4
Juniperus communis	Juniper	1750	2
Juniperus conferta	Shore juniper	1915	6–8
Juniperus horizontalis	Creeping juniper	1836	3–9
Juniperus horizontalis 'Douglasii'	Douglas juniper	1855	4
Juniperus horizontalis 'Plumosa'	'Plumosa' Chinese juniper	1907	3–9
Juniperus horizontalis 'Wiltonii'	Blue rug juniper	1914	3–9
Juniperus procumbens	Japanese garden juniper	1843	5
Juniperus rigida	Needle juniper	1861	5
Juniperus sabina	Savin juniper	1800	4
Juniperus scopulorum	Rocky Mountain juniper	1836	5
Juniperus squamata	Singleseed juniper	1836	4–8
Juniperus squamata 'Meyeri'	Meyer's juniper	1914	4
Juniperus virginiana 'Kosteri'		1870	4
Juniperus virginiana 'Tripartita'	Fountain red cedar	1867	2
Kalmia angustifolia	Sheep laurel	1736	2
Kalmia latifolia	Mountain laurel	1734	4
Kerria japonica	Japanese kerria	1834	4
Kolkwitzia amabilis	Beautybush	1901	5
Lantana camara	Yellow sage	1800	8
Lavandula angustifolia	English lavender	1800	5
Lavandula stoechas	French lavender	1800	7
Ledum groenlandicum	Labrador tea	1763	2–5
Ledum palustre	Wild rosemary, crystal tea	1800	3
Leiophyllum buxifolium	Box sand myrtle	1736	5
Lespedeza bicolor	Shrub bush clover	1856	4–7
Leucothoe fontanesiana	Drooping leucothoe	1793	4
Leucothoe keiskei	Keisk's leucothoe	1915	5
Leucothoe populifolia	Florida leucothoe	1765	7

Botanical Name	Common Name	Year of Introduction	Zone
Leucothoe racemosa	Sweetbells leucothoe	1736	5–9
Ligustrum amurense	Amur privet	1860	3
Ligustrum × ibolium	Ibolium privet	1910	4
Ligustrum japonicum	Japanese privet	1845	7
Ligustrum japonicum 'Rotundifolium'	'Rotundifolium' Japanese privet	1860	7
Ligustrum lucidum	Wax-leaf privet	1794	8
Ligustrum obtusifolium	Border privet	1860	3
Ligustrum ovalifolium	California privet	1847	5
Ligustrum sinense	Chinese privet	1852	7
Ligustrum vulgare	European privet	1750	4–7
Ligustrum vulgare 'Lodense'	'Lodense' privet	1800	5
Lindera benzoin	Spicebush	1800	4
Lindera obtusiloba	Japanese spicebush	1880	6
Lonicera alpigena	Dwarf Alps honeysuckle	1600	5
Lonicera canadensis	Fly honeysuckle	1800	4
Lonicera etrusca	Etruscan honeysuckle	1750	7
Lonicera fragrantissima	Winter honeysuckle	1845	4–8
Lonicera hildebrandiana	Giant honeysuckle	1888	9
Lonicera maackii	Amur honeysuckle	1860	2
Lonicera maximowiczii var. sachalinensis	Sakhalin honeysuckle	1917	4
Lonicera nitida	Boxleaf honeysuckle	1908	7–9
Lonicera pileata	Privet honeysuckle	1900	6
Lonicera tatarica	Tatarian honeysuckle	1752	3
Lonicera xylosteum	European fly honeysuckle	1850	4
Loropetalum chinense		1880	7–9
Lycium barbarum	Matrimony vine	1900	8
Lycium halimifolium	Boxthorn	1800	5
Lyonia ligustrina	Male blueberry	1800	4
Lyonia lucida	Tetterbush	1800	7
Mahonia aquifolium	Oregon grape holly	1823	6
Menziesia pilosa	Allegany menziesia	1800	6
Myrica gale	Sweet gale	1750	1
Myrica pensylvanica	Northern bayberry	1800	3
Myrtus communis	Myrtle	1800	8–9
Nandina domestica	Heavenly bamboo	1804	6–9
Neillia sinensis	Chinese neillia	1910	5
Nerium oleander	Oleander	1750	8
Neviusia alabamensis	Snow wreath	1860	4–8
Nyssa ogeche	Ogeechee tupelo	1806	7
Osmanthus americanus	Osmanthus	1758	7–9

Botanical Name	Common Name	Year of Introduction	Zone
Osmanthus × fortunei	Fortune's osmanthus	1856	7
Osmanthus heterophyllus	Holly osmanthus	1856	7–9
Osmanthus heterophyllus 'Purpureus'	Purple holly osmanthus	1900	7–9
Paeonia suffruticosa	Tree peony	1800	5
Parrotiopsis jacquemontiana		1879	5–7
Paxistima canbyi	Canby paxistima	1880	3–8
Philadelphus coronarius	Sweet mock orange	1700	4–8
Philadelphus × cymosus	Cymosus mock-orange	1900	5
Philadelphus × cymosus 'Bannière'		1907	5
Philadelphus × cymosus 'Conquette'		1903	5
Philadelphus × cymosus 'Norma'		1914	5
Philadelphus × cymosus 'Perle Blanche'		1900	5
Philadelphus inodorus	Scentless mock orange	1800	5
Philadelphus × lemoinei	Lemoine mock orange	1900	5
Philadelphus × lemoinei 'Avalanche'		1896	5
Philadelphus × lemoinei 'Boule d'Argent'		1894	5
Philadelphus × lemoinei 'Erectus'		1894	5
Philadelphus × lemoinei 'Fleur de Neige'		1916	5
Philadelphus × lemoinei 'Girandole'		1916	5
Philadelphus × lemoinei 'Mont Blanc'		1894	5
Philadelphus purpurascens	Purplecup mock orange	1904	5
Philadelphus × purpureomaculatus 'Sirene'	'Sirene' mock orange	1910	5
Philadelphus schrenkii var. *jackii*	Jack mock orange	1905	5
Philadelphus × splendens	Splendens mock orange	1900	5
Philadelphus × virginalis	Virginalis mock orange	1900	5
Philadelphus × virginalis 'Albâtre'		1914	5
Philadelphus × virginalis 'Argentine'		1914	5
Philadelphus × virginalis 'Bouquet Blanc'		1894	5
Philadelphus × virginalis 'Glacier'		1914	5
Phillyrea vilmoriniana	Lanceleaf phillyrea	1867	6
Photinia glabra	Japanese photinia	1914	7
Photinia serrulata	Chinese photinia	1804	7–9
Photinia villosa	Oriental photinia	1865	4–7
Physocarpus monogynus	Mountain ninebark	1879	5
Physocarpus opulifolius	Ninebark	1800	2–7

Botanical Name	Common Name	Year of Introduction	Zone
Pieris floribunda	Mountain andromeda	1800	5
Pieris japonica	Japanese andromeda	1870	5
Pinus nigra 'Pygmaea'	Dwarf Austrian pine	1860	4
Pinus strobus 'Brevifolia'		1855	3
Pinus strobus 'Nana'		1855	3
Pinus strobus 'Prostrata'		1893	3
Pinus strobus 'Umbraculifera'	Umbrella eastern white pine	1855	3
Pittosporum tobira	Japanese pittosporum	1804	8
Poncirus trifoliata	Hardy orange	1850	6
Potentilla fruticosa	Bush cinquefoil	1850?	2
Potentilla fruticosa 'Friedrichsenii'		1895	2
Potentilla fruticosa 'Ochroleuca'		1902	3
Potentilla fruticosa 'Veitchii'		1900	3
Prinsepia sinensis	Cherry prinsepia	1896	4
Prunus armeniaca (many cvs.)	Apricot	1800	5
Prunus × cistena	Purple-leaf sand cherry	1910	2–8
Prunus japonica	Nakai Chinese bush cherry	1910	2
Prunus maritima	Beach plum	1800	4
Prunus pumila	Dwarf cherry	1800	3
Prunus tenella	Dwarf Russian almond	1683	2
Prunus tomentosa	Nanking cherry	1870	2
Prunus triloba var. *multiplex*	Double flowering plum	1885	3
Prunus virginiana	Chokecherry	1724	2
Ptelea trifoliata	Hop tree, water ash	1724	3–9
Pyracantha atalantioides	Gibbs firethorn	1910	6
Pyracantha coccinea	Scarlet firethorn	1629	6
Pyracantha coccinea 'Lalandei'	Lelande firethorn	1874	6
Pyracantha crenulata var. *rogersiana*	Rogers firethorn	1911	7
Pyracantha fortuneana	Chinese firethorn	1906	7
Quercus prinoides	Chinquapin oak	1800	5
Rhamnus caroliniana	Indian cherry	1727	5–9
Rhamnus cathartica	Common buckthorn	1800	2–7
Rhamnus davurica	Dahurian buckthorn	1817	2–7
Rhamnus frangula	Tall hedge	1800?	3
Rhapiolepis indica	Indian hawthorn	1806	8
Rhapiolepis umbellata	Yeddo rhapiolepis	1864	7
Rhododendron albrechtii	Albrecht azalea	1892	5
Rhododendron arborescens	Sweet azalea	1875	5
Rhododendron atlanticum	Coast azalea	1916	5–8
Rhododendron austrinum	Florida azalea	1914	7–9
Rhododendron calendulaceum	Flame azalea	1800	5
Rhododendron canadense	Rhodora	1800	2

Botanical Name	Common Name	Year of Introduction	Zone
Rhododendron canescens	Piedmont azalea	1730	5–9
Rhododendron carolinianum	Carolina rhododendron	1815	5
Rhododendron catawbiense	Catawba rhododendron	1819	4
Rhododendron decorum	Sweetshell rhododendron	1904	5
Rhododendron discolor	Mandarin rhododendron	1900	6
Rhododendron flammeum	Oconee azalea	1787	5–8
Rhododendron fortunei	Fortune rhododendron	1859	6
Rhododendron × *gandavense*	Ghent hybrid azaleas	1890	4
Rhododendron indicum	Indian azalea	1700	5
Rhododendron japonicum	Japanese azalea	1861	5
Rhododendron keiskei	Keisk rhododendron	1905	5
Rhododendron × *kosteranum*	Mollis hybrid azaleas	1872	5
Rhododendron luteum	Rosebay rhododendron	1792	5
Rhododendron maximum	Rosebay rhododendron	1736	4
Rhododendron mucronatum	Snow azalea	1819	5
Rhododendron mucronatum 'Narcissiflorum'		1850	5
Rhododendron mucronatum 'Plenum'		1819	5
Rhododendron mucronulatum	Korean rhododendron	1882	5
Rhododendron nudiflorum	Pinxter flower	1800	3
Rhododendron prinophyllum	Roseshell azalea	1812	4–8
Rhododendron prunifolium	Plumleaf azalea	1918	7
Rhododendron racemosum	Mayflower rhododendron	1889	5
Rhododendron roseum	Roseshell azalea	1800	3
Rhododendron schlippenbachii	Royal azalea	1893	6
Rhododendron smirnowii	Smirnow rhododendron	1886	4
Rhododendron vaseyi	Pinkshell azalea	1900	4
Rhododendron viscosum	Swamp azalea	1731	4
Rhododendron yedoense	Yodogawa azalea	1884	5
Rhododendron yedoense var. *poukhanense*		1905	4
Rhus aromatica	Fragrant sumac	1759	3–9
Rhus chinensis	Chinese sumac	1784	5
Rhus copallina	Shining sumac	1688	4–9
Rhus glabra	Smooth sumac	1620	2–9
Rhus glabra 'Laciniata'		1875	2–9
Rhus trilobata	Skunkbush sumac	1877	4
Rhus typhina	Staghorn sumac	1629	3–8
Rhus typhina 'Dissecta'		1900	4
Rhus typhina 'Laciniata'	Cut-leaf sumac	1750	4
Ribes alpinum	Alpine currant	1700	2–7
Ribes alpinum 'Aureum'		1881	2–7

Botanical Name	Common Name	Year of Introduction	Zone
Ribes odoratum	Clove currant	1812	4
Robinia hispida	Rose acacia	1800	5
Rosa × alba	White rose	1800	5
Rosa × alba 'Incarnata'	Cottage rose	1800	4
Rosa amblyotis	Kamchatka rose	1917	2
Rosa banksiae	Banks rose	1870	7
Rosa canina	Dog rose	1800	3
Rosa carolina	Carolina rose	1800	4
Rosa centifolia	Cabbage rose	1800	5
Rosa centifolia var. *muscosa*	Moss rose	1800	5
Rosa centifolia var. *parvifolia*	Burgundian rose	1800	5
Rosa damascena	Damask rose	1800	4
Rosa eglanteria	Sweetbrier	1750	5
Rosa foetida	Austrian brier	1800	5
Rosa foetida 'Persiana'	Yellow rose	1800	5
Rosa gallica	French rose	1750	5
Rosa gallica 'Officinalis'	Apothecary rose	1750	5
Rosa gallica 'Versicolor'	Thorny rose	1800	5
Rosa × harisonii	Harison's yellow rose	1830	4
Rosa helenae	Helen rose	1907	5
Rosa hugonis	Father Hugo rose	1899	5
Rosa laevigata	Cherokee rose	1804	7
Rosa moschata	Musk rose	1800	5
Rosa moyesii	Moyes rose	1894	5
Rosa multiflora	Japanese rose	1886	5
Rosa odorata	Tea rose	1810	7
Rosa omeiensis	Omei rose	1901	4
Rosa palustris	Swamp rose	1800	4
Rosa pendulina	Alpine rose	1789	5
Rosa primula	Primrose rose	1910	5
Rosa roxburghii	Roxburgh rose	1828	5
Rosa rubrifolia	Redleaf rose	1814	2
Rosa rugosa	Rugosa rose	1845	4
Rosa spinosissima	Scotch rose	1800	4
Rosa virginiana	Virginia rose	before 1900	3
Rosa wichuraiana	Memorial rose	1891	5
Rubus idaeus	Flowering raspberry	1800	3
Rubus odoratus	Rose-flowering raspberry	1800	3
Ruscus aculeatus	Butcher's broom	1750	7
Salix caprea	Goat willow	1800	4–8
Salix caprea 'Pendula'	Weeping pussy willow	1860	4–8
Salix melanostachys	Black pussy willow	1900?	5

Botanical Name	Common Name	Year of Introduction	Zone
Sambucus canadensis	American elder	1761	3–9
Sambucus pubens	Scarlet elder	1812	4
Sambucus racemosa	European red elder	1700	3–6
Sarcococca ruscifolia	Fragrant sarcococca	1901	7
Sedum populifolium	Poplar sedum	1850	3
Shepherdia argentea	Buffalo berry	1850	2
Shepherdia canadensis	Russet buffalo berry	1850	2
Solanum pseudocapsicum	Jerusalem cherry	1800	9
Sorbaria aitchisonii	Kashmir false spirea	1895	5
Sorbaria arborea	Tree false spirea	1908	5
Sorbaria sorbifolia	Ural false spirea	1759	2–7
Sorbus tianshanica	Turkestan mountain ash	1895	5
Sorbus vilmorinii	Vilmorin mountain ash	1889	5
Spartium junceum	Spanish broom	1800	?
Spiraea albiflora	Japanese white spirea	1868	4
Spiraea × billiardi	Billiard spirea	1854	3
Spiraea bullata	Crispleaf spirea	1880	4
Spiraea × bumalda	Bumald spirea	1890	3–8
Spiraea × bumalda 'Anthony Waterer'		1890	5
Spiraea cantoniensis 'Lanceata'	Double Reeves spirea	1824	6–9
Spiraea × cinerea 'Grefsheim'		1884	4
Spiraea japonica	Japanese spirea	1870	5
Spiraea japonica 'Atrosanguinea'	Mikado spirea	1870	5
Spiraea × margaritae	Margarita spirea	1890	4
Spiraea × multiflora	Snow garland spirea	1884	4
Spiraea nipponica var. *rotundifolia*	Big Nippon spirea	1882	7
Spiraea prunifolia var. *plena*	Double-flowering bridal wreath	1843	4
Spiraea × superba	Striped spirea	1873	4
Spiraea thunbergii	Thunberg spirea	1863	4
Spiraea tomentosa	Steeplebush	1736	5
Spiraea trilobata	Three-lobe spirea	1801	3
Spiraea × vanhouttei	Van Houtte spirea	1866	4
Spiraea veitchii	Veitch spirea	1900	5
Spiraea wilsonii	Wilson spirea	1900	5
Stachyurus praecox		1865	6
Staphylea trifolia	American bladdernut	1640	3–8
Stephanandra incisa	Cutleaf stephanandra	1872	5
Stephanandra tanakae	Tanaka stephanandra	1893	5
Stranvaesia davidiana	Chinese stranvaesia	1917	7
Symphoricarpos albus	White hedge snowberry	1812	4
Symphoricarpus orbiculatus	Indian currant coralberry	1727	2–7

Botanical Name	Common Name	Year of Introduction	Zone
Symplocos paniculata	Sapphire berry	1875	4–8
Symplocos tinctoria	Horse-sugar	1780	7–9
Syringa amurensis var. *japonica*	Japanese tree lilac	1876	4
Syringa × *chinensis*	Chinese lilac	1800	6
Syringa × *henryi* 'Lutece'	'Lutece' lilac	1891	2
Syringa × *hyacinthiflora*		1876	3–8
Syringa josikaea	Hungarian lilac	1830	2
Syringa meyeri	Korean lilac	1908	4
Syringa microphylla	Littleleaf lilac	1910	4–8
Syringa oblata	Early lilac	1856	3
Syringa oblata var. *dilatata*		1917	3
Syringa patula	Manchurian lilac	1902	3–8
Syringa pekinensis	Pekin lilac	1881	3–7
Syringa × *persica*	Persian lilac	1614	4
Syringa potaninii	Daphne lilac	1905	6
Syringa villosa	Late lilac	1802	2–7
Syringa vulgaris	Common lilac	1700	3
Syringa vulgaris 'Adelaide Dunbar'		1916	3
Syringa vulgaris 'Alba'		1900	3
Syringa vulgaris 'Alphonse Lavellée'		1885	3
Syringa vulgaris 'Belle de Nancy'		1891	3
Syringa vulgaris 'Capitaine Baltet'		1919	3
Syringa vulgaris 'Cavour'		1910	3
Syringa vulgaris 'Charles Joly'		1896	3
Syringa vulgaris 'Charles X'		1830	3
Syringa vulgaris 'Congo'		1896	3
Syringa vulgaris 'Cristophe Colomb'		1905	3
Syringa vulgaris 'Decaisne'		1910	3
Syringa vulgaris 'De Miribel'		1903	3
Syringa vulgaris 'De Saussure'		1903	3
Syringa vulgaris 'Edith Cavell'		1916	3
Syringa vulgaris 'Ellen Willmott'		1903	3
Syringa vulgaris 'Jacques Callot'		1876	3
Syringa vulgaris 'Jan Van Tol'		1916	3
Syringa vulgaris 'Jeanne d'Arc'		1902	3
Syringa vulgaris 'Léon Gambetta'		1907	3
Syringa vulgaris 'Lucie Baltet'		1888	3
Syringa vulgaris 'Ludwig Spaeth'		1883	3
Syringa vulgaris 'Macrostachya'		1844	3
Syringa vulgaris 'Marc Micheli'		1898	3
Syringa vulgaris 'Maréchal Lannes'		1916	3
Syringa vulgaris 'Marie Legraye'		1879	3

Botanical Name	Common Name	Year of Introduction	Zone
Syringa vulgaris 'Mme. Antoine Buchner'		1909	3
Syringa vulgaris 'Mme. Casimir Perier'		1894	3
Syringa vulgaris 'Mme. Florent Stepman'		1908	3
Syringa vulgaris 'Mme. F. Morel'		1892	3
Syringa vulgaris 'Mme. Lemoine'		1890	3
Syringa vulgaris 'Monge'		1913	3
Syringa vulgaris 'Mont Blanc'		1910	3
Syringa vulgaris 'Olivier de Serres'		1909	3
Syringa vulgaris 'Paul Hariot'		1902	3
Syringa vulgaris 'Paul Thirion'		1915	3
Syringa vulgaris 'President Carnot'		1890	3
Syringa vulgaris 'Président Grévy'		1886	3
Syringa vulgaris 'President Lincoln'		1916	3
Syringa vulgaris 'Président Poincaré'		1913	3
Syringa vulgaris 'Reamur'		1904	3
Syringa vulgaris 'Victor Lemoine'		1906	3
Syringa vulgaris 'Violetta'		1916	3
Syringa vulgaris 'Waldeck-Rosseau'		1904	3
Tamarix parviflora	Small-flowered tamarix	1853	4
Tamarix ramosissima	Five-stamen tamarix	1883	2
Taxus baccata	English yew	1775	6
Taxus baccata 'Adpressa'		1830	6
Taxus baccata 'Dovastoniana'		1800	6
Taxus baccata 'Fastigiata'		1800	6
Taxus baccata 'Lutea'		1830	6
Taxus baccata 'Pygmaea'		1912	6
Taxus canadensis	Canadian yew	1800	2–6
Taxus cuspidata	Spreading Japanese yew	1853	4
Taxus cuspidata 'Densa'	Dwarf yew	1900	4
Taxus × *media*	Anglojap yew	1900	5
Taxus × *media* 'Hicksii'	Hick's yew	1920?	4
Thuja occidentalis 'Compacta'	Douglas pyramidal arborvitae	1850	4
Thuja occidentalis 'Hoveyi'		1859	4
Thuja occidentalis 'Pumila'		1900	4
Thuja occidentalis 'Umbraculifera'		1891	4
Thuja occidentalis 'Wareana'		1860	4
Thuja occidentalis 'Woodwardii'		1860	4
Vaccinium angustifolium	Lowbush blueberry	1772	2
Vaccinium corymbosum	Highbush blueberry	1765	5

Botanical Name	Common Name	Year of Introduction	Zone
Vaccinium macrocarpon	American cranberry	1760	2–6
Vaccinium vitis-idaea	Cowberry	1800	6
Vaccinium vitis-idaea var. *minus*	Mountain cranberry	1900?	2
Viburnum acerifolium	Maple-leaved viburnum	1800	3
Viburnum alnifolium	Alder-leaved viburnum	1800	3
Viburnum × *burkwoodi*	Burkwood viburnum	1924	5
Viburnum carlesii	Mayflower or Korean spice viburnum	1902	5
Viburnum davidii	David viburnum	1904	7
Viburnum dentatum	Arrowwood viburnum	1800	2
Viburnum dilatatum	Linden viburnum	1845	5
Viburnum farreri	Fragrant viburnum	1910	5
Viburnum grandiflorum		1914	7
Viburnum henryi	Henry viburnum	1901	7
Viburnum japonicum	Japanese viburnum	1859	7
Viburnum lantana	Wayfaring tree	1800	3
Viburnum lentago	Sweet viburnum	1800	2
Viburnum lobophyllum		1901	5
Viburnum macrocephalum	Chinese snowball	1844	6
Viburnum nudum	Possum haw	1800	6
Viburnum opulus	European cranberry bush	1800	5
Viburnum opulus 'Sterile'	Snowball bush, Guelder rose	1800	?
Viburnum plicatum	Japanese snowball	1814	6
Viburnum prunifolium	Black haw	1738	4
Viburnum rhytidophyllum	Leatherleaf viburnum	1900	5
Viburnum sargentii 'Flavum'	Yellow Sargent cranberry bush	1904	4
Viburnum setigerum 'Aurantiacum'	Tea viburnum	1907	6
Viburnum sieboldii	Siebold viburnum	1880	5
Viburnum tinus	Laurustinus	1800	7
Viburnum trilobum	American cranberry bush	1800	2
Viburnum wrightii	Wright viburnum	1892	6
Weigela florida	Old-fashioned weigela	1845	5
Weigela florida var. *venusta*		1905	5
Weigela middendorffiana	Middendorff weigela	1850	4
Xanthoceras sorbifolium	Shinyleaf yellowhorn	1866	5
Zanthoxylum clava-herculis	Southern prickly ash	1744	8

Trees

Botanical Name	Common Name	Year of Introduction	Zone
Abies alba	Silver fir	1761	5
Abies balsamea	Balsam fir	1696	3–5
Abies concolor	White fir	1872	3–7
Abies fraseri	Fraser fir	1811	4–7
Abies lasiocarpa	Alpine fir	1900	3
Abies pinsapo	Spanish fir	1837	6
Abies procera	Noble fir	1900	5
Acacia nilotica ssp. *tomentosa*	Gum-arabic tree	1800	9
Acer barbatum	Southern sugar maple	1800	7–9
Acer circinatum	Vine maple	1900	5
Acer griseum	Paperbark maple	1901	5
Acer japonicum	Full-moon maple	1864	5
Acer negundo	Box elder	1800	2
Acer palmatum (and many later cvs.)	Japanese maple	1820	6
Acer palmatum 'Atropurpureum'	Redleaf Japanese maple	1890	6
Acer pensylvanicum	Striped maple	1755	3
Acer platanoides	Norway maple	1762	4
Acer platanoides 'Columnare'	Column maple	1855	4
Acer pseudoplatanus	Planetree maple	1750	4–7
Acer rubrum	Red maple	1860	3–9
Acer saccharinum	Silver maple	1725	3–9
Acer saccharum	Sugar or rock maple	1753	3–8
Acer spicatum	Mountain maple	1750	2
Aesculus glabra	Ohio buckeye	1800	3
Aesculus hippocastanum	Common horse chestnut	1576	3
Aesculus octandra	Sweet buckeye	1764	3–8
Ailanthus altissima	Tree of heaven	1784	4–8
Albizia julibrissin	Albizia	1745	6–9
Ambrosia eliator	Oak of Cappadocia	1750	?
Annona reticulata	Bullock's heart	1800	10
Aralia elata	Japanese angelica tree	1830	3
Aralia spinosa	Devil's walking stick	1688	4–9
Arbutus unedo	Strawberry tree	1800	8
Asimina triloba	Pawpaw	1736	5–9
Betula albo-sinensis	Chinese paper birch	1910	5
Betula davurica	Dahurian birch	1883	5
Betula lenta	Sweet birch	1800	3–8
Betula maximowicziana	Monarch birch	1888	5
Betula nana	Dwarf birch	1789	2

Botanical Name	Common Name	Year of Introduction	Zone
Betula nigra	River birch	1800	5
Betula occidentalis	Water birch	1874	4
Betula papyrifera	Canoe birch	1800	2
Betula pendula	European white birch	1750	4
Betula populifolia	Gray birch	1780	3–6
Betula schmidtii	Schmidt birch	1896	5
Carpinus betulus	European hornbeam	1750	5
Carpinus caroliniana	American hornbeam, ironwood	1800	3
Carpinus cordata	Heartleaf hornbeam	1879	5
Carpinus japonica	Japanese hornbeam	1879	4
Carpinus orientalis	Oriental hornbeam	1739	5
Carya aquatica	Bitter pecan	1800	7
Carya cordiformis	Bitternut hickory	1689	4
Carya glabra	Pignut or red hickory	1750	4
Carya illinoinensis	Pecan	1760	5
Carya laciniosa	Shellbark hickory	1800	5
Carya ovata	Shagbark hickory	1629	4
Carya tomentosa	Mockernut hickory	1800	4
Castanea crenata	Japanese chestnut	1876	6
Castanea dentata	American chestnut	1800	4
(now almost extinct)			
Castanea mollissima	Chinese chestnut	1903	5
Castanea pumila	Chinquapin chestnut	1800	6
Castanea sativa	Spanish chestnut	1853	6
Catalpa bignonioides	Southern catalpa	1728	5
Catalpa speciosa	Northern catalpa	1754	4
Cedrus atlantica	Atlas cedar	1840	6
Cedrus deodara	Deodar cedar	1831	7
Cedrus libani	Cedar of Lebanon	c. 1740	6
Celtis occidentalis	Nettle tree	1636	2–9
Cercidiphyllum japonicum	Katsura tree	1865	5
Cercis canadensis	Eastern redbud	1641	4
Cercis chinensis	Chinese redbud	1850	6
Chamaecyparis nootkatensis	Alaska cedar	1853	6
Chamaecyparis obtusa	Hinoki false cypress	1861	6
Chamaecyparis pisifera	Sawara cypress	1861	4
Chamaecyparis thyoides	White cedar	1800	3
Chionanthus virginicus	Fringe tree	1735	5
Cinnamomum camphora	Camphor tree	1800	9
Citrus × limonia	Lemon	1800	10
Cladrastis lutea	American yellowwood	1812	3
Clerodendrum trichotomum	Harlequin glorybower	1880	6

Botanical Name	Common Name	Year of Introduction	Zone
Cornus alternifolia	Pagoda dogwood	1760	3
Cornus amomum	Silky dogwood	1658	5
Cornus controversa	Giant dogwood	1880	5
Cornus controversa 'Variegata'	Variegated giant dogwood	1893	5
Cornus florida	Flowering dogwood	1731	4
Cornus florida 'Pendula'	Weeping white dogwood	1880	6
Cornus kousa	Kousa dogwood	1875	6
Cornus mas	Cornelian cherry	1750	4–8
Cornus mas 'Aureo-elegantissima'	'Elegantissima' cornelian cherry	1872	4–8
Cornus racemosa	Gray dogwood	1800	4
Corylus americana	American filbert	1800	4
Corylus avellana	European filbert	1800	3
Corylus colurna	Turkish filbert	1700	4–7
Corylus cornuta	Beaked filbert	1745	4
Crataegus crus galli	Cockspur hawthorn	1656	3–7
Crataegus laevigata	English hawthorn	1750	4
Crataegus mollis	Downy hawthorn	1800	3
Crataegus monogyna	Singleseed hawthorn	1800	4–7
Crataegus nitida	Glossy hawthorn	1883	4
Crataegus phaenopyrum	Washington hawthorn	1738	3–8
Crataegus viridis	Green hawthorn	1800?	5
Cryptomeria japonica	Cryptomeria	1861	6–8
Cudrania tricuspidata	Silkworm tree	1862	7
Cunninghamia lanceolata	Common China fir	1804	7–9
Cupressus sempervirens	Italian cypress	1800	7–8
Cydonia oblonga	Quince	1850	5
Davidia involucrata	Dove tree	1904	6–8
Diospyros virginiana	Persimmon	1800	4
Elaeagnus angustifolia	Russian olive	1850	4
Elaeagnus pungens	Thorny elaeagnus	1830	4
Elaeagnus umbellata	Autumn olive	1830	4
Elliottia racemosa	Georgia plume	1813	5–8
Erythrina corallodendrum		1800	10
Eucommia ulmoides	Hardy rubber tree	1896	5
Evodia daniellii	Korean evodia	1905	4–8
Fagus grandiflora	American beech	1800	4
Fagus grandifolia	American beech	1800	3–9
Fagus sylvatica	European beech	1750	4–7
Fagus sylvatica 'Dawyck'	'Dawycle' European beech	1913	5
Fagus sylvatica f. *laciniata*	Cutleaf European beech	1792	5
Fagus sylvatica f. *pendula*	Weeping beech	1900	5
Fagus sylvatica f. *purpurea*	Purple beech	1772	5

Botanical Name	Common Name	Year of Introduction	Zone
Fagus sylvatica 'Purpurea pendula'	Weeping purple beech	1870	5
Fagus sylvatica 'Riversii'	Rivers purple beech	1869	5
Fagus sylvatica 'Rohanii'	Rohan European beech	1894	5
Fagus sylvatica 'Tortuosa'		1845	5
Fagus sylvatica 'Zlatia'	Golden beech	1890	5
Feijoa sellowiana	Guava	1819	8
Ficus carica	Common fig	1800	8
Ficus pumila	Climbing fig	1759	8
Firmiana simplex	Chinese parasol tree	1757	7–9
Franklinia alatamaha	Franklin tree	1770	5–8
Fraxinus americana	White ash	1724	3–9
Fraxinus angustifolia	Narrowleaf ash	1800	5
Fraxinus nigra	Black ash	1800	2
Fraxinus ornus	Flowering ash	1700	5
Fraxinus pennsylvanica	Green ash	1824	3–9
Fraxinus quadrangulata	Blue ash	1823	4–7
Ginkgo biloba	Maidenhead tree	1784	5
Gleditsia aquatica	Water locust	1800	8
Gleditsia triacanthos	Common honey locust	1700	4
Gleditsia triacanthos var. *inermis*	Thornless common honey locust	1700	5
Gordonia lasianthus	Loblolly bay gordonia	1800	8
Grevillea robusta	Silk oak	1900	10
Gymnocladus dioca	Kentucky coffee tree	1748	3–8
Halesia carolina	Carolina silverbell	1756	5
Halesia diptera	Two-winged silverbell	1758	5
Halesia monticola	Mountain silverbell	1897	5
Halimodendron halodendron	Salt tree	1779	2
Hovenia dulcis	Japanese raisin tree	1850	5
Ilex aquifolium	English holly	1750	6
Ilex cassine	Dahoon	1800	7
Juglans cinerea	Butternut	1633	3–7
Juglans nigra	Black walnut	1686	4
Juglans regia	Persian or English walnut	1750	6
Juniperus chinensis 'Keteleerii'		1905	4
Juniperus chinensis 'Pyramidalis'	Hollywood juniper	1907	7
Juniperus drupacea	Alligator juniper	1853	7
Juniperus excelsa	Greek juniper	1836	7
Juniperus virginiana	Eastern red cedar	1664	2–9
Juniperus virginiana 'Canaertii'		1868	2–9
Juniperus virginiana var. *glauca*	Silver red cedar	1850	2–9
Juniperus virginiana var. *pendula*	Weeping red cedar	1855	2–9
Juniperus virginiana var. *venusta*		1915	2–9

Botanical Name	Common Name	Year of Introduction	Zone
Kalopanax pictus	Castor aralia	1865	4
Keteleeria fortunei	Fortune keteleeria	1845	7
Koelreuteria paniculata	Goldenrain tree	1763	5
Laburnum alpinum	Scotch laburnum	1750	4
Laburnum anagyroides	Golden-chain tree	1700	5
Laburnum × watereri	Golden-chain tree	1864	6
Lagerstroemia indica	Crape myrtle	1747	7
Larix decidua	European larch	1750	2–6
Larix kaempferi	Japanese larch	1861	5
Larix laricina	Eastern larch	1737	1–4
Laurus nobilis	Bay, sweet bay, laurel	1750	7
Liquidambar formosana	Formosan sweet gum	1907	6
Liquidambar styraciflua	American sweet gum	1681	5
Liriodendron tulipifera	Tulip poplar	1664	4–9
Maackia amurensis	Amur maackia	1864	5
Maclura pomifera	Osage orange	1818	5
Magnolia acuminata	Cucumber tree	1736	3–8
Magnolia cordata	Yellow cucumber tree	1800	5
Magnolia dawsoniana	Dawson magnolia	1908	7
Magnolia fraseri	Fraser magnolia	1776	5
Magnolia grandiflora	Southern magnolia	1734	6–9
Magnolia heptapeta	Yulan magnolia	1789	5
Magnolia hypoleuca	Whiteleaf Japanese magnolia	1865	5
Magnolia kobus	Kobus magnolia	1865	4
Magnolia macrophylla	Bigleaf magnolia	1800	5
Magnolia nitida	Shinyleaf magnolia	1917	8
Magnolia rostrata		1917	9
Magnolia sieboldii	Oyama magnolia	1865	6
Magnolia × soulangiana	Saucer magnolia	1820	6
Magnolia × soulangiana 'Alba'		1867	6
Magnolia × soulangiana 'Alexandrina'		1851	6
Magnolia × soulangiana 'André LeRoy'		1851	6
Magnolia × soulangiana 'Lennei'		1852	6
Magnolia × soulangiana 'Rustica'		1893	6
Magnolia × soulangiana 'Speciosa'		1830	6
Magnolia sprengeri	Sprenger magnolia	1901	7
Magnolia stellata	Star magnolia	1862	6
Magnolia tripetala	Umbrella magnolia	1752	4–7
Magnolia virginiana	Sweetbay magnolia	1688	5–9
Malus × arnoldiana	Arnold crab apple	1883	4

Botanical Name	Common Name	Year of Introduction	Zone
Malus × *atrosanguinea*	Carmine crab apple	1889	4
Malus baccata	Siberian crab apple	1800	2
Malus × 'Bob White'		1876	4
Malus 'Dolgo'		1917	3
Malus floribunda	Japanese flowering crab apple	1862	4
Malus halliana 'Parkmanii'	Parkman crab apple	1861	5
Malus hupehensis	Tea crab apple	1900	5
Malus ioensis 'Plena'	Bechtel crab apple	1888	2
Malus × *robusta*	Cherry crab apple	1815	3
Malus × *scheideckeri*	Scheidecker crab apple	1888	4
Malus sieboldii var. *arborescens*	Tree Toringo crab apple	1892	5
Malus spectabilis 'Riversii'	River's crab apple	1883	4
Malus toringoides	Cutleaf crab apple	1904	5
Malus × *zumi* var. *calocarpa*	Redbud crab apple	1892	5
Melia azedarach	Chinaberry tree	1700	7
Mespilus germanica	Medlar	1800	5
Michelia figo	Banana shrub	1789	7–9
Morus alba	White mulberry	1650	4–8
Morus nigra	Black mulberry	1800	6
Morus rubra	Red mulberry	1629	5–9
Myrica cerifera	Wax myrtle	1699	7
Myroxylon pereirae		1800	8
Nyssa aquatica	Water tupelo	1735	6–9
Nyssa sylvatica	Sour gum	1750	3–9
Olea europaea	European olive	1900	9
Ostrya virginiana	American hop hornbeam	1690	3–9
Oxydendrum arboreum	Sourwood	1747	5
Parrotia persica	Persian parrotia	1840	6
Paulownia tormentosa	Royal paulownia	1834	5–9
Persea americana	American avocado	1900	10
Persea borbonia	Red bay	1800	7
Phellodendron amurense	Amur cork tree	1856	4
Philesia magellanica	Magellan box lily	1847	8
Phillyrea latifolia	Tree phillyrea	1800	7
Phoenix dactylifera	Date palm	1900	10
Picea abies	Norway spruce	1776	2–7
Picea abies 'Clanbrassiliana'	Barry spruce	1836	4
Picea breweriana	Brewer spruce	1897	5
Picea engelmannii	Engelmann spruce	1862	2
Picea glauca	White or Canadian spruce	1700	2
Picea glauca 'Conica'	Dwarf Alberta spruce	1904	3
Picea koyamai	Koyama spruce	1914	4

Botanical Name	Common Name	Year of Introduction	Zone
Picea mariana	Black spruce	1700	2
Picea omorika	Serbian spruce	1880	4
Picea orientalis	Oriental spruce	1837	4–7
Picea pungens	Colorado spruce	1862	3
Picea rubens	Red spruce	1750	2
Picea smithiana	Himalayan spruce	1818	5
Picea wilsonii	Wilson spruce	1901	5
Pinckneya pubens	Feverbark	1800	8
Pinus aristata	Bristlecone pine	1861	5
Pinus banksiana	Jack pine	1783	3
Pinus bungeana	Lacebark pine	1846	4
Pinus canariensis	Canary pine	1850	8
Pinus cembra	Swiss stone pine	1875	3
Pinus densiflora 'Oculus-draconis'	Japanese red pine	1854	5
Pinus echinata	Shortleaf pine	1800	6–9
Pinus flexilis	Limber pine	1861	4
Pinus halepensis	Aleppo pine	1800	9
Pinus jeffreyi	Jeffrey pine	1853	5
Pinus koraiensis	Korean pine	1861	4
Pinus monticola	Western white pine	1900	6
Pinus mugo var. *mugo*	Mugo pine	1779	3
Pinus nigra	Austrian pine	1759	4
Pinus palustris	Southern yellow pine	1800	7
Pinus parviflora	Japanese white pine	1861	6
Pinus peuce	Balkan pine	1863	4
Pinus pinaster	Cluster pine	1800	7
Pinus ponderosa	Ponderosa pine	1827	3–7
Pinus pumila	Dwarf Siberian pine	1807	5
Pinus pungens	Prickly pine	1800	6
Pinus resinosa	Red pine	1756	3
Pinus rigida	Pitch pine	1759	5
Pinus strobus	White pine	1705	3
Pinus sylvestris	Scotch pine	1775	3
Pinus taeda	Loblolly pine	1800	6
Pinus thunbergii	Japanese black pine	1855	5
Pinus virginiana	Jersey pine	1800	4
Pinus wallichiana	Himalayan pine	1827	5
Pistacia chinensis	Chinese pistache	1890	6–9
Platanus × *acerifolia*	London plane tree	1750	6
Platanus occidentalis	Plane tree	1800	4–9
Populus alba	White poplar	1784	3
Populus balsamifera		1800	2

Botanical Name	Common Name	Year of Introduction	Zone
Populus candicans		1800	2
Populus deltoides	Northern cottonwood, white poplar	1800	2
Populus grandidentata	Bigtooth aspen	1772	3
Populus heterophylla	Black cottonwood	1800	2
Populus nigra	Black poplar	1800	2
Populus nigra 'Italica'	Lombardy poplar	1800	3–9
Populus tremula	European aspen	1800	2
Populus tremuloides	Quaking aspen	1812	1
Prunus amygdalus	Almond	1750	3
Prunus avium	Bird or sweet cherry	1750	3
Prunus avium 'Plena'	Double-flowered mazzard cherry	1878	3
Prunus × *blireiana*	Blireiana plum	1906	5
Prunus campanulata	Taiwan cherry	1899	6–9
Prunus caroliniana	Carolina cherry laurel	1800	7
Prunus cerasifera 'Atropurpurea'	Pissard plum	1890	4
Prunus cerasus	Sour cherry, morello cherry	1750	3
Prunus domestica	Garden plum	1800	5
Prunus glandulosa	White flowering almond	1835	6
Prunus laurocerasus 'Zabeliana'		1898	5
Prunus lusitanica	Portuguese laurel	1648	7–9
Prunus maackii	Amur chokecherry	1878	2–6
Prunus mahaleb	Mahaleb cherry	1800	6
Prunus maximowiczii	Miyama cherry	1892	4
Prunus mume	Japanese apricot	1844	6
Prunus nipponica	Nipponese cherry	1915	5
Prunus padus	European bird cherry	1776	3
Prunus pensylvanica	Pin cherry	1773	2
Prunus persica	Common peach	1750	5
Prunus persica 'Semiplena'	Double-flowering peach	1800	6
Prunus persica var. *nucipersica*	Nectarine	1800	?
Prunus serotina	Black cherry	1629	3–9
Prunus serrula		1908	5
Prunus serrulata	Japanese flowering cherry	1900	6
Prunus subhirtella 'Autumnalis'	Autumn-flowering Higan cherry	1894	6
Prunus subhirtella 'Pendula'	Weeping Higan cherry	1862	6
Prunus yedoensis	Yoshino cherry	1902	5–8
Pseudocydonia sinensis	Chinese quince	1800	5
Pseudolarix kaempferi	Golden larch	1854	5
Pseudotsuga menziesii	Douglas fir	1827	4–6
Pterocarya fraxinifolia	Caucasian wingnut	1782	5–8
Pterocarya × *rehderana*	Rehder wingnut	1879	5–8
Petrocarya stenoptera	Chinese wingnut	1860	6

Botanical Name	Common Name	Year of Introduction	Zone
Pterostyrax hispidus	Fragrant epaulette tree	1875	4–8
Punica granatum	Pomegranate	1700	7
Punica granatum 'Nana'	Pomegranate	1750	7
Pyrus calleryana	Callery pear	1908	5
Pyrus communis	Common pear	1800	4–8
Pyrus salicifolia	Willowleaf pear	1780	4
Pyrus ussuriensis	Ussurian pear	1855	3
Quercus acutissima	Sawtooth oak	1862	6
Quercus agrifolia	California live oak	1900	9
Quercus alba	White oak	1750	4
Quercus cerris	Turkey oak	1735	6
Quercus coccinea	Scarlet oak	1800	5
Quercus engleriana	Engler's oak	1900	7
Quercus falcata	Spanish oak	1800	5
Quercus glauca	Blue Japanese oak	1878	8–9
Quercus ilex	Holly oak	1776	9
Quercus ilicifolia	Scrub oak	1800	5
Quercus laurifolia	Laurel oak	1786	6
Quercus libani	Lebanon oak	1855	5
Quercus lyrata	Overcup oak	1786	5–10
Quercus marilandica	Blackjack oak	1800	6
Quercus muehlenbergii	Chinquapin oak	1822	5
Quercus myrsinifolia	Chinese evergreen oak	1854	7–9
Quercus nigra	Black oak	1723	6–9
Quercus palustris	Swamp oak	1770	4–8
Quercus phellos	Willow oak	1736	5–9
Quercus prinus	Chestnut oak	1688	4
Quercus robur	English oak	1750	4–8
Quercus rubra	Red oak	1800	3
Quercus stellata	Post oak	1819	5
Quercus suber	Cork oak	1825	7
Quercus velutina	Yellow-bark oak	1800	4
Quercus virginiana	Live oak	1800	7
Robinia pseudoacacia	False acacia	1800	3–8
Robinia pseudoacacia 'Aurea'		1864	3–8
Robinia pseudoacacia 'Bessoniana'		1871	3–8
Robinia pseudoacacia 'Decaisneana'		1863	3–8
Robinia pseudoacacia 'Semperflorens'		1874	3–8
Robinia viscosa	Clammy locust	1800	3
Sabal palmetto	Palmetto	1800	8
Salix alba	White willow	1750	2

Botanical Name	Common Name	Year of Introduction	Zone
Salix alba 'Chermesina'	Redstem willow	1850	2
Salix alba 'Vitellina Tristis'		1814	2
Salix babylonica	Weeping willow	1730	6
Salix gracilistyla	Rosegold pussy willow	1900	5
Salix matsudana 'Tortuosa'	Corkscrew willow	1923	4
Salix purpurea	Purple osier willow	1900	3
Sassafras albidum	Sassafras	1800	4
Sophora japonica	Scholar tree	1747	5
Sorbus alnifolia	Korean mountain ash	1892	5
Sorbus americana	American ash	1811	2
Sorbus aria	White beam mountain ash	1830	5
Sorbus aucuparia	European mountain ash, rowan	1750	3
Sorbus domestica	Service tree	1800	6
Stewartia koreana	Japanese stewartia	1917	6
Stewartia malacodendron	Silky stewartia	1800	7–9
Stewartia ovata	Mountain stewartia	1800	5–9
Stewartia pseudocamellia	Japanese stewartia	1874	5–8
Stewartia sinensis	Chinese stewartia	1901	5
Styrax americanus	Carolina storax tree	1756	5
Styrax japonicus	Japanese snowbell	1862	5
Styrax obassia	Fragrant snowbell	1878	5
Swietenia mahagoni	West Indian mahogany	1800	10
Syringa reticulata	Japanese tree lilac	1881	4
Taxodium ascendens	Pond bald cypress	1789	4–9
Taxodium distichum	Bald cypress	1640	5
Thuja occidentalis	Common arborvitae	1700	5
Thuja occidentalis 'Lutea'	George Peabody arborvitae	1873	4
Thuja orientalis	Oriental arborvitae	1737	6
Thuja plicata	Giant or western arborvitae	1900	5
Thuja standishii	Japanese arborvitae	1860	5
Thujopsis dolabrata	Hiba false arborvitae	1861	6
Tilia americana	Linden	1752	2–8
Tilia cordata	Littleleaf linden	1775	4
Tilia × *euchlora*	Crimean linden	1860	3–7
Tilia × *europaea*	Common linden	1750	3–7
Tilia heterophylla	Bee-tree linden	1752	5–9
Tilia mongolica	Mongolian lime	1880	4
Tilia petiolaris	Pendent silver linden	1840	5
Tilia platyphyllos	Bigleaf linden	1800	3
Tilia tomentosa	Silver linden	1800	4
Torreya nucifera	Japanese torreya	1860	5
Tsuga canadensis	Canadian hemlock	1800	4

Botanical Name	Common Name	Year of Introduction	Zone
Tsuga canadensis 'Dawsoniana'		1920	5
Tsuga canadensis 'Macrophylla'		1891	5
Tsuga canadensis 'Pendula'	Sargent weeping hemlock	1870	4
Tsuga caroliniana	Carolina hemlock	1800	5
Tsuga diversifolia	Japanese hemlock	1861	5
Ulmus alata	Winged elm	1820	6–9
Ulmus americana	American white elm	1785	2
Ulmus carpinifolia	Smoothleaf elm	1850	4
Ulmus glabra	Scotch elm	1800	5
Ulmus glabra 'Camperdownii'	Camperdown elm, umbrella tree	1800	5
Ulmus parvifolia	Chinese elm	1794	5
Ulmus procera	English elm	1800	5
Ulmus pumila	Siberian elm	1860	3
Ulmus rubra	Slippery elm	1830	3–9
Zanthoxylum americanum	Prickly ash, toothache tree	1800	4
Zelkova serrata		1860	5–8

Vines

Botanical Name	Common Name	Year of Introduction	Zone
Actinidia arguta	Bower actinidia	1874	4
Actinidia kolomikta	Kiwi vine	1855	5
Adlumia fungosa	Climbing fumitory	1850	annual
Akebia quinata	Fiveleaf akebia	1845	4 or 5
Ampelopsis aconitifolia	Monk's hood vine	1868	4
Ampelopsis arborea	Peppervine	1700	7–9
Ampelopsis brevipedunculata	Porcelain ampelopsis	1870	4–8
Apios tuberosa (americana)	Groundnut	1750	4
Aristolochia durior	Dutchman's pipe	1750	4
Aristolochia serpentaria	Virginia snakeroot	1900	4
Bignonia capreolata	Cross vine	1750	6
Campsis grandiflora	Chinese trumpet vine	1800	7
Campsis radicans	Trumpet vine	1750	4
Campsis × *tagliabuana* 'Madame Galen'	'Madam Galen' trumpet creeper	1858	4
Celastrus scandens	American bittersweet	1800	2
Clematis heracleifolia	Solitary blue clematis, bush clematis	1868	?
Clematis × *jackmanii*	Jackman clematis	c. 1860	6
Clematis montana 'Rubens'	Pink anemone clematis	1900	5
Clematis paniculata	Sweet autumn clematis	1864	5
Clematis tangutica	Golden clematis	1890	5
Clematis virginiana	Virgin's bower	1720	4
Clematis vitalba (and many hybrids)	Traveler's joy	1820	6
Epigaea repens	Trailing arbutus, mayflower	1700	2
Gelsemium sempervirens	Evening trumpet flower	1640	6–9
Hedera helix	English ivy	1750	5–9
Hydrangea anomala ssp. *petiolaris*	Climbing hydrangea	1865	4
Ipomoea coccinea	Scarlet starglory	1800	annual
Jasminum grandiflorum	Catalonian jasmine	1800	8
Jasminum mesnyi	Primrose jasmine	1900	8
Jasminum nudiflorum	Winter jasmine	1844	6–10
Kadsura japonica	Scarlet kadsura	1846	7
Lonicera flava	Yellow honeysuckle	1750	5
Lonicera heckrotti	Goldflame honeysuckle	1895	5
Lonicera japonica	Honeysuckle	1860	5
Lonicera korolkowii	Blueleaf honeysuckle	1880	4
Lonicera sempervirens	Trumpet honeysuckle	1800	3
Menispermum canadense	Common moonseed	1646	4–8
Mina lobata	Crimson starglory	1900	annual

Botanical Name	Common Name	Year of Introduction	Zone
Momordica balsamina	Balsam apple	1800	?
Parthenocissus henryana	Silvervein creeper	1895	7–9
Parthenocissus quinquefolia	Woodbine	1800	3–4
Parthenocissus tricuspidata	Boston ivy	1862	5
Periploca graeca	Grecian silk vine	1763	6
Phaseolus coccineus	Scarlet runner bean	1800	annual
Phaseolus coccineus 'Albus'	White runner bean	1825	annual
Polygonum aubertii	Chinese fleece vine	1899	4 or 5
Thunbergia alata	Clock vine	1850	annual
Trachelospermum jasminoides	Confederate or star jasmine	1880	8
Tripterygium regelii	Regels threewingnut	1904	4
Wisteria floribunda	Japanese wisteria	1830	5
Wisteria × *formosa*	Formosa wisteria	1905	5
Wisteria frutescens	American wisteria	1800	5
Wisteria sinensis	Chinese wisteria	1816	5
Wisteria sinensis 'Alba'	White Chinese wisteria	1900?	5

Historic Gardens of Interest to the Old-Garden Enthusiast

The following is a short list of some of the gardens I have found to be of interest to the old-garden enthusiasts throughout the United States. While not all of these gardens have period plantings, many contain traditional features and plant materials that will be of great interest to the home gardener. If you don't find your favorite garden on this list, don't be offended. Instead, let us know, and we will be happy to add it to the list on our Web site (www.traditionalgardening.com.), which is constantly being expanded and updated and contains much more detailed information on some of these gardens, including pictures, hours, directions, and admission fees.

ALABAMA

Bellingrath Gardens
12401 Bellingrath Gardens Rd.
Theodore, AL 36582
334-973-2217, fax: 334-973-0540, Web site: bellingrath.org/gardens/
Renowned throughout the South, this 905-acre garden includes 65 acres arranged in a formal style, with numerous collections of flowers, trees, and native plants.

Ordeman Shaw House and Garden
310 North Hull St.
Montgomery, AL 36104
334-240-4500, fax: 334-240-4519
A fine example of southern urban architecture, the house is surrounded by period grounds and outbuildings typical of the 1850s.

ARIZONA

Boyce Thompson Southwest Museum
37615 U.S. 60
Superior, AZ 85273
520-689-2723, fax: 520-689-5858, Web site: ag.arizona.edu/BTA
Founded in 1925, this 1,000-acre site also doubles as a research center for desert plants. The arboretum was designed by Franklin Jacob Crider and was the first of its kind in the Southwest.

Century House Museum and Gardens
240 Madison Ave.
Yuma, AZ 85364
520-782-1841, fax: 520-783-0680, E-mail: azhist.yuma@juno.edu
Established in 1890, the gardens here feature a huge variety of plants and flowers as well as adobe buildings and an exotic-bird aviary.

Desert Botanical Garden
5800 E. Van Buren and 6400 E. McDowell Rds.
Phoenix, AZ 85008
602-941-1217, fax: 602-754-8124
A showcase for varieties of cacti and other succulents from around the world, this garden, begun in 1935, is located on 150 acres of natural desert.

CALIFORNIA

Balboa Park
1549 El Prado
San Diego, CA 92101
619-239-0512, fax: 619-235-3065
Dating to 1868, Balboa is famous for its diverse gardens: a Spanish garden, a traditional English garden, the Alcazar garden (which is modeled on a Moorish palace in Spain), and a desert garden. The park also contains a conservatory with various collections and offers exhibits.

Descanso Gardens
1418 Descanso Dr.
La Canada Flintridge, CA 91011
818-952-4400, fax: 818-790-3291, E-mail: descanso.com
Famous for its collections of roses and camellias (some 100,000 of the latter), Descanso also houses a Japanese garden as well as a rare Chinese garden. Although the estate gardens were private when built in 1930, visitors today have the option to view the gardens either from a hiking trail or by a train tour.

Filoli
Canada Rd.
Woodside, CA 94062
650-364-2880, fax: 650-366-7836, Web site: filoli.com
Citrus fruit trees, indigenous plants, and a 16-acre formal garden are among the highlights of this 1917 estate, whose name is an acronym for *fidelity, love, and life*. It is now the property of the National Trust for Historical Preservation.

Golden Gate Park and Strybing Arboretum
9th Ave. and Lincoln Way
San Francisco, CA 94122
415-661-1316, fax: 415-661-7427
Originally, the site of this 1,000-acre landmark was a sandy waste, which was

completely transformed in 1870 by William H. Hall into a lush and exotic landscape. Specialty gardens in the arboretum include the Shakespeare Garden, the Garden of Fragrance, and the Japanese Tea Garden, whose authenticity was assured with the help of several Japanese designers.

Huntington Botanical Gardens
1151 Oxford Rd.
San Marino, CA 91108
626-405-2160, fax: 626-405-2260, Web site: henry.huntington.org
Founded in 1905 by philanthropist Henry E. Huntington, this 200-acre garden's claim to fame rests on the fact that it houses the world's largest collection of outdoor desert plants. It also contains (to name but a few) cycad specimens, an Australian garden, and an herb garden, as well as the Huntington Library and Art Gallery.

J. Paul Getty Museum and Gardens
17895 Pacific Coast Hwy.
Malibu, CA 90265
310-459-7611, fax: 310-440-7723
The gardens and architecture have been re-created via archaeological research of the Roman Villa dei Papiri, complete with statuary, mosaics, and a reflecting pool. The plants featured were used in classical times, thus imbuing the gardens with an authentic feel.

La Purisima
2295 Purisima Rd.
Lompoc, CA 93436
805-733-1303, fax: 805-733-2497, E-mail: lapurmis@lapurisima.sbceo
.k12.ca.us
Built in the 1930s, this restoration of a Spanish Colonial garden may not be historically accurate, but it is one of the most popular garden attractions in the state, and deservedly so.

Octagon House
2645 Gough St.
San Francisco, CA 94123
415-441-7512
Showcasing this country's foremost examples of a 19th-century octagon plan, the site features a meticulous period garden.

Santa Barbara Mission
2201 Laguna St.
Santa Barbara, CA 93105
805-682-4713, fax: 805-687-7841
Founded in 1786, the mission offers a restored cloister garden and walled cemetery.

COLORADO

Denver Botanic Gardens
909 York St.
Denver, CO 80206
303-331-4000, fax: 303-331-4013, Web site: botanicgardens.org
Cacti and tropical plants, water gardens, annuals, and a children's garden are just some of the attractions of this botanical garden, which is actually divided into two principal areas within a 50-mile radius: the 50-acre Denver garden and the 150 acres on Mount Goliath. The latter includes native alpine plants at a 12,000-foot elevation.

CONNECTICUT

Bates-Scofield House
45 Old King's Highway 7 N.
Darien, CT 06820
203-655-9233
The gardens of this restored 18th-century house were designed in 1968. Authentic to the times, the gardens feature shrub roses, herbs, and medicinal plants. The site is also the headquarters of the Darien Historical Society.

Bowen Cottage
Rt. 169
Woodstock, CT 06281
860-928-4074
One of the oldest parterre gardens in New England is featured in this Gothic Revival house.

Brookfield Craft Center and Historical Museum
Brookfield Ctr.
Brookfield, CT 06804
203-740-8140
Carefully re-created from Colonial-era designs, the center features a true-to-period herb and flower garden.

Mark Twain House and Nook Farm
351 Farmington Ave.
Hartford, CT 06105
860-247-0998, fax: 860-278-8148
This site features a meticulously restored 18th-century Victorian house and grounds.

Putnam Cottage
243 E. Putnam Ave.
Greenwich, CT 06830
203-869-9697
The authentic 18th-century kitchen garden has fruits, plants, and herbs that can be dated back to 1690, when the original cottage was built.

DELAWARE

Nemours Mansion and Gardens
1600 Rockland Rd.
Wilmington, DE 19803
302-651-6912, fax: 302-651-6933
This early 1900s Louis XIV mansion sits on 300 acres surrounded by equally sumptuous gardens in the French Renaissance style.

Winterthur Gardens
Winterthur, DE 19735
302-888-4865, fax: 302-888-4960, Web site: udel.edu/winterthur
One of the loveliest gardens in the United States, Winterthur was the home of Henry Francis du Pont and is famous for its naturalistically styled gardens.

DISTRICT OF COLUMBIA

Dumbarton Oaks and Gardens
1703 32nd St., NW
Washington, DC 20007
202-339-6410, fax: 202-339-6419, Web site: doak.org
With spectacular gardens designed by Beatrix Farrand, this 1922 Georgetown estate is now owned by Harvard University. The gardens contain numerous areas of rare beauty and interest and were created to be particularly brilliant in spring and fall.

Audubon House and Garden
205 Whitehead St.
Key West, FL 33040
305-294-2116, fax: 305-294-4513, Web site: audubonhouse.com
Rare, exotic plants flank John James Audubon's 1830 house, which was restored in 1958.

Thomas A. Edison Winter Home and Botanical Gardens
2350 McGregor Blvd.
Fort Myers, FL 33901
941-334-7419, fax: 941-332-6684, Web site:
naples.net/~nfn.04538/home_i.htm
Between 1890 and 1930, Edison collected thousands of tropical trees and plants from the world over. These are on display in the 14-acre botanical garden.

Vizcaya Gardens
3251 S. Miami Ave.
Miami, FL 33129
305-856-4866, fax: 305-285-2004
A walled, secret garden can be found amidst the 10 acres of this re-creation of an Italian Renaissance villa. Built in 1912, the estate also possesses a large, Italianate formal garden.

GEORGIA

Atlanta Historical Museum
130 W. Paces Ferry Rd. NW
Atlanta, GA 30305
404-814-4000, fax: 404-814-4186, Web site: atlhist.org
The museum is part of a 26-acre historic complex of homes and gardens, which include Quarry Garden, Swan House and Gardens, and the Tullie Smith House. Featured are everything from an authentic 19th-century Georgia farmhouse and garden to the elegant, 1920s Palazzo Corsini–inspired Swan House, with its cascade, formal vistas, and nature trail.

Green-Meldrim House
14 W. Macon St.
Savannah, GA 31401
912-233-3845, fax: 912-232-5559
The house is an 1856 Gothic Revival with an authentic Victorian garden.

Isaiah Davenport House
324 E. State St.
Savannah, GA 31401
912-236-8097, fax: 912-233-7938
The 1821 house possesses a restored period garden.

Owens-Thomas House
124 Abercorn St.
Savannah, GA 31401
912-233-9743, fax: 912-233-0102
Regency architecture flanks an 1820s garden complete with tabby walls.

Savannah
111 Barnard St.
Savannah, GA 31401
912-233-7787, fax: 912-233-7706
Although not a garden per se, in reality the entire city is one lovely garden, with 22 gorgeous squares and numerous gardens, public and private. A garden lover's dream, and a must-see. (Address and phone/fax numbers are for the Historic Savannah Foundation.)

HAWAII

Foster Botanical Gardens
180 N. Vineyard Blvd.
Honolulu, HI 96817
808-522-7065, Web site: alohapostcard.com/focus/foster.html
Purchased by Capt. Foster in 1867 from William Hilebrand (who originally bought it from Queen Kalama in 1855), the site was given to the city of Honolulu in 1930. The gardens house thousands of species of tropical and rare indigenous flora.

Liliuokalani Garden Park
Banyon Dr. and Lihiwani St.
Hilohoi, HI 96720
808-961-5797
This 30-acre Japanese garden was built in 1914 and is counted among the most notable landscapes in the United States.

Abraham Lincoln Memorial Garden and Nature Center
2301 E. Lake Dr.
Springfield, IL 62707
217-529-1111, fax: 217-529-0134, E-mail: lmg2301@inw.net
The garden contains 80 acres, with a 5-mile trail featuring native plant life from Lincoln's childhood.

Chicago Botanic Garden
1000 Lake Cook Rd.
Glencoe, IL 60022
847-835-5440, fax: 847-835-0832, Web site: chicagobotanic.org
The gardens in this 300-acre site feature aquatic displays, native Illinois plant landscapes, and a prairie restoration area.

Dawes Garden
225 Greenwood St.
Evanston, IL 60201
847-492-7951
The 19th-century residence of former vice president Charles Dawes, the property offers chateau-style terraces and gardens as well as a historical museum.

Lincoln Park
2400 N. Stockton Dr.
Chicago, IL 60614
312-742-7736, fax: 312-742-5619
The park's conservatory has five glass buildings featuring a variety of plants and seasonal displays. There are also 6 acres of outdoor gardens as well as a zoo, all spread out along the lovely Lake Michigan shore.

Pettengil-Morron House Gardens
1212 W. Moss Ave.
Peoria, IL 61606
309-674-1921
Hosta and fragrance gardens as well as a wildflower walk are the memorable features of this 1868 Second Empire house and grounds.

INDIANA

James F. Lanier House and Garden
511 W. First St.
Madison, IN 47250
812-265-3526, fax: 812-265-3501
The grounds were laid out in 1840 and feature a rare 19th-century greenhouse.

Sullivan House Garden
304 W. Second St.
Madison, IN 47250
812-265-2967, fax: 812-273-3941, E-mail: hmihmfi@seidata.com
This 1818 Federal-style estate features one of the first large-scale domestic gardens along the Ohio River.

IOWA

Old-World Gardens
Amana, IA 52203
319-622-7622, fax: 319-622-6395, E-mail: /accvb@netins.com
The town, famous for its artisans and craftspeople, contains an interesting collection of small gardens nestled among brick cottages.

Terrace Hill
2300 Grand Ave.
Des Moines, IA 50312
515-281-3604, fax: 515-281-7267
This fabulous 1869 mansion features a landscape of native trees and shrubs, as well as flower gardens, pools, and fountains.

Vander Veer Park
215 W. Central Park
Davenport, IA 52803
319-326-7812, fax: 319-326-7815
The site contains a conservatory that houses an unusual mixture of tropical and subtropical plants and cacti, as well as several outdoor gardens of note.

KANSAS

University Gardens
17th and Anderson Sts.
Manhattan, KS 66502
785-776-4222, fax: 785-776-8979, Web site: mbiproperties.com
This site comprises a display of five individual gardens, all suited to the Kansas climate.

KENTUCKY

Farmington
3033 Bardstown Rd.
Louisville, KY 40205
502-452-9920, fax: 502-546-1976
Built from a design by Thomas Jefferson in 1810, the house features an extensive landscape of 14 acres, including a garden showcasing pre-1820 plant materials.

Liberty Hall
West Main and Wilkinson Sts.
Frankfort, KY 40601
502-227-2560
Old roses and boxwoods are the main attraction at this 18th-century garden, which was restored in the 1930s by the Garden Club of Kentucky.

Locust Grove
561 Blankenbaker Ln.
Louisville, KY 40207
502-897-9845, fax: 502-897-0103
This 1790 estate features restored gardens authentic to the era.

LOUISIANA

Afton Villa
U.S. 61
Saint Francisville, LA 70775
504-635-6773
Sunken gardens and a boxwood maze are part of this former estate of a mid-19th-century senator.

City Park
Lelong and City Park Aves.
New Orleans, LA 70124
504-483-9386
This is the home of the New Orleans Botanical Garden and the New Orleans Museum of Art. The park itself is 15,000 acres filled with boating lagoons; a Victorian carousel; rose, camellia, and azalea gardens; and a floral clock.

Longue Vue Gardens
7 Bamboo Rd.
New Orleans, LA 70124
504-488-5488, fax: 504-486-7015, Web site: longuevue.com
The small gardens dispersed throughout this stylized, 8-acre area are organized by color schemes. Other notable attractions are the wildflowers, a pastoral wooded area, and especially the Spanish Court. This city estate was built in the early 1940s.

Rosedown Plantation and Gardens
12501 Hwy. 10
Saint Francisville, LA 70775
504-635-3332, Web site: cimarron.net/usa/la/rosedown.html
The 1835 house features an opulent landscape, reflecting the oftentimes elaborate lifestyle of the steamboat era. Today it serves as a charming bed-and-breakfast.

Shadows-on-the-Teche
117 E. Main St.
New Iberia, LA 70560
318-369-6446, fax: 318-365-5213
Owned by the National Trust for Historical Preservation, this is a fine example of a lush, pre–Civil War plantation.

MARYLAND

Hampton National Historic Site
535 Hampton Ln.
Towson, MD 21286
410-823-1309, fax: 410-823-8394, Web site: nps.gov/hmp/
European styles from French to English to Italian have left their mark on this 1820s estate. Garden features include three descending terrace levels that hold six parterres and a restored Classic Revival orangerie.

Ladew Topiary Gardens
3535 Jarretsville Pike
Monkton, MD 21111
410-557-9570, fax: 410-557-7763
Noted for its elaborate topiaries, this 22-acre garden is a must-see.

William Paca House and Garden
1 Martin St.
Annapolis, MD 21401
410-267-6656, fax: 410-267-6189, Web site: annapolis.org
Designed by William Paca (a signer of the Declaration of Independence), the house features a restored, meticulously researched 18th-century garden.

MASSACHUSETTS

Arnold Arboretum of Harvard University
125 Arborway
Jamaica Plain, MA 02130
617-524-1717, fax: 617-524-1418, Web site: arboretum.harvard.edu
One of the oldest centers of horticultural research in the United States, this 265-acre area was established in 1872. It houses a library, an herbatorium, and diverse specimens of plants, trees, and flowering shrubs.

Chesterwood
4 Williamsville Rd., P.O. Box 827
Stockbridge, MA 01262
413-298-3579, fax: 413-298-3973
Sculptor Daniel Chester French believed that a garden should be a natural continuation of the house, and that's how he developed the gardens at his summer home from 1898 until his death in 1931. His records, containing extensive plant notes, have helped researchers restore the grounds, which are now part of the National Trust for Historical Preservation.

Garden in the Woods
Hemenway Rd.
Framingham, MA 01701
508-877-7630, fax: 508-877-3658, Web site: newfs.org/~newfs/
Native plants and a 42-acre botanical garden are the main attraction here, the headquarters of the New England Wild Flower Society.

King Caesar's Garden
King Caesar's Rd.
Duxbury, MA 02332
781-934-2378
When restoration of the garden was begun back in 1886 (the original dates to 1808), the owner found rare *Iris reticulata* from Asia Minor (which was brought to these shores by Ezra Weston, a.k.a. "King Caesar," a powerful shipping tycoon and the builder of the house). The plants still flourish today and are the main attraction of this well-restored estate.

Mount Auburn Cemetery
580 Mt. Auburn St.
Cambridge, MA 02138
617-547-7105, fax: 617-876-4405
Famous botanists are honored at the Asa Gray Memorial Garden in this, the oldest garden cemetery in the country. The beautiful headstones, tombs, and mausoleums are surrounded by hundred-year-old trees, many rare and all labeled.

Naumkeag Gardens
The Choate Estate, Prospect Hill Rd.
Stockbridge, MA 01262
413-298-3239, fax: 413-298-5239, Web site: ttor.org
This Stanford White–designed Victorian summer estate dating from 1885 features gardens that are large and formal, offering a magnificent view of the Berkshires.

Old Sturbridge Village
1 Sturbridge Rd.
Sturbridge, MA 01566
508-347-3362, fax: 508-347-0375, Web site: osv.org
This historic village re-creates the era between 1790 and 1830 and features many period plants and gardens.

Rotch-Jones-Duff House and Garden
396 Country St.
New Bedford, MA 02740
508-997-1401, fax: 508-997-6846
Surrounding this 1834 Greek Revival mansion is a restored formal garden.

MICHIGAN

W. J. Beal-Garfield Botanical Gardens
412 Olds Hall
East Lansing, MI 48825
517-355-9582, fax: 517-432-1090, Web site: ccp.msu.edu/beal.htm
In operation since 1873, this is one of the oldest botanical gardens in the United States. Containing thousands of plant species, the grounds also house a teaching and research facility.

MINNESOTA

Minnesota Zoological Gardens
12101 Johnny Cake Ridge Rd.
Apple Valley, MN 55124
612-431-9200, fax: 612-431-9300, Web site: mnzoo.com
A showcase for the plant and animal life from all over the Northern Hemisphere, the gardens contain everything from North American boggy marshes to areas of prairie land, as well as six tropical ecosystems.

MISSISSIPPI

Governor's Mansion
300 E. Capitol St.
Jackson, MS 39201
601-359-6421, fax: 601-359-6473
Extensive restoration in 1972, including work on the gazebo and the formal perennial beds, has brought this 1838 Greek Revival back to full charm. It still serves as the governor's residence today.

Mynelle Gardens
4736 Clinton Blvd.
Jackson, MS 39209
601-960-1894, fax: 601-922-5759
Japanese, English, and rustic are among the varied garden styles to be found on the 6-acre grounds.

The Oakes
823 N. Jefferson St.
Jackson, MS 39202
601-353-9339
Occupied by General Sherman during the siege of 1863, this Greek Revival cottage and its garden have been restored.

MISSOURI

Missouri Botanical Garden
P.O. Box 299
St. Louis, MO 63166
314-577-5150, fax: 314-577-9598, Web site: mobot.org
The gardens themselves were founded in 1859 by Henry Shaw, whose restored country residence still stands on the grounds. Famous for the Climatron geodesic dome, considered to be the largest of its kind in the country, the gardens also contain an arboretum and nature preserve, among many other features. It is one of the most complete horticultural centers to be found anywhere, and a must-see.

NEBRASKA

General Crook House
30th and Fort Sts.
Omaha, NE 68111
402-455-9990, fax: 402-453-9448
A Victorian garden is maintained on the grounds of this 1878 Italianate house, the former headquarters of Fort Omaha's commanding officer.

NEW HAMPSHIRE

Fuller Gardens
10 Willow Ave.
North Hampton, NH 03862
603-964-5414, fax: 603-964-8901
An interesting Colonial Revival garden, this features formal areas, a Japanese garden, a wildflower walk, a conservatory, and a hedge topiary, all with a spectacular ocean view.

Gilman Garrison House
12 Water St.
Exeter, NH 03833
603-778-7183, fax: 603-436-4651, Web site: spnea.org
This log house was built in the 17th century and has 18th-century additions.
The restored grounds feature several period gardens.

Governor John Langdon Mansion
143 Pleasant St.
Portsmouth, NH 03801
603-436-3205, fax: 603-436-4651, Web site: spnea.org
The gardens of this 1784 Colonial estate are extensive, with everything from
wildflowers to more-formal areas.

NEW JERSEY

Acorn Hall Memorial Garden
68 Morris Ave.
Morristown, NJ 07960
973-267-3465, fax: 973-267-8773
This site offers an authentically restored Victorian garden.

Frelinghuysen Arboretum
53 E. Hanover Ave.
Morristown, NJ 07962
973-326-7600, fax: 973-644-2726, Web site: parks.morris.nj.us
Dating back to the 19th century, the arboretum features orchards, a pignut,
and formal and informal gardens.

Israel Crane House Gardens
110 Orange Rd.
Montclair, NJ 07042
973-744-1796, fax: 973-783-9419
Features include a 17th-century kitchen garden, a period herb area, and pleasure gardens.

Tempe Wicke House
Jockey Hollow, Tempe Wicke Rd.
Morristown, NJ 07960
973-539-2016, fax: 973-539-8361
The house includes a restored Colonial garden.

NEW YORK

Boscobel
1601 Rt. 90
Garrison-on-Hudson, NY 10524
914-265-3638, fax: 914-265-4405
Built in 1805 and restored in 1960, the 36-acre garden offers a large formal garden, including a rose garden and perennial beds.

Brooklyn Botanic Garden
1000 Washington Ave.
Brooklyn, NY 11225
718-622-4433, fax: 718-857-2430, Web site: bbg.org
This must-see 50-acre area is divided into specialized gardens—Japanese, iris, magnolia, fragrance, and herb. It also contains a beautiful cherry esplanade. All this in the heart of Brooklyn.

The Cloisters—Metropolitan Museum of Art
Fort Tryon Park, North Ave. and Cabrini Circle
Manhattan, NY 10040
212-923-3700, fax: 212-795-3640, Web site: metmuseum.com
The museum contains several fascinating medieval gardens in its inner courtyards.

George Ellwanger Perennial Garden
625 Mount Hope Ave.
Rochester, NY 14620
716-546-7029
Established by the cofounder of the famous Ellwanger and Barry Nursery in 1867, the one-acre garden is at its peak flowering period in early May.

New York Botanical Garden
Bronx Park, One E. 200th St.
Bronx, NY 10458
718-817-8700, fax: 718-562-8474, Web site: nybg.org
Lying on a 230-acre site, the magnificent landscape features a hemlock forest as well as herb, rock, rose, and aquatic gardens. The conservatory is open year-round and contains plants from every part of the world.

Old Westbury Gardens
P.O. Box 430
Westbury, NY 11568
516-333-0048, fax: 516-333-6807
This pre–World War II Long Island estate is one of the last survivors of its type. The magnificent site features an avenue of linden and beech trees, five gardens, and several lakes.

Sonnenberg Gardens
151 Charlotte St.
Canandaigua, NY 14424
716-394-4922, fax: 716-394-2192, Web site: sonnenberg.org
Sonnenberg is a turn-of-the-century estate complete with gardens ranging from Japanese to Italian, as well as a rose garden, a rock garden, and blue and white gardens. Also featured are a reflecting pool and a conservatory.

NORTH CAROLINA

Biltmore Estate and Gardens
One N. Pack Square
Asheville, NC 28801
808-274-6333, fax: 828-274-6213, Web site: biltmore.com
The grounds, covering 12,000 acres, were designed for G. W. Vanderbilt and are unique in the United States for their scope and beauty. They feature extensive formal gardens, a spectacular azalea collection, a walled garden, an Italian garden, and a glen.

Sarah P. Duke Memorial Gardens
Duke University
Box 90341
Durham, NC 27708
919-684-3698, fax: 919-684-8861, Web site: hrduke.edu/dukegardens
The site includes formal gardens with extensive perennial and flowering-shrub plantings.

Tyron Palace Gardens
610 Pollack St.
New Bern, NC 28562
252-514-4900, fax: 252-514-4876
The lovely grounds belong to the site of North Carolina's first Colonial

capital. The Maud Moore Latham Garden is particularly ornate, with clipped hedges and floral parterres. Also featured are the Green Garden and a kitchen garden.

OHIO

Western Reserve Herb Society Garden
11030 E. Blvd.
Cleveland, OH 44106
216-721-1600, fax: 216-721-2056, Web site: cbgarden.org
An interesting re-creation of a medieval monastery garden, this is part of the Cleveland Botanical Garden.

OKLAHOMA

Oklahoma Heritage Center
201 NW 14th St.
Oklahoma City, OK 73103
405-235-4458
The grounds of this 1920s mansion feature well-tended gardens flanked by fountain pools.

Will Rogers Park and Horticultural Center
3500 NW 36th St.
Oklahoma City, OK 73112
405-943-0827
The formal rose garden contains 5,000 varieties. Rock gardens, display areas, and a conservatory are among the features of the center.

OREGON

Bybee-Howell House and Territorial Garden
13901 NW Howell Park Rd.
Portland, OR 97231
503-621-344
The house and grounds, built in 1856, have been restored to their original mid-19th-century appearance, featuring a unique period orchard.

John Bartram House and Gardens
54th St. and Lindbergh Blvd.
Philadelphia, PA 19143
215-729-5281, fax: 215-729-1047, Web site: libertynet.org/~bartram
Naturalist John Bartram's 1700s house and barn still remain amidst the
country's first (and possibly most fascinating) botanic garden.

Longwood Gardens
P.O. Box 501
Kennett Square, PA 19348
610-388-1000, fax: 610-388-2078, Web site: longwoodgardens.org
One of the nation's most impressive gardens, this showplace includes over
1,000 acres of water gardens and display gardens, as well as conservatories,
an arboretum, and an open-air theater.

Old Economy Village and Gardens
14th and Church Sts.
Ambridge, PA 15003
724-266-4500, fax: 724-266-7506
The beautiful 19th-century gardens, ranging from formal to kitchen, testify
to one of the earliest examples of communal living in America.

Pennsbury Manor
400 Pennsbury Memorial Rd.
Morrisville, PA 19067
215-946-0400, fax: 215-295-2936, Web site: pennsburymanor.org
This late-17th-century country manor, originally the property of William
Penn, features formal paths, a kitchen garden, fruit trees, and flower gardens.

Wyck
6026 Germantown Ave.
Philadelphia, PA 19144
215-848-1690, fax: 215-848-1690
The site of the oldest house in the city, the 3 acres of grounds have been in
the continual care of generations of Quakers since the 1820s. The gardens are
adorned by boxwood borders, old-fashioned roses, and original 18th-century
outbuildings. There is also a vegetable garden.

RHODE ISLAND

Chateau Sur Mer
747 Bellevue Ave.
Newport, RI 02840
401-847-1000, Web site: newportmansions.org
The grounds of this magnificent 1852 mansion are in the landscape style typical of the period and include a collection of rare and unusual landscape trees and shrubs.

John Brown House and Courtyard Garden
52 Power St.
Providence, RI 02906
401-331-8575, fax: 401-751-2307
The house and grounds of this 1786 historic house overlook the harbor, making this quite a scenic visit.

Wanton-Lyman-Hazard House
17 Broadway
Newport, RI 02840
401-846-0813, fax: 401-846-1853, Web site: newportmansions.org
The house and gardens of this fine 1675 Jacobean house (the oldest in Newport) have been restored.

SOUTH CAROLINA

Drayton Hall
3380 Ashley River Rd.
Charleston, SC 29414
843-766-0188, fax: 843-766-0878
Established in the 1730s, this great plantation estate (now owned by the National Trust for Historical Preservation) has one of the best-laid gardens of any plantation from the era.

Middleton Place
4300 Ashley River Rd.
Charleston, SC 29414
843-556-6020, fax: 843-766-4460, Web site: middletonplace.org
Renowned for their unique terraces, butterfly lakes, and camellia gardens, the grounds of this estate date to the early 1740s.

The Hermitage
4580 Rachel's Ln.
Nashville, TN 37076
615-889-2941, fax: 615-889-9289, Web site: thehermitage.com
The 625 acres of Andrew Jackson's Hermitage constitute one of the best-maintained historic sites in the nation, with fine gardens restored with help of documents from the president's papers.

Tipton-Haynes Living Farm
2620 S. Roan St.
Johnson City, TN 37601
423-926-3631, Web site: pages.preferred.com/~compress/tipton
The Colonial farmstead of Col. John Tipton is on the National Register.

TEXAS

Alamo Gardens
955 S. Alamo
San Antonio, TX 78205
210-225-7363
The historic site features attractive gardens.

San Antonio Botanical Garden
555 Funston Pl.
San Antonio, TX 78209
210-207-3255, fax: 210-207-3274, Web site:
stic.net/users/gloriadr/sabs.html
Opened in 1980, the 33-acre site features old-fashioned gardens, native Texas plants, a garden for the blind, and a conservatory.

VERMONT

Park-McCullough House and Gardens
P.O. Box 388
North Bennington, VT 05257
802-442-5441, fax: 802-442-5442
The house (built in 1865) and grounds are meticulously restored examples of Victorian domestic taste.

VIRGINIA

Mount Vernon House and Gardens
P.O. Box 110
Mount Vernon, VA 22121
703-780-2000, fax: 703-799-8609
George Washington's beloved home and grounds (including flower gardens, kitchen gardens, and an orchard) have been carefully researched and preserved.

Stratford Hall Plantation
Stratford, VA 22558
804-493-8038, fax: 804-493-0333, Web site: arthes.com
This 1725 mansion is a striking example of Georgian architecture, and the garden is a perfect example of Colonial Revival restoration.

WASHINGTON

Drug Plant Gardens
University of Washington College of Pharmacy
17th Ave. N
Seattle, WA 98107
206-543-1126
These formal gardens exclusively feature medicinal and culinary plants, representing one of the largest collections in the nation.

WISCONSIN

Alfred E. Boerner Botanical Gardens
Whitnall Park, 5879 S. 92nd St.
Hales Corner, WI 53130
414-425-1132, fax: 414-425-8679
This 450-acre park, built in 1932 and opened to the public in 1939, features native flowers, plants, and trees as well as extensive formal and trial gardens. It also offers a wide range of horticultural lessons, exhibits, and classes.

Hazelwood Garden
1008 S. Monroe St.
Green Bay, WI 54301
920-437-1840, fax: 920-437-1840
This historic 1837 house is flanked by a Victorian garden and is a good example of 19th-century tastes in architecture and landscape.

Old World Wisconsin
S. 103 W. 3789 Hwy. 67
Eagle, WI 53119
414-594-6300, fax: 414-595-6342
Historic buildings from all over the state have been relocated to this 576-acre area. The result is a diverse ethnic community, featuring a variety of herb and cutting gardens.

Villa Louis
P.O. Box 65
Prairie du Chien, WI 53821
608-326-2721, fax: 608-326-5507, E-mail: villalouis@mhtc.net
Extensive grounds surround this unique 19th-century mansion.

Suppliers of *Period* Garden Materials

For a continually updated and expanded list, please see our Web site at www.traditionalgardening.com

ANTIQUE BOOKS

The American Botanist
P.O. Box 532, 1103 W. Truitt
Chillicothe, IL 61523
309-274-5254
Catalog cost: $2

Barbara Farnsworth, Bookseller
P.O. Box 9, Rt. 128
West Cornwall, CT 06796
860-672-6571

Calendula Horticultural Books
P.O. Box 930
Picton, ON K0K 2T0 Canada
613-476-3521

Carol Barnett—Books
3562 NE Liberty St.
Portland, OR 97211
503-282-7036

Elizabeth Woodburn
P.O. Box 398, Booknoll Farm
Hopewell, NJ 08525
609-466-0522
Catalog cost: $2

Garden Street Books
P.O. Box 1811
Geelong, Victoria 3220 Australia
011-615-229-1667

Lloyd's of Kew
9 Mortlake Terrace
Kew, Surrey TW9 3DT England
+44 01-940-2512
Catalog cost: $1(US)

Quest Rare Books
774 Santa Ynez
Stanford, CA 95305
415-324-3119
Catalog cost: $3

St. Ann's Books
Rectory House
26 Priory Rd.
Great Malvern, Worcester
WR14 3DR, England
+44 1684 526 818

BEEKEEPING SUPPLIES

Bee-Commerce.com
203-222-2368
Web site: www.bee-commerce.com

Brushy Mountain Bee Farm, Inc.
Rt. 1, Box 135
Moravian Falls, NC 28654
1-800-BEESWAX

Sunstream Bee Supply
P.O. Box 225
Eighty Four, PA 15330
412-222-3330
Catalog cost: $1

Daveco Bee Supply
60 Breakneck Hill Road
Southborough, MA 01772
508-485-8112

FENCING

Central Exchange
P.O. Box 839
Decatur, TX 76234
940-627-2718

Custom Ironworks Inc.
10619 Big Bone Rd., P.O. Box 180
Union, KY 41091
606-384-4122

Iron Fencing & Gates
10619 Big Bone Rd., P.O. Box 180
Union, KY 41091
606-384-4122

Stewart Iron Works Company
P.O. Box 2612
20 West 18th Street
Covington, KY 41012
606-431-1985

FRUIT TREES

Applesource
1716 Apples Rd.
Chapin, IL 62628
1-800-588-3854

Classical Fruits Nursery
8831 AL Hwy. 157
Moulton, AL 35650
205-974-8813

Lawson's Nursery
2730 Yellow Creek Rd.
Ball Ground, GA 30107
770-893-2141

Southmeadow Fruit Gardens
15310 Red Arrow Hwy.
Lakeside, MI 49116
Catalog cost: $10

Stark Bro's
P.O. Box 10
Louisiana, MO 63353
1-800-325-4180
Catalog cost: $4

GARDEN BOOKS

The Book Tree
12 Pine Hill Rd
Englishtown, NJ 07726
732-446-3853

Garden Book & Magazine
   Publishers
10210 Leatherleaf Ct.
Manassas, VA 20111
703-257-1032

Mailorder Gardening Association
P.O. Box 2129
Columbia, MD 21045
Catalog cost: $2

Raymond M. Sutton, Jr.
P.O. Box 330, 430 Main St.
Williamsburg, KY 40769
606-549-3464

GARDEN FURNITURE

Adirondack Designs
350 Cypress St.
Fort Bragg, CA 95437
1-800-222-0343

Charleston Gardens
61 Queen St.
Charleston, SC 29401
1-800-469-0118

Country Casual
17317 Germantown Rd.
Germantown, MD 20874-2999
1-800-284-8325
Catalog cost: $5

Cumberland Woodcraft
P.O. Drawer 609
Carlisle, PA 17013
1-800-367-1884
Catalog cost: $5

David Robinson/Natural Edge
515 Tuxford Ct.
Trenton, NJ 08638
609-737-8996

French Wyres
P.O. Box 131655
Tyler, TX 75713
903-597-8322

Green Enterprises
43 S. Rogers St.
Hamilton, VA 22068
703-338-3606
Catalog cost: $1

The Plow & Hearth
P.O. Box 830
Orange, VA 22960
1-800-627-1712

A Proper Garden
225 S. Water St.
Wilmington, NC 28401
919-763-7177
Catalog cost: $1

Romancing the Woods
33 Raycliffe Dr.
Woodstock, NY 12498

Windsor Designs
37 Great Valley Pkwy.
Malvern, PA 19355
215-640-1212

Woodbrook Furniture
    Manufacturing Co.
P.O. Box 175
Trussville, AL 35173
205-655-4041

GARDEN ORNAMENTS

The Artisan's Group
1039 Main St.
Dublin, NH 03444
1-800-528-2035
Catalog cost: $1

Carruth Studio
1178 Farnsworth Rd.
Waterville, OH 43566
1-800-225-1178

Design Toscano, Inc.
17 E. Campbell St.
Arlington Heights, IL 60005
1-800-525-0733

The Garden Concepts Collection
P.O. Box 241233, 6621 Poplar
    Woods Circle S
Memphis, TN 38124
901-756-1649
Catalog cost: $5

Gateways
849 Hannah Branch Rd.
Burnsville, NC 28714
704-675-5286

Glass House
50 Swedetown Rd.
Pomfret Center, CT 06259
1-800-222-3065

Handcrafted Copper
RR 2, Box 294
Colebrook, NH 03576
603-237-8326

Hardwicke Gardens
Rt. 9 East
Westborough, MA 01581
508-366-5478
Catalog cost: $2

Lake Creek Garden Features Inc.
200 N. Illinois St.
Lake City, IA 51449
712-464-8924

Lazy Hill Farm Designs
P.O. Box 235
Colerian, NC 27924
919-356-2828
Catalog cost: $1

New England Garden Ornaments
P.O. Box 235, 38 Brookfield Rd.
North Brookfield, MA 01535
508-867-4474

Old Carolina Brick Company
475 Majolica Rd.
Salisbury, NC 28147
704-636-8850

Ornate Products International
26-27 Clivemont Rd.—Cordwallis
    Estate
Maidenhead, Berkshire
SL6 7BZ, UK
44-0-628-2561

Pompeian Studios
90 Rockledge Rd.
Bronxville, NY 10708
914-337-5595
Catalog cost: $10

Robinson Iron
P.O. Box 1119
Alexander City, AL 35010
205-329-8486

Sailor Creek Woodcrafts
W6959 Dam Rd.
Fifield, WI 54524
715-762-4180

Stewart Ironworks Company
P.O. Box 2612, 20 W. 18th St.
Covington, KY 41012
606-431-1985

The Stone Yard
66 North St.
Groton, MA 01450
1-800-231-2200

Sycamore Creek
P.O. Box 16
Ancram, NY 12502

Syracuse Pottery
6551 Pottery Rd.
Warners, NY 13164
1-800-448-2313

The Victoriana Collection
906 Line St.
Easton, PA 18042
1-800-361-9807

Yanzum—Art for Gardens
1285 Peachtree St. NE
Atlanta, GA 30309
404-874-8063

GARDEN PROTECTION

Benner's Gardens
P.O. Box 875
Bala Cynwyd, PA 19004
1-800-244-3337

The Bug Store
113 W. Argonne
St. Louis, MO 63112
314-966-2287

GARDEN STRUCTURES

Bow House, Inc.
P.O. Box 900, 92 Randall Rd.
Bolton, MA 01740
508-779-6464
Catalog cost: $3

Heritage Garden Houses
311 Seymour Ave.
Lansing, MI 48933
517-372-3385
Catalog cost: $3

S & H Architectural Supply Co.
906 Line St.
Easton, PA 18042
1-800-361-9807

Vintage Wood Works
P.O. Box R, Hwy. 34 S
Quinlan, TX 78624
903-356-2158
Catalog cost: $2

Vixen Hill Gazebos
Main St.
Elverson, PA 19520
1-800-423-2766
Catalog cost: $3

GARDEN TOOLS

A. M. Leonard
241 Fox Dr., P.O. Box 816
Piqua, OH 45356
1-800-433-0063
Catalog cost: $1

Forestry Suppliers, Inc.
P.O. Box 8397
Jackson, MS 39284
1-800-647-5368

Gardener's Supply Company
128 Intervale Rd.
Burlington, VT 05401
1-800-863-1700

Home & Garden Innovations
130 Intervale Rd.
Burlington, VT 05401
1-800-944-5580

Little's Good Garden Gloves
P.O. Box 808
Johnstown, NY 12095
1-888-967-5548

Smith & Hawken
117 E. Strawberry Dr.
Mill Valley, CA 94941
1-800-776-3336

Stillbrook Horticultural Supplies
P.O. Box 600
Bantam, CT 06750
1-800-414-4468

GREENHOUSES

Charley's
1599 Memorial Hwy.
Mt. Vernon, WA 98273
1-800-322-4707

Gardener's Supply Company
128 Intervale Rd.
Burlington, VT 05401
1-888-833-1412

Gothic Arch Greenhouses
P.O. Box 1564
Mobile, AL 36633
Catalog cost: $5

HERBS

Le Jardin de Gourmet
P.O. Box 75
St., Johnsbury Center, VT 05836
1-800-748-1446
Catalog cost: $1

Southern Exposure Seed Exchange
P.O. Box 170
Earlysville, VA 22936
804-973-4703
Catalog cost: $2

Sunnyboy Gardens, Inc.
3314 Earlysville Rd.
Earlysville, VA 22936
1-800-974-7350

LANDSCAPE DESIGN

GardenWorks, Ltd.
189 Cordaville Rd.
Southborough, MA 01772
508-485-3637

PERIOD PLANTS

The Antique Rose Emporium
9300 Lueckemeyer Rd.
Brenham, TX 77833
1-800-441-0002

Argyle Acres—Joe and Donna
   Spears
910 Pioneer Circle
Argyle, TX 76226
817-464-3680
Cost: Two 1st-class stamps for list

Blanchette Gardens
223 Rutland St.
Carlisle, MA 01741
508-369-2962
Catalog cost: $3

Bluebird Haven Iris Garden—Mary
   Hess
6940 Fairplay Rd.
Somerset, CA 95684
209-245-5017
Cost: $1 (specify Antique List)

Bluebird Nursery, Inc.
P.O. Box 460
519 Bryan St.
Clarkson, NE 68629
402-892-3457

Burpee Gardens
300 Park Ave.
Warminster, PA 18974
1-800-888-1447

Charles H. Mueller Co.
7091 N. River Rd.
New Hope, PA 18938
215-862-2033

Colorblends by Schipper
Box 7584
Greenwich, CT 06836
1-888-TIP-TOES
Catalog cost: $2

Cricket Hill Garden
670 Walnut Hill Rd.
Thomaston, CT 06787
860-283-1042
Catalog cost: $3.00

Crystal Palace Perennials, Ltd.
P.O. Box 154
St. John, IN 46373
219-374-9419

Dirk Visser & Co.
P.O. Box 295, 201 High St.
Ipswich, MA 01938
1-800-582-3650

Dutch Gardens
P.O. Box 200
Adelphia, NJ 07710-0200
1-800-818-3861

Fanfare Daylilies
54 Beltran St.
Malden, MA 02148
617-321-3786
Catalog cost: $2.50

Five Acre Farm Greenhouse
108 Hinsdale Rd.—Rt. 63
Northfield, MA 01360
1-800-221-2049

Forest Farm
990 Tetherow Rd.
Williams, OR 97544
541-846-7269
Catalog cost: $4

The Fragrant Path
P.O. Box 328
Fort Calhoun, NE 68023
Catalog cost: $2

Gossler Farms Nursery
1200 Weaver Rd.
Springfield, OR 97478-9691
541-744-7924
Catalog cost: $2

Graceful Gardens
Box 100
Mecklenburg, NY 14863

Heirloom Seeds
P.O. Box 245
West Elizabeth, PA 15088
412-384-0852
Catalog cost: $1

Heronswood Nursery Ltd.
7530 NE 288th St.
Kingston, WA 98346
360-297-4172
Catalog cost: $5

Hydrangeas Plus
P.O. Box 345
Aurora, OR 97002
503-651-2887

J. W. Jung Seeds & Nursery
335 S. High St.
Randolph, WI 53957-0001
414-326-4100

John Scheepers, Inc.
23 Tulip Dr.
Bantam, CT 06750
860-567-0838

K. Van Bourgondien & Sons
245 Rt. 109, P.O. Box 1000
Babylon, NY 11702
1-800-552-9996

Klehm Nursery
4210 North Duncan Rd.
Champaign, IL 61821
1-800-553-3715

Logee's Greenhouses, Ltd.
141 North St.
Danielson, CT 06239
860-774-8038
Catalog cost: $3

Milaeger's Gardens
4838 Douglas Ave.
Racine, WI 53402-2498
414-639-2371
Catalog cost: $1

Miller Nurseries
5060 West Lake Rd.
Canandaigua, NY 14424
1-800-836-9630

Old House Gardens
536 Third St.
Ann Arbor, MI 48103-4957
313-995-1486

Old Sturbridge Village Museum
Gift Shop Seed Program
Sturbridge, MA 01566

Park Seed Company
1 Parkton Ave.
Greenwood, SC 29647-0002
1-800-845-3366

Perennial Pleasures Nursery
2 Brick House Rd.
East Hardwick, VT 05836
Catalog cost: $3

R. Seawright
201 Bedford Rd., P.O. Box 733
Carlisle, MA 01741-0733
508-369-2171
Catalog cost: $2

Ros-Equus (Heritage Rose
Gardens)
40350 Wilderness Rd.
Branscomb, CA 95417

The Roseraie at Bayfields
P.O. Box R
Waldoboro, ME 04572
207-832-6330

Sandy Mush Herb Nursery
316 Surrett Cove Rd.
Leicester, NC 28748
704-683-2014
Catalog cost: $4

Schreiner's Iris Gardens
3625 Quinaby Rd. NE
Salem, OR 97303
1-800-525-2367
Catalog cost: $4

Select Seeds
180 Stickney Hill Rd.
Union, CT 06076
860-684-9310

Shepherd Hill Farm
200 Peekskill Hollow Rd.
Putnam Valley, NY 10579
914-528-5917

Siskiyou Rare Plant Nursery
2825 Cummings Rd.
Medford, OR 97501
541-772-6846
Catalog cost: $3

Skittone Bulb Company
1415 Eucalyptus Dr.
San Francisco, CA 94132
415-753-3332

Spring Hill Nurseries
110 W. Elm St.
Tipp City, OH 45371
1-800-582-8527
Catalog cost: $2.50

Thompson & Morgan
P.O. Box 1308
Jackson, NJ 08527
1-800-274-7333

Van Engelen Inc.
23 Tulip Dr.
Bantam, CT 06750
860-567-8734

Wayside Gardens
1 Garden Ln.
Hodges, SC 29695
1-800-845-1124

We-Du Nurseries
Rt. 5, Box 724
Marion, NC 28752
704-738-8300
Catalog cost: $2

Weir Meadow Nursery
Weir Meadow Rd.
Wayland, MA 01778
508-358-2472

Well-Sweep Herb Farm
205 Mount Bethel Rd.
Port Murray, NJ 07865
908-852-5390
Catalog cost: $2

Weston Nurseries
East Main St., Rt. 135, P.O. Box
    186
Hopkinton, MA 01748
1-800-322-2002

Wilkerson Mill Gardens
9595 Wilkerson Mill Rd.
Palmetto, GA 30268
770-463-2400

SEED SAVER PROGRAMS

Eastern Native Seed Conservancy
P.O. Box 451
Great Barrington, MA 01230

Heritage Seed Program
RR 3
Uxbridge, ON L9P 1R3 Canada

KUSA Research Foundation
P.O. Box 761
Ojai, CA 93023
Catalog cost: $2

Landis Valey Museum Heirloom
    Seed Project
2541 Kissel Hill Rd.
Lancaster, PA 17601
Catalog cost: $2.50

Native Seeds/SEARCH
2509 N. Campbell Ave. #325
Tucson, AZ 85719
Catalog cost: $1

Seed Savers Exchange
3076 N. Winn Rd.
Decorah, IA 52101

Seed Shares
P.O. Box 226
Earlysville, VA 22936
Catalog cost: $1

Thomas Jefferson Center for
Historic Plants
P.O. Box 316
Charlottesville, VA 22902
Catalog cost: $1

SEEDS

Abundant Life Seed Foundation
P.O. Box 772, 109 Lawrence St.
Port Townsend, WA 98368
206-385-7192
Catalog cost: $2

Bountiful Gardens
18001 Shafer Ranch Rd.
Willits, CA 95490
707-459-6410
Catalog cost: $3

The Cook's Garden
P.O. Box 5010
Hodges, SC 29653-5010
1-800-457-9703

CORNS—Carl and Karen Barnes
Rt. 1, Box 32
Turpin, OK 73950

D. L. Landreth Seed Co.
P.O. Box 6426
Baltimore, MD 21230
301-727-3922
Catalog cost: $2

Goodwin Creek Gardens
P.O. Box 83
Williams, OR 97544
541-846-7357

Harris Seeds
P.O. Box 22960
Rochester, NY 14692-2960
1-800-514-4441

Johnny's Selected Seeds
Foss Hill Rd.
Albion, ME 04910-9731
207-437-4395

Raintree Nursery
391 Butts Road
Morton, WA 98356
360-496-6400

Ronniger's Seed Potatoes
Star Route
Moyie Springs, ID 83845
509-925-6025
Catalog cost: $2

Seeds of Change
P.O. Box 15700
Santa Fe, NM 87506
1-888-762-7333

Shepherd's Garden Seeds
30 Irene St.
Torrington, CT 06790
860-482-3638

Stokes Seeds, Inc.
Box 548
Buffalo, NY 14240
1-800-396-9238

Territorial Seed Company
P.O. Box 157
Cottage Grove, OR 97424
541-942-9547

Tomato Growers Supply Company
P.O. Box 2237
Fort Myers, FL 33902
1-888-478-7333

Vermont Bean Seed Company
Garden Ln.
Fair Haven, VT 05743
802-273-3400

WATER-GARDEN SUPPLIES

Beckett
2521 Willowbrook Rd.
Dallas, TX 75220
214-357-6421

Fiber Tech Garden Pools
833 Main St.
Southbridge, MA 01550
508-764-7501

Lilypons Water Gardens
6800 Lilipons Rd., P.O. Box 10
Buckeystown, MD 21717
1-800-999-5459
Catalog cost: $5

Moore Water Gardens
P.O. Box 70
Port Stanley, ON N5L 1J4 Canada
519-782-4052

North American Pond Source
1301 Mermaid Ln.
Wyndmoor, PA 19038
215-836-4206
Catalog cost: $1

Paradise Water Gardens
14 May St.
Whitman, MA 02382
617-447-4711

Bibliography

Adams, William H. *Grounds for Change: Major Gardens of the Twentieth Century.* Boston: Little, Brown, 1993.

———. *Nature Reflected: Gardens Through History.* New York: Abbeville Press, 1991.

Alexander, Rosemary, and Anthony du Gard Pasley. *The English Gardening School.* New York: Weidenfeld & Nicolson, 1987.

Appleton, Bonnie Lee. *Landscape Rejuvenation.* Pownal, Vt.: Garden Way/Storey Communications, 1988.

Bailey, Liberty Hyde, and Ethel Zoe Bailey. *Hortus Third: A Concise Dictionary of Plants*

Cultivated in the United States and Canada. Rev. by the Staff of the Liberty Hyde Bailey Hortorium. New York: Macmillan Publishing Company, 1976.

Banks, Elizabeth. *Creating Period Gardens*. Washington, D.C.: Preservation Press, 1991.

Barn Plans and Outbuildings. New York: Orange Judd Company, 1894.

Barton, Barbara J. *Gardening by Mail*, 5th ed. Boston: Houghton Mifflin, 1997.

Beale, Galen, and Mary Rose Boswell. *The Earth Shall Blossom: Shaker Herbs and Gardening*. Woodstock, Vt.: Countryman Press, 1991.

Benjamin, Asher. *The American Builder's Companion*. Reprint of 1872 ed. New York: Dover Publications, 1969.

Bessette, Alan E., and William K. Chapman, eds. *Plants and Flowers: 1,761 Illustrations for Artists and Designers*. New York: Dover Books, 1992.

Betts, Edwin, and Hazelhurst Bolton Perkins. *Thomas Jefferson's Flower Garden at Monticello*. Charlottesville, Va.: University Press of Virginia, 1971.

Billington, Jill. *Architectural Foliage*. London: Ward Lock, 1991.

Blajan, Daniel. *Foxgloves & Hedgehog Days*. Boston: Houghton Mifflin, 1997.

Blomfield, Reginald, and F. Inigo Thomas. *The Formal Garden in England*. London: Macmillan & Co., 1892.

Boggs, Kate Doggett. *Prints and Plants of Old Gardens*. Richmond, Va.: Garrett & Massie, 1932.

Boisset, Caroline. *Gardening in Time*. New York: Prentice-Hall, 1990.

Bonney, Richard E. *Beekeeping: A Practical Guide*. Pownal, Vt.: Storey Communications, 1993.

Bowles, E. A. *My Garden in Spring*. Reprint of 1914 ed. Portland, Or.: Timber Press, 1997.

———. *My Garden in Summer*. Reprint of 1914 ed. Portland, Or.: Timber Press, 1998.

Breck, Joseph. *Annual Catalogue of the New England Agricultural Warehouse and Seed Store*. Boston: Joseph Breck & Co., 1840.

———. *The Flower Garden*. Boston: J. P. Jewett, 1851.

Bremness, Lesley. *The Complete Book of Herbs*. London: Viking Studio Books, 1988.

Brinkley, M. Kent, and Gordon W. Chappell. *The Gardens of Colonial Williamsburg*. Williamsburg, Va.: Colonial Williamsburg Foundation, 1996.

Brookes, John. *The Small Garden Book*. New York: Crown, 1989.

Brookes, John, Kenneth A. Beckett, and Thomas H. Everett. *The Gardener's Index of Plants & Flowers*. New York: Collier Books, 1987.

Brown, Jane. *Sissinghurst: Portrait of a Garden*. New York: Abrams, 1990.

Buchanan, Rita. *The Shaker Herb and Garden Book*. Boston: Houghton Mifflin, 1996.

Buczacki, Stefan. *Creating a Victorian Flower Garden*. New York: Weidenfeld & Nicolson, 1988.

Burpee's Farm Annual. Philadelphia: W. Atlee Burpee & Co., 1894.

Calhoun, Creighton Lee. *Old Southern Apples*. Blacksburg, Va.: McDonald & Woodwark, 1995.

Callaway, Dorothy J. *The World of Magnolias*. Portland, Oreg.: Timber Press, 1994.

Carter, Brian, ed. *The Gardener's Palette*. New York: Doubleday, 1986.

Christopher, Thomas. *In Search of Lost Roses.* New York: Summit Books, 1989.

Clarke, Ethne. *Herb Garden Design.* New York: Macmillan, 1995.

Clarke, H. P. *Wet Days at Edgewood.* New York: Charles Scribner, 1865.

Clausen, Ruth Rogers, and Nicolas H. Ekstrom. *Perennials for American Gardens.* New York: Random House, 1989.

Coats, Alice M., and Dr. John L. Creech. *Garden Shrubs and Their Histories.* New York: Simon & Schuster, 1992.

Coffin, David R. *The English Garden: Meditation and Memorial.* Princeton, N.J.: Princeton University Press, 1994.

Colborn, Nigel. *The Old-Fashioned Gardener.* London: Lorenz Books, 1995.

Cole, Brenda, ed. *Shade Gardens.* Ontario, Can.: Firefly Press, 1995.

Colonial Gardens: The Landscape and Architecture of George Washington's Time. Prepared by the American Society of Landscape Architects. Issued by the United States George Washington Bicentennial Commission, Washington, D.C., 1933.

Cook, Ferris, ed. *Invitation to the Garden.* New York: Stewart, Tabori & Chang, 1991.

Copeland, Morris. *Country Life: A Handbook of Agriculture, Horticulture, and Landscape Gardening.* Boston: John P. Jewett and Company, 1860.

Cox, James A. D., and N. Jane Isley. *Savannah: Tour of Homes & Gardens.* Savannah, Ga.: Historical Savannah Foundation, 1996.

Crisp, Sir Frank. *Mediaeval Gardens,* Vols. 1–2, ed. by Catherine Childs Paterson. London: John Lane, 1924.

Cruso, Thalassa. *Making Things Grow Indoors.* New York: Knopf, 1977.

———. *Making Things Grow Outdoors.* New York: Knopf, 1976.

———. *Making Vegetables Grow.* New York: Knopf, 1975.

———. *To Everything There Is a Season.* New York: Knopf, 1974.

Culpepper's Color Herbal. New York: Sterling Publishing, 1983.

D'Andrea, Jeanne. *Ancient Herbs.* Malibu, Calif.: J. Paul Getty Museum, 1982.

Davis, Brian. *The Gardener's Illustrated Encyclopedia of Trees & Shrubs.* Emmaus, Pa.: Rodale Press, 1987.

de Bray, Lys. *Borders: A Guide to Spring, Summer & Autumn Colour.* London: Ward Lock, 1987.

Dezallier d'Argenville, Antoine-Joseph. *The Theory and Practice of Gardening,* trans. by John James. London: G. James, 1712.

Dirr, Michael A. *Manual of Woody Landscape Plants.* Champaign, Ill.: Stipes Publishing Company, 1983.

Doell, M. Christine Klim. *Gardens of the Gilded Age.* Syracuse, N.Y.: Syracuse University Press, 1986.

Dorra, Mary Tonetti. *Beautiful American Vegetable Gardens.* New York: Clarkson Potter, 1997.

Downing, A. J. *The Architecture of Country Houses.* Reprint of 1850 ed. New York: Dover Publications, 1969.

———. *A Treatise on the Theory and Practice of Landscape Gardening Adapted to North America.* New York: Orange Judd Company, 1865.

Downing, Andrew Jackson. *Cottage Residences.* Reprint of 1873 ed. New York: Dover Publications, 1981.

———. *Fruits and Fruit Trees of America*, rev. ed. New York: John Wiley & Son, 1867.

———. *Victorian Cottage Residences.* New York: Dover, 1981.

Druse, Ken. *The Collector's Garden.* New York: Clarkson Potter, 1996.

Duncan, Frances. *Home Vegetables and Small Fruits.* New York: Charles Scribner's Sons, 1918.

Dutton, Joan Parry. *Plants of Colonial Williamsburg.* Williamsburg, Va.: Colonial Williamsburg Foundation, 1997.

Eck, Joe, and Wayne Winterrowd. *A Year at North Hill.* New York: Henry Holt & Co., 1995.

Elder, Walter. *The Cottage Garden of America.* Philadelphia: Moss and Brother, 1850.

Elliott, Brent. *The Country House Garden.* London: Mitchell Beazley, 1995.

———. *Victorian Gardens.* Portland, Or.: Timber Press, 1986.

Elliott, F. R. *Handbook of Practical Landscape Gardening.* Rochester, N.Y.: D. M. Dewey, 1885.

Ely, Helena Rutherford. *A Woman's Hardy Garden.* New York: Grossett & Dunlap, 1903.

Emmet, Alan. *So Fine a Prospect: Historic New England Gardens.* Hanover, N.H.: University Press of New England, 1996.

Endersby, Elric, Alexander Greenwood, and David Larkin. *Barn: The Art of a Working Building.* Boston: Houghton Mifflin, 1992.

Erler, Catriona T., and Derek Fell. *550 Home Landscaping Ideas.* New York: Simon & Schuster, 1991.

Evans, Catherine. *Cultural Landscape Report for Longfellow National Historic Site,* Vol. I. Boston: National Park Service, 1993.

Favretti, Rudy J., and Joy P. Favretti. *For Every House a Garden.* Hanover, N.H.: University Press of New England, 1990.

Favretti, Rudy J., and Joy Putman Favretti. *Landscapes and Gardens for Historic Buildings,* 2nd ed. Nashville, Tenn.: American Association for State and Local History, 1991.

Fiala, John L. *Flowering Crabapples: The Genus* Malus. Portland, Or.: Timber Press, 1994.

Galle, Fred C. *Hollies: The Genus* Ilex. Portland, Or.: Timber Press, 1997.

Gallup, Barbara, and Deborah Reich. *The Complete Book of Topiary.* New York: Workman Publishing, 1987.

Gardner, Jo Ann. *The Heirloom Garden.* Pownal, Vt.: Storey Communications, 1992.

Garnock, Jamie. *Trellis.* New York: Rizzoli, 1991.

Girouard, Mark. *The Victorian Country House.* New Haven, Conn.: Yale University Press, 1979.

Greenberg, David B., ed. *Countryman's Companion,* illus. by Jack Wilson. New York: Harper & Brothers Publishers, 1947.

Greenoak, Francesca. *Glorious Gardens.* New York: Congdon & Weed, 1989.

———. *Water Features for Small Gardens.* London: CoranOctopus, 1996.

Griswold, Mac, and Eleanor Weller. *The Golden Age of American Gardens.* New York: Abrams, 1991.

Gunn, Fenja. *Lost Gardens of Gertrude Jekyll.* New York: Macmillan, 1991.

Hagan, Joan, and David Hagan. *The Farm: An American Living Portrait.* Westchester, Pa.: Schiffer Publishing, 1990.

Hale, Jonathan. *The Old Way of Seeing Things.* Boston: Houghton Mifflin, 1994.

Harris, John, ed. *The Garden: A Celebration of One Thousand Years of British Gardening.* London: New Perspectives Publishing, 1979.

Harris, Cyril M. *Illustrated Dictionary of Historic Architecture.* New York: Dover Books, 1977.

Harrison, Peter Joel. *Brick Pavements.* Richmond, Va.: Dietz Press, 1994.

———. *Fences.* Richmond, Va.: Dietz Press, 1993.

———. *Fences of Cape Cod.* Richmond, Va.: Dietz Press, 1996.

———. *Gazebos.* Richmond, Va.: Dietz Press, 1995.

Hatch, Peter J. *The Fruits and Fruit Trees of Monticello.* Charlottesville, Va.: University Press of Virginia, 1988.

Hatton, Richard G. *1001 Plant and Floral Illustrations from Early Herbals.* New York: Dover Books, 1996.

Heatherly, Ana Nez. *Healing Plants: A Medicinal Guide to Native American Plants and Herbs.* New York: Lyons Press, 1998.

Henderson, Peter. *Gardening for Pleasure.* New York: Orange Judd Company, 1893.

———. *Gardening for Profit.* New York: Orange Judd Company, 1908.

Henslow, T. Geoffrey. *Ye Sundial Booke.* London: Edward Arnold, 1914.

Hill, Lewis. *Fruits and Berries for the Home Garden.* Pownal, Vt.: Storey Communications, 1992.

———. *Pruning Made Easy.* Pownal, Vt.: Storey Publishing, 1988.

———. *Secrets of Plant Propagation.* Pownal, Vt.: Garden Way Publishing, 1985.

Hindermyer, Gilbert. "Wyck, an Old House and Garden at Germantown, Philadelphia." *House & Garden*, vol. 2 (November 1902).

Hobhouse, Penelope. *Borders.* London: Pavilion, 1989.

———. *Gardening Through the Ages.* New York: Simon & Schuster, 1992.

Howells, John Meade. *Architectural Heritage of the Piscataqua.* Washington, D.C.: Whalesback Books, 1988.

Hunt, John Dixon. *Gardens and the Picturesque: Studies in the History of Landscape Architecture.* Cambridge, Mass.: MIT Press, 1992.

Hurley, Judith Benn. *The Good Herb.* New York: Morrow, 1995.

Jacobs, Betty E. M. *Growing & Using Herbs Successfully.* Pownal, Vt.: Garden Way/Storey Communications, 1981.

Janson, H. Frederic. *Pomona's Harvest.* Portland, Or.: Timber Press, 1997.

Jaworski, Henry. *Summer Bulbs.* Boston: Houghton Mifflin, 1998.

Jekyll, Gertrude. *The Illustrated Gertrude Jekyll.* Boston, Toronto: Little, Brown, 1988.

Jekyll, Gertrude, and Lawrence Weaver. *Arts and Crafts Gardens.* Suffolk, UK: Garden Art Press, 1981.

Jones, Louisa. *The Art of French Vegetable Gardening.* New York: Artisan, 1995.

Journal of the New England Garden History Society, Vols. 1–5. Boston: Massachusetts Horticultural Society, 1991, 1992, 1993, 1996, 1997.

Kalman, Bela. *Flowers.* Boston: Houghton Mifflin, 1997.

Karson, Robin. *Fletcher Steele, Landscape Architect.* New York: Abrams/Sagapress, 1989.

Kellaway, Herbert J. *How to Lay Out Suburban Home Grounds.* New York: John Wiley & Sons, 1915.

Kelso, William M., and Rachel Most, eds. *Earth Patterns: Essays in Landscape Archaeology.* Charlottesville, Va.: University Press of Virginia, 1990.

Kemp, Edward. *Landscape Gardening: How to Lay Out a Garden.* New York: John Wiley & Sons, 1911.

Kimball, Fiske. *Mr. Samuel McIntire, Carver, the Architect of Salem.* Portland, Maine: Southworth-Anthoensen Press, 1940.

King, Peter, Carole Ottesen, and Graham Rose. *Gardening with Style.* London: Bloomsbury, 1988.

Kingsbury, Noel. *The New Perennial Garden.* New York: Henry Holt & Co., 1996.

Kylloe, Ralph. *Rustic Garden Architecture.* Salt Lake City, Utah: Gibbs Smith, 1997.

Lacy, Allen. *The Garden in Autumn.* New York: Atlantic Monthly Press, 1990.

Lambeth, William Alexander, and Warren H. Manning. *Thomas Jefferson as an Architect and a Designer of Landscapes.* Boston: Houghton Mifflin, 1913.

Landsberg, Sylvia. *The Medieval Garden.* New York: Thames & Hudson, 1996.

Larkin, David. *Country Wisdom.* Boston: Houghton Mifflin, 1997.

Lasdun, Susan. *The English Park.* New York: Vendome Press, 1992.

Lawrence, Elizabeth. *Through the Garden Gate.* Chapel Hill, N.C.: University of North Carolina Press, 1990.

Lawson-Hall, Toni, and Brian Rothera. *Hydrangeas: A Gardener's Guide.* Portland, Or.: Timber Press, 1996.

Ledward, Daphne. *The Victorian Garden Catalogue.* London: Studio Editions, 1995.

Leighton, Ann. *American Gardens in the Eighteenth Century.* Amherst, Mass.: University of Massachusetts Press, 1986.

———. *American Gardens of the Nineteenth Century.* Amherst, Mass.: University of Massachusetts Press, 1987.

———. *Early American Gardens.* Amherst, Mass.: University of Massachusetts Press, 1986.

Lennox-Boyd, Arabella. *Traditional English Gardens.* New York: Weidenfeld & Nicolson, 1987.

Leopold, Allison Kyle. *The Victorian Garden.* New York: Clarkson Potter, 1995.

Lewis, Arnold. *American Country Houses of the Gilded Age.* New York: Dover, 1982.

Lillie, Rupert B. *The Gardens and Homes of the Loyalists,* Vol. 26. Cambridge, Mass.: Cambridge Historical Society, 1941.

Lloyd, Christopher. *The Well-Tempered Garden.* New York: Penguin Books, 1987.

Lloyd, Christopher, and Richard Bird. *The Cottage Garden.* New York: Prentice-Hall, 1990.

Lockwood, Alice. *Gardens of Colony and State,* Vol. I. New York: Charles Scribner's Sons, 1931.

Loewer, Peter. *The Annual Garden.* Emmaus, Pa.: Rodale Press, 1988.

Long, Elias A. *Ornamental Gardening for Americans.* New York: Orange Judd Company, 1896.

Lowery, Woodbury. *Spanish Settlements in the United States: Florida from 1513 to 1561.* New York: Putnam, 1905.

Macoboy, Stirling. *The Ultimate Rose Book.* New York: Abrams, 1993.

Major, Judith K. *To Live in the New World: A. J. Downing and American Landscape Gardening.* Cambridge, Mass.: MIT Press, 1997.

Mayall, R. Newton, and Margaret L. Mayall. *Sundials: How to Know, Use, and Make Them.* Boston: Hale, Cushman & Flint, 1938.

Maynard, Samuel T. *Landscape Gardening as Applied to Home Decoration.* New York: John Wiley & Sons, 1903.

McAlester, Virginia, and Lee McAlester. *A Field Guide to American Houses.* New York: Knopf, 1995.

McDonald, Elvin, Barbara Grubman, and Peter Lower. *Everything You Need to Know About Growing House Plants . . . Successfully.* New York: Popular Library, 1971.

McGourty, Frederick. *The Perennial Gardener.* Boston: Houghton Mifflin, 1989.

Menten, Theodore. *Plant and Floral Woodcuts for Designers & Craftsmen.* New York: Dover Books, 1974.

Michalak, Patricia A. *Rodale's Successful Organic Gardening: Herbs.* Emmaus, Pa.: Rodale Press, 1993.

Mitchell, Donald G. *Rural Studies.* New York: Charles Scribner & Co., 1867.

M'Mahon, Bernard. *The American Gardener's Calendar.* Reprint of 1806 ed. Charlottesville, Va.: Thomas Jefferson Memorial Foundation, 1997.

Moore, Barbara W., and Gail Weesner, eds. *Hidden Gardens of Beacon Hill,* photographs by Southie Burgin. Boston: Beacon Hill Garden Club, 1987.

Morris, Alistair. *Antiques from the Garden.* Wappingers Falls, N.Y.: Garden Art Press, 1996.

Mosser, Monique, and George Teyssot, eds. *The Architecture of Western Gardens.* Cambridge, Mass.: MIT Press, 1991.

Munting, Abraham. *Floral Engravings for Artists and Craftspeople.* New York: Dover Books, 1975.

Murphy, Wendy B. *Beds and Borders.* Boston: Houghton Mifflin, 1990.

Nitschke, Robert. *Choice and Unusual Fruits for the Connoisseur and Home Gardener.* Lakeside, Mich.: Southmeadow Fruit Gardens, 1976.

Nuese, Josephine. *The Country Garden.* New York: Scribners, 1970.

Old Southborough: A Photographic Essay. Southborough, Mass.: Yankee Colour Corp, 1981.

Ondra, Nancy J. *Soil and Composting*. Boston: Houghton Mifflin, 1997.

Ottesen, Carole. *The New American Garden*. New York: Macmillan, 1987.

Ottewill, David. *The Edwardian Garden*. New Haven, Conn.: Yale University Press, 1989.

Otto, Stella. *The Backyard Berry Book*. Maple City, Mich.: OttoGraphics, 1995.

———. *The Backyard Orchardist*. Maple City, Mich.: OttoGraphics, 1993.

Page, Russell. *The Education of a Gardener*. London: Harvill/HarperCollins, 1994.

Parsons, Samuel. *Landscape Gardening*. New York: G. P. Putnam, 1891.

Phillips, Roger, and Martyn Rix. *Shrubs*. New York: Random House, 1989.

Platt, Charles A., and Keith N. Morgan. *Italian Gardens*. Reprint of 1894 ed. Portland, Or.: Timber Press, 1993.

Pollan, Michael. *Second Nature: A Gardener's Education*. New York: Atlantic Monthly Press, 1991.

Rainwater, Hattie, ed. *Garden History of Georgia 1733–1933*. Atlanta, Ga.: Peachtree Garden Club, Walter Brown Publishing, 1933.

Reader's Digest Practical Guide to Home Landscaping. Pleasantville, N.Y.: Reader's Digest Association, 1972.

Reich, Lee. *Uncommon Fruits Worthy of Attention: A Gardener's Guide*. Reading, Mass.: Addison-Wesley Publishing Company, 1991.

Reilly Smith, Mary. *The Front Garden: New Approaches to Landscape Design*. Boston: Houghton Mifflin, 1991.

Reily, H. Edward. *Success with Rhododendrons and Azaleas*. Portland, Or.: Timber Press, 1992.

Rice, Graham. *Plants for Problem Places*. Portland, Or.: Timber Press, 1988.

Riotte, Louise. *Successful Small Food Gardens*. Pownal, Vt.: Garden Way/Storey Communications, 1993.

Robinson, Peter. *Pool and Waterside Gardening*. Middlesex, UK: CollinGridge, 1987.

Robinson, William. *The English Flower Garden*. Portland, Or.: Sagapress, 1995.

Rodale's Illustrated Encyclopedia of Herbs. Emmaus, Pa.: Rodale Press, 1987.

Rohr, René R. J. *Sundials: History, Theory, and Practice*. Toronto: University of Toronto Press, 1970.

Root, Amos Ives. *The ABC & XYZ of Bee Culture*. Medina, Ohio: Root Publishing, 1991.

Root, R. R., and G. R. Forbes. "Notes upon a Colonial Garden at Salem, Massachusetts." *Landscape Architecture*, vol. 2 (October 1911).

Schinz, Marina, and Gabrielle van Zuylen. *The Gardens of Russell Page*. New York: Stewart, Tabori & Chang, 1991.

Schuler, Stanley. *American Barns*. Atglen, Pa.: Schiffer Publishing, 1984.

Schuyler, David. *Village & Farm Cottages*. Cleaveland, Henry W. & Backus Bros. (William & Samuel D.) 1856. Watkins Glen, N.Y.: American Life, 1982.

Scott, Frank J. *The Art of Beautifying Suburban Home Grounds*. New York: D. Appleton & Co., 1870.

Shaudys, Phyllis V. *Herbal Treasures.* Pownal, Vt.: Garden Way/Storey Communications, 1993.

Shurtleff, Arthur A. "The Design of Colonial Places in Virginia." *Landscape Architecture,* vol. 19 (April 1929).

———. "A New Hampshire Farm Group of 1805." *Landscape Architecture,* vol. 8 (October 1917).

Smith, Shane. *Greenhouse Gardener's Companion.* Golden, Colo.: Fulcrum, 1992.

Spencer, Darrell. *The Gardens of Salem: The Landscape History of a Moravian Town in North Carolina.* Winston-Salem, N.C.: Old Salem Books, 1987.

Stamets, Paul. *Growing Gourmet & Medicinal Mushrooms.* Berkeley, Calif.: Ten Speed Press, 1993.

Stamets, Paul, and J. S. Chilton. *The Mushroom Cultivar.* Olympia, Wash.: Agarikon Press, 1983.

Stearn, William T. *Botanical Latin.* London: David & Charles, 1989.

Stickland, Sue. *Heirloom Vegetables.* New York: Fireside/Simon & Schuster, 1998.

Stiles, David, and Jeanie Stiles. *Rustic Retreats.* Pownal, Vt.: Storey Books, 1998.

Stell, Elizabeth P. *Secrets to Great Soil.* Pownal, Vt.: Storey Publishing, 1988.

Strong, Roy. *Successful Small Gardens.* New York: Rizzoli, 1995.

Stuart, David. *The Garden Triumphant.* New York: Harper & Row, 1988.

Tabor, Grace. *Old-Fashioned Gardening: A History and a Reconstruction.* New York: McBride, Nast and Co., 1913.

Tanner, Ogden. *Gardening in America.* London: Viking Studio Books, 1990.

Taylor, Albert D., and Gordon D. Cooper. *The Complete Garden.* New York: Garden City Publishing, 1921.

Thomas, Graham S. *The Art of Gardening with Roses.* New York: Holt, 1991.

Thomas, John. *The American Fruit Culturist.* New York: William Wood and Company, 1867.

Thompson, Peter. *Creative Propagation.* Portland, Or.: Timber Press, 1992.

Tice, Patricia M. *Gardening in America 1830–1910.* Rochester, N.Y.: Strong Museum, 1984.

Tooley, Michael, and Primrose Arnander, eds. *Gertrude Jekyll: Essays on the Life of a Working Amateur.* Durham, UK: Michaelmas Books, 1995.

Turner, Carole B. *Seed Sowing and Saving.* Pownal, Vt.: Storey Publishing, 1988.

Vaughan's Seed Store Chicago Illustrated Catalog. Chicago: Vaughan, 1891, 1896.

Verrier, Suzanne. *Rosa Gallica.* Deer Park, Wis.: Capability's Books, 1995.

———. *Rosa Rugosa.* Deer Park, Wis.: Capability's Books, 1991.

Vick's Illustrated Monthly Magazine, vols. 1–5 (January 1878–December 1882). Rochester, N.Y.: James Vick, 1878–1888.

Vivian, John. *Building Stone Walls.* Pownal, Vt.: Garden Ways/Storey Communications, 1993.

Watson, Benjamin. *Heirloom Vegetables.* Boston: Houghton Mifflin, 1993.

Waugh, Albert. *Sundials: Their Theory and Construction.* New York: Dover, 1973.

Waugh, F. A. *Formal Design in Landscape Architecture.* New York: Orange Judd Publishing Co., 1927.

———, ed. *Kemp's Landscape Gardening.* New York: John Wiley & Sons, 1911.

Weaver, Lawrence. *Houses and Gardens by E. L. Lutyens.* Reprint of 1913 ed. Suffolk, UK: Antique Collectors' Club, 1994.

Weidenmann, Jacob. *Beautifying Country Homes: A Handbook of Landscape Gardening.* New York: Orange Judd & Company, 1870.

Whaley, Emily, and William Baldwin. *Mrs. Whaley and Her Charleston Garden.* Chapel Hill, N.C.: Algonquin Books, 1997.

Whiteside, Katherine, and Mick Hales. *Classic Bulbs: Hidden Treasures for the Modern Garden.* New York: Villard Books, 1991.

Whitner, Jan K. *Stonescaping: A Guide to Using Stone in Your Garden.* Pownal, Vt.: Garden Way/Storey Communications, 1992.

Wilder, Marshall P. *The Horticulture of Boston and Vicinity.* Boston: Tolman and White, 1881.

Williams, Bunny. *On Garden Style,* with Nancy Drew. New York: Simon & Schuster, 1998.

Wood, Christopher. *Paradise Lost: Paintings of English Country Life and Landscape 1850–1914.* Avenel, N.J.: Crescent, 1993.

Wright, Richardson. *The Story of Gardening.* New York: Dodd, Mead & Company, 1934.

Wyman, Donald. "Introductory Dates of Familiar Trees, Shrubs and Vines." In *Origins of American Horticulture, A Handbook,* vol. 23, no. 3. New York: Brooklyn Botanic Garden, 1967.

———. "Plants and Gardens." In *Origins of American Horticulture, A Handbook,* vol. 23, no. 3. New York: Brooklyn Botanic Garden, 1967.

———. *Shrubs and Vines for American Gardens.* New York: Macmillan Publishing Company, 1969.

———. *Trees for American Gardens,* 3rd ed. New York: Macmillan Publishing Company, 1990.

———. *Wyman's Gardening Encyclopedia.* New York: Macmillan Publishing Company, 1986.

Wysocki, Karen, and David Wysocki. *Wonderful World of Garden Structures.* Hillsborough, N.C.: Hummer Press, 1992.

Yetter, George H. *Williamsburg: Before and After.* Williamsburg, Va.: Colonial Williamsburg Foundation, 1996.

The magazine that started it all, Michael Weishan's

TRADITIONAL GARDENING

America's only practical guide to:

Authentic American Gardens
Classic Ornamentation
Traditional Planning and Planting
Garden Renovation and Restoration
Topiaries
Heirloom Plants
Historic Designs, Patterns, and Planting Plans

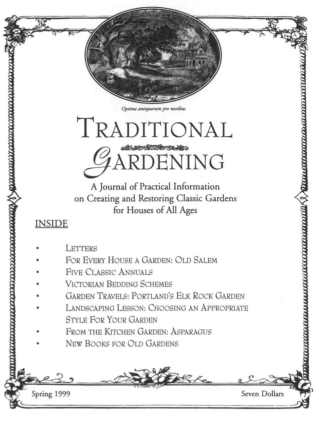

Optima antiquorum pro novibus

TRADITIONAL GARDENING

A Journal of Practical Information
on Creating and Restoring Classic Gardens
for Houses of All Ages

INSIDE

- LETTERS
- FOR EVERY HOUSE A GARDEN: OLD SALEM
- FIVE CLASSIC ANNUALS
- VICTORIAN BEDDING SCHEMES
- GARDEN TRAVELS: PORTLAND'S ELK ROCK GARDEN
- LANDSCAPING LESSON: CHOOSING AN APPROPRIATE STYLE FOR YOUR GARDEN
- FROM THE KITCHEN GARDEN: ASPARAGUS
- NEW BOOKS FOR OLD GARDENS

Spring 1999   Seven Dollars

Preview us on-line and subscribe at
www.traditionalgardening.com

SEND MY SUBSCRIPTION TO:

TO SUBSCRIBE TO TRADITIONAL GARDENING™

Send this order form, along with
your check, money order, or
charge information to:
Traditional Gardening
189 Cordaville Road
Southborough, MA 01772
e-mail:
Editorial@traditionalgardening.com

*US subscribers only; $28 in Canada; $30 overseas

Name ....

Address ....

City .... State .... Zip ....

❏ Payment enclosed   ❏ Credit Card

MasterCard /VISA# ....

Expiration Date:................................ Signature: ....

❏ Two years $45   ❏ One year $24